AN INTRODUCTION TO CHAUCER

AN INTRODUCTION TO CHAUCER

Derek Brewer

LONGMAN
London and New York

Longman Group Limited
Longman House, Burnt Mill, Harlow
Essex CM20 2JE, England
Associated companies throughout the world

*Published in the United States of America
by Longman Inc., New York*

First published 1984
Second impression 1985

BRITISH LIBRARY CATALOGUING IN PUBLICATION DATA

Brewer, Derek
  An introduction to Chaucer.
  1. Chaucer, Geoffrey—Criticism and
  interpretation
  I. Title
  821'.1   PR1924
  ISBN 0-582-49356-0

LIBRARY OF CONGRESS CATALOGING IN PUBLICATION DATA

Brewer, Derek, 1923-
  An introduction to Chaucer.

  Bibliography: p.
  Includes index.
  1. Chaucer, Geoffrey, d. 1400. 2. Poets, English—
Middle English, 1100–1500—Biography. 3. Great Britain—
Court and courtiers—Biography. I. Title.
PR1905.B72 1984   821'.1 [B]   84-899
ISBN 0-582-49356-0 (pbk.)

Set in Linotron 202 10/11pt Times

Produced by Longman Singapore Publishers (Pte) Ltd.
Printed in Singapore.

CONTENTS

PREFACE

The original idea for this book was to update and combine two much reprinted books *Chaucer* (1953) and *Chaucer in his Time* (1963) still in print. Not surprisingly, so simple a plan proved impossible. The present book is newly written, with a very much larger and fresh account of all the poetry, except that some passages of later biographical documentation, and a few other passages, have been taken over with modifications from *Chaucer*; and a substantial part of one chapter, on the court, has been adapted from *Chaucer in his Time*.

Since this is virtually a new book it has a new title. I believe it to be now more useful than its predecessors, as well as up to date. My ideas about Chaucer's work have deepened, and I am conscious of the great flood of books about Chaucer to so many of which I must be consciously or unconsciously indebted, if only by my disagreements. The Select Bibliography, however extensive, could not do justice to the amount of work that has been done, and it is limited to a few basic books which if consulted will themselves lead the reader further. The interest of Chaucer's own work can only increase the better one knows it, and the more clearly one sees it in its cultural context, both English and European.

Chapter 1

IN THE BEGINNING

THE NEW AND THE OLD, ARCHAIC AND MODERN

Geoffrey Chaucer, the most varied of our half-dozen greatest poets, is well documented as a courtier, customs officer, diplomat, occupant of a flat over Aldgate in London Wall, traveller to France and Italy, married, with children, and so forth. His poetry tells us about him as a poet. Put together the records, the poetry, and the history of the fascinating fourteenth century, and we find a remarkably full and interesting picture of a man and an age. It was a great creative period. Many new things were starting or, having started, were gaining strength. The modern world was beginning. Towns were established, capitalist enterprise raised standards of living, serfdom was being eroded, new inventions such as clockwork and a new numeracy and power to calculate, were developing. New feelings, for the family, for the individual, a new tenderness for suffering, were being experienced. These have to be seen against a background of special sorrows and troubles. Things went badly for England in much of Chaucer's lifetime, even when they prospered for him personally, and he was fully responsive to the sadness of life. Ancient sorrows continued: those caused by mankind, the savage warfare, the brutal rapine of cities; and those caused by nature, starvation and disease from poor harvests, illnesses unmitigated by medicine, and plague, culminating but not ceasing with the fearful Black Death which ravaged Europe 1348–9. Religion ancient and new offered consolations. The message of Christianity has always been the conquest of suffering and death, the triumph of love and significance. Religious experience increased the emphasis on the individual's internal values. The very success of Christianity in preaching higher ideals, more gentleness, more pity, led to men judging the Church unfavourably by its own divinely inspired ideals as inefficient and corrupt. On the

1

other hand the higher value which was being set on secular life gave that more vividness, more splendour, and consequently, because it was so swiftly passing and so full of suffering, gave it more pathos.

One of the driving engines of all these developments was the spread of schooling derived from the Church, which created literacy and the multiplication of books. Books were still in manuscript, painfully copied with many errors, for the last great medieval invention, printing, was still a century away. But there were many books, the more powerful ones in Latin – the Bible, the great theological tomes, and the classics of Antiquity themselves, still used as schoolbooks. There were also many books in French, which was still, since William of Normandy's Conquest in 1066, one of the main languages of England, though it was now more of a local dialect, limited to the upper classes, and losing its hold. There was a rapidly increasing flow of books in English; sermons, romances, encyclopaedias, works of instruction, often translated, but with more original work also. The steady advance of literacy had been at first limited to the clergy. To be literate was indeed to be a cleric, a clerk. But now in the second half of the fourteenth century the literate layman, secular, advanced in thought, appears, and his supreme manifestation is Geoffrey Chaucer.

For all his advanced interests, Chaucer was solidly a part of traditional culture. The mixture of tradition and innovation which he supremely illustrates is one of his great qualities. Literate, son of a citizen of London, numerate, secular in his occupations, and thus a part of what was new, he was also a 'courtman all his life', as one of his characters says. The court, with its fierce loyalties and betrayals, its focus on the king, its basis in the ethos of fighting, its interest in sexual love, was a flourishing example of traditional archaic patterns of thought and feeling. The court flourished partly because it was so well allied with the city. The court at Westminister, and two miles away the City of London, with the law courts on the way, sum up the spread of Chaucer's life, an axis which gave unique opportunities to a unique genius.

THE LIFE OF A PAGE AT COURT

Chaucer first appears in a court record. Medieval England is notably rich in administrative records of many kinds, but this record has survived by a marvellous accident. It is a couple of pages which were later used for binding up another book and were preserved by pure chance. They are pages from the accounts, kept as usual in a curious mixed jargon of Anglified Latin and French, mingled with actual

English words, of the household of Elizabeth, Countess of Ulster, wife of Lionel, Duke of Clarence, who was the third son of the glamorous and long-reigning King Edward III. From these scraps we learn that various people were given ribbons and robes worth so much, and that 'Galfridus' (Latin for Geoffrey) Chaucer was given, on Monday 4 April 1357 a 'paltok' or short cloak, costing four shillings, plus a pair of red and black breeches and a pair of shoes which cost his lady a further three shillings. He must have been a page, probably now seventeen years old, and was being set up in bright new clothing for Easter, which fell on 9 April. His outfit was quite expensive to the Countess. Twelve pence made a shilling, and twenty shillings a pound. One would have to multiply these sums by three or four hundred times to get their rough modern equivalents, though on the other hand labour was terribly cheap and the gap between rich and poor immensely greater than in modern Britain. A ploughman was paid about twelve shillings a year, while the Black Prince when at war drew pay of twenty shillings a day, and an archer sixpence a day.

Our sight of Chaucer in this princely household shows his connection, at his most impressionable age, with all the splendour, elegance and sophistication of Edward III's court – the most magnificent in Europe, and also the most efficiently run, to be discussed more fully in a later chapter. Chaucer's lady, the Countess Elizabeth, travelled about the country a great deal, and probably took Chaucer with her. London, Southampton, Reading, Hatfield, Windsor, Hertford Castle, Anglesey, Liverpool all saw her and her train in those four years, some places several times. State weddings and funerals held at Edward's court, as well as the normal feasts of the year, were duly kept by her, and no doubt by Chaucer in her train. As her page he helped to serve her at table, and attend her at various ceremonies, according to the strict and elaborate etiquette of a great household, which he had to learn. Some slight care would be taken of his general education, as well as of his manners. Much of what he learned, of politeness, of good manners, of noble behaviour (as well, doubtless, as scandalous talk and comic stories) came to him by watching and waiting at table, talking with his fellow pages and the older squires, and so forth. The chaplain might supervise his serious reading. He picked up an interest in music. He listened to, and read for himself, the current songs and romances, both English and the fashionable French ones. French was losing its domination as the language of the court, but the royal family spoke it. However, Chaucer learnt Continental French, the 'French of Paris', and he shows no interest in, or significant influence from Anglo-French. Chaucer had a remarkable memory for the poems of the fashionable Continental French poet Machaut, as *The Book of the Duchess* shows. The last item of this courtly education by living was instruction in military

exercises, given by the knight or gentleman in the Countess Elizabeth's household to whom this important duty was assigned. Chaucer
is never cynical about fighting.

What was Chaucer's background for this courtier's life?

CHAUCER'S FAMILY

Chaucer came, like a number of other courtiers, from a well-to-do
merchant family whose progress can be traced from modest beginnings in Ipswich, and whose increasing prosperity depended on
being equally at home, in a modest way, in both Court and City.

Both Chaucer's father and grandfather were prosperous men, with
varying amounts of property, whose principal income came from
their connection with the wine trade. Apart from their own business
as wholesale importers and wine merchants, they were both (like
Chaucer himself) employed at various times in the collection of the
king's customs. The family had property in Ipswich and had probably
lived there, but before Chaucer was born his father had moved to
London. He was drawn, doubtless, by that city's increasing importance as a financial and business centre, and by its nearness to the
king's court and administrative offices.

About the poet's grandfather, Robert, little is known. He owned
property in Ipswich, and was a vintner. In 1308 and 1310, he was
deputy to the king's chief butler (an important official, who was
sometimes a man of considerable wealth). Part of the butler's duties
was the collection of taxes on imported wines, and this was Robert
Chaucer's department. His wife Mary came from the prosperous
Ipswich family of the Westhales, and when he married her she was
already a widow, presumably with property.

Robert and Mary Chaucer had a son, John Chaucer (who became
the poet's father), born in 1313. He inherited his father's Ipswich
property and carried on the family business as a vintner. A curious
sidelight is thrown on the fourteenth century by an incident in his
childhood, when at eleven years of age his aunt (Robert Chaucer's
sister), and others, abducted him with the intention of marrying him
to her daughter Joan, thereby joining his Ipswich property to hers.
This was no unusual event at the time, but fortunately for us she and
her accomplices were prevented. They were then sued at law. Her
principal accomplice was very heavily fined. Having escaped this
early marriage, John Chaucer is next seen at the age of twenty-five, as
a member of the great and splendid retinue which the king took to
the Continent in 1338, though we do not know in what capacity John
Chaucer travelled. Probably around this time he married a widow,

Agnes Northwell, who also owned property. John Chaucer prospered. He became one of the main vintners in the City of London; for two years he, like his father, was deputy to the king's chief butler in the collection of duty on wines, and he was also deputy to the same person in April 1347 in the collection of export duties on woollen cloths. By this time he was an important figure in the general affairs of the City. To this wealthy wine merchant, man of affairs, connected with the court, Geoffrey Chaucer was born; perhaps in his father's house in Thames Street, probably in 1340.

THE CITY OF LONDON

London was Geoffrey Chaucer's earliest experience and it will be worth pausing to imagine what it was like. London was unique among English cities, being the centre of commercial power, with a special relationship to the king. It was that square mile on the north bank of the Thames, still called in English *the* City, and thus near the main seat of the royal power, which was the city of Westminster, further along the river. London was the biggest of English cities with a population of about 45,000. (Estimates for other towns are: York, about 11,000; Bristol, about 10,000; Plymouth and Coventry, about 7,000; no other town is thought to have had above 6,000; by contrast, contemporary Florence, one of the biggest cities in Europe, had about 90,000.) London also had substantial suburbs south of the Thames, especially at Southwark, by London Bridge. From Southwark, just over the river, the Dover Road, and the Pilgrim's Way to Canterbury began. In Southwark was the Tabard Inn, at which Chaucer's pilgrims gathered, and the church (now the Cathedral) where the effigy of the poet John Gower, a friend of Chaucer, can still be seen. North of the river, the road which is still called the Strand (or Bankside) ran between London and the palace of Westminster, passing the law courts, and then the large town houses owned by rich merchants and nobles. The most famous of these was the Savoy, John of Gaunt's palace, built by his father-in-law Henry, Duke of Lancaster, crowded with beautiful treasures, and totally destroyed in the Revolt of 1381. (Its situation is now marked by the Savoy Hotel.) The houses faced the road, and had long gardens at the back running down to the river. St Martin's then, was truly 'in the fields'. To get to Westminster you could go along the Strand from London, but the Exchequer and Privy Seal clerks, like Chaucer's younger friend and poetic follower Hoccleve, who worked at Westminster and usually lodged in London, often preferred, like many others, to go by water, especially in winter when the roads were so

5

muddy. The River Thames was a fine highway, though the famous bridge, with houses on it (like the Ponte Vecchio still to be seen in Florence) was a dangerous hazard with its great supports which caused a six-foot drop in the water level when the tide was running strong. It also bore grim reminders of the rough punishments of the times, with its rotting heads of offenders stuck upon spikes. Within the city many houses had their gardens, often with vegetable plots and fruit trees. Since the houses were mostly of no more than two storeys it must have been easy to see the blossom in spring, and church towers everywhere, with over all the Gothic spire of Old St Paul's, destroyed in the seventeenth-century Great Fire of London. There were big markets, and masses of shops, all governed by complex laws. There was a sewage-system, advanced for the times, a number of public latrines, and despite arrangements for street-cleaning, much filth in the streets, with pigs rooting about in the rubbish, and streams that were open sewers. It must have smelt like a farmyard in summer. We cannot estimate the city by our own standards of comfort and cleanliness; the great medieval European cities, of which London was a small example, were a remarkable achievement, with all their faults, in the art of living, won against heavy odds: of physical difficulty in an age without machines; of administrative difficulty in an age when communication was slow and limited; of disciplinary difficulty in an age when men were often as violent, unruly and unstable as children; and of sheer difficulty of survival in an age of primitive medical science, ignorant of microbes. The fourteenth century saw the growth of some great cities such as Hamburg, Paris, Florence, on the Continent. London, alone of all English cities in the fourteenth century, achieved something of their quality. So at least thought one poet, writing in the later fifteenth century, when the city was much as it was in the later fourteenth century. I quote a modernised form of part of his poem (which was once attributed to Dunbar).

> London, thou art of townés A per se,
> Sovereign of cities, seemliest in sight....
>
> Above all rivers thy river hath renown,
> Whose boreal stremés, pleasant and preclare   [*crystal; illustrious*
> Under thy lusty wallés runneth down,
> Where many a swan doth swim with wingés fair,
> Where many a barge doth row and sail with air,
> Where many a ship doth rest with top royal.
> O town! of towns patron and not compeer;   [*superior; equal*
> London, thou art the flower of cities all.
>
> Upon the lusty bridge of pillars white
> Be merchantés full royal to behold;
> Upon thy streets goth many a seemly knight

In velvet gown and chainés of fine gold.
By Julius Caesar thy Tower founded of old
May be the house of Mars victorial,
Whose artillery with tongue may not be told;
London, thou art the flower of cities all.

Strong be thy wallés that about thee stands;
Wise be the people that within thee dwells;
Fresh is thy river with his lusty strands;
Blithe be thy churches; well sounding be thy bells;
Rich be thy merchantés in substance that excels;
Fair be thy wives, right lovesome, white and small:
Clear be thy virgins, lusty under kells;   [*caps*
London, thou art the flower of cities all.

Thy famous Mayor, by princely governance,
With sword of justice thee ruleth prudently.
No Lord of Paris, Venice, or Florence
In dignity or honour goeth to him nigh;
He is exemplar, loadé-star and guy,   [*guide*
Principal patron and rose original,
Above all Mayors as master most worthy;
London, thou art the flower of cities all.

In the great cities of Europe in the fourteenth century a new urban
consciousness was developing, of which we are the direct heirs. Many
of the things we now take for granted in cities and towns, like the
common services of street-cleaning and sewerage, and complex
matters of shopping regulations, uniformity of measures, proper
time-keeping, were being established. They relied on a greater
communal sense, a certain amount of democratic self-government,
and created more privacy, less domination of the collective over the
individual.

There were many other influences encouraging the privacy of the
individual. Many came from religion, and the education in literacy
that the Church gave, and some came from the court, especially in
the sentiment of love, 'derne' (secret) love, as the poets called it. But
the sense of privacy and individuality in Chaucer must be considerably due to his rich bourgeois background. The city was the place of
trade, of specialised work, of regular time, and a serious concern for
this world. We shall see that Chaucer became a kind of accountant,
and with this urban numeracy we can associate what eventually
became his strong sense of regular metre, and his unusual sensitivity
to the passage of time in his poetry. Chaucer's secular humanism and
realism, which were not at all anti-religious (for the cities were very
pious in their worldliness) must be related in a general way to that
strand in his make-up represented by his City background, as were
his rationalism, his individualism, and his self-awareness. All of these
aspects will be summed up in that great original work of a series of

portraits, *The General Prologue* to *The Canterbury Tales*. Wordliness, work, social experience, a concentration on the rich centre of society (the middle classes), privacy, a loosening of feudal personal bonds, and at the end a certain loneliness; these are the gifts of the city. In addition there must have been an emphasis on vernacular English, to be discussed later.

The gifts of the city must be seen in context, especially in the case of Chaucer. The countryside with its alternating seasons of harshness and joy was never far away. There was a certain social mobility among all classes, much of it prompted by the presence of cities and towns, leading to a general mingling of country, city and court. It was becoming possible for peasants to enrich themselves and to rise in society, even apart from the Church which had for long offered the only chance of escape from the ignorant, sweated poverty which was the lot of the peasantry. Even a knight might have a serf as ancestor, while at the end of the century John Greyndor, a yeoman from the Forest of Dean, rose by his capacity as a ruthless captain (he beheaded 300 captives after a battle with the Welsh in 1405) to become Member of Parliament, sheriff of Glamorgan and of Gloucester, and constable of four border castles. In later life he turned merchant of Bristol (and was in fact guilty of something like piracy), and this is yet another example of the way in which, among the upper classes in England, trade and the professions (including that of war), merchants and the nobility, found it easy to mix. When Gaunt, the greatest noble in England (and about this time the most hated), was pursued by the mob in 1381, he was having dinner with a great merchant, Sir John Ypres. Sir John Montague, later Earl of Salisbury, was the third husband of a rich mercer's daughter. Nicholas Brembre, the grocer, was rich enough to make loans to Richard II and John of Gaunt. He was knighted for his bold behaviour during the Revolt, and was closely associated with the ruling court faction which was displaced by the barons in 1388. He paid for his social mobility and his financial and political power by being executed for political reasons.

The older upper classes often resisted the new tendency to move from class to class, and Parliament in 1363 passed a 'sumptuary' law, regulating the food and clothing that each class should have. Naturally, it was not obeyed. A chronicler says that yeomen dress like squires, squires like knights, knights like dukes, and dukes like kings. Chaucer, in his description of those social climbers *par excellence*, the city merchants, or gildsmen, describes them, no doubt deliberately, as wearing clothing above their station.

All this shows that along with much unease (there were often riots in London), and much oppression, English society by the second half of the century was reasonably well mixed and united, if not harmonious. The legal distinction between a crime committed by an

Englishman, and one committed by a Norman, introduced by
William the Conqueror for holding down a defeated English nation
with a small Norman-French force, had long been out of date when it
was abolished by Parliament in 1340. Of this sense of unity London
was a signal example. That did not mean that it was not often in
conflict with the Court. But neither Court nor City could do without
each other.

Chapter 2

CHAUCER'S SCHOOLING

There is first-class evidence that Chaucer went to school – his poetry. It is full of school-learning, like the passage from the Latin author Claudian, used as a school-text, in *The Parliament of Fowls*, 99–105, and dozens of others, including school jokes, like the reference to 'dulcarnoun' put in Criseyde's mouth, with Pandarus's tart reply (*Troilus and Criseyde*, III, 930–5). Chaucer's references in *The Prioress's Tale* to the 'song-school', that is, the primary school for choirboys attached to a cathedral, suggest personal knowledge. Chaucer's own knowledge of Latin is likely to have been acquired at a grammar school. Unfortunately we lack documentary evidence. No school registers were kept.

There were at least three schools in London at the time; St Paul's (a grammar school, with an almonry or song-school as a semi-independent attachment), the Arches (at St Mary le Bow), and St Martin's le Grand. St Paul's was nearest his father's house in Lower Thames Street, and he may well have gone there. The hours were long, and the holidays none except the festivals of the Church, which would, however, have amounted to at least one day a week, apart from Sundays. The instruction at such a school may be summed up in one word: Latin. Latin was the language of the Church, and of much of the country's administration (which was largely run by clerics). It was the language of the Holy Bible; it was the language of philosophy, and of science; and in it was also the most impressive single body of literature known to the Middle Ages, the Classics of Antiquity. First, however, at the most elementary level of teaching (which they were supposed to have passed through before they came to a grammar school), children were taught to read in English the Ave Maria ('Hail Mary', which is the beginning of the Annunciation of the birth of Christ to the Virgin Mary, Luke I, 28, used as a prayer); the Lord's Prayer; and the Creed (the essentials of belief), with a few psalms. Such might be learnt from a primer which would contain first the alphabet in large and small letters, then the exorcism, and the

Lord's Prayer, followed by the Ave Maria, the Creed, the Ten Commandments, and the Seven Deadly Sins. The child thus learnt to read Latin, often without being able to understand it – like the little boy in *The Prioress's Tale*, who had just started at such a school.

Chaucer would have learnt his 'grammar' at the grammar school. Grammar meant something more than it does nowadays. Not only did it signify grammar in the modern sense of 'the structure of the language', but also, when this was acquired, much information of various kinds. The commonest way of starting the actual Latin grammar was for the master to dictate it, and the children to write it down, and learn it off by heart. There were versified Latin grammars to help this. This method of learning and of acquiring books was in use even in the university. The extreme shortage of books in the fourteenth century has always to be remembered. Memory had to play a far larger part in all schooling and all scholarship than it need do now. Proper dictionaries were not available, and although there were several vocabularies in circulation, only one of them had an alphabetical arrangement. As soon as children had acquired some knowledge of Latin an attempt was made, in some schools, to enforce Latin speaking at all times. Some of the better pupils at any rate acquired some fluency in speaking Latin. Some simple textbooks, such as Aesop's *Fables*, were read after the elements of grammar, and then some classical authors, especially parts of Virgil and Ovid. Few classical authors were read thoroughly; apart from Virgil, who was considered to be almost a Christian, they were still looked upon with a little suspicion by some and Christian authors were often preferred. The extremely pious nature of the educational system is one of its most notable characteristics. This is noticeable in some Rules for Conduct for the boys of Westminster School, which, although written in the thirteenth century, probably applied in the fourteenth, and were similar to those in other schools.

> In the morning let the boys upon rising sign themselves with the holy cross, and let each one say the creed, namely, I believe in God, etc., and the Lord's prayer three times, and the salutation to the Blessed Virgin five times, without shouting and confusion; and if anyone neglects these good things, let him be punished.
>
> Then, after they have made up the beds properly, let them leave their room together quietly, without clattering, and approach the church modestly, and with washed hands, not running, or skipping, or even chattering, or having a row with any person or animal; not carrying bow or staff, or stone in the hand, or touching anything with which another could be harmed; but marching along simply and honestly and with ordered step. ...
>
> Whether they are standing or sitting in the choir, let them not have their eyes turned aside to the people, but rather towards the altar; not grinning, or chattering, or laughing aloud; not making fun of another if he does not read or sing psalms well; not hitting one another secretly or openly, or

answering rudely if they happen to be asked a question by their elders. Those who break these rules will feel the rod without delay. ...

Likewise, if anyone who knows Latin dares to speak English or French with his companion, or with any clerk, for every word he shall have a blow with the rod. ...

Again, who ever at bedtime has torn to pieces the bed of his companions, or hidden the bed clothes, or thrown shoes or pillows from corner to corner, or roused anger, or thrown the school into disorder, shall be severely punished in the morning.

(Quoted by E. Rickert, *Chaucer's World*, 1948, pp. 116–17)

Choirboys clearly have not changed much.

A certain impression of violence is increased by what we can guess of outdoor sports. Here again, there is little direct fourteenth-century evidence. But things changed slowly in the Middle Ages, and boys' games also are largely traditional. The picture given by a twelfth-century account of some games is indirectly confirmed by what we know or can guess about the fourteenth century.

On holidays all the summer the boys play at archery practice, running, jumping, wrestling, putting the stone, sending missiles attached with thongs beyond a mark, and duelling with bucklers. The girls Cytherea leads in dancing until moonrise, and the earth is beaten with the lively foot.

In winter on almost all holidays before dinner, foaming boars and pigs armed with gleaming teeth are made to fight for their heads so that they may be added to the flitches of bacon, or fat hooved bulls or huge bears are made to fight with dogs set upon them.

When the great swamp that borders the northern wall of the city is frozen over, crowds of boys go out for fun on the ice. Some take long runs and slide far across toward the other side. Others make themselves seats out of lumps of ice like great stones; and many running ahead, hand in hand, draw the one who is seated thus. With such a slippery speed of movement, sometimes they all lose their balance and fall headlong. Some know how to have [still] better sport on the ice: they fit to their feet and bind about their ankles bones, such as the thigh bones of animals, and take in their hands stakes tipped with iron; when they strike these on the ice, they are carried with the speed of a flying bird or of a dart from a sling. Sometimes from a great distance, by agreement, two advance [in this way] from opposite sides; they come together, they lift their sticks, they strike at one another; one falls or both, not without bodily hurt; for after the fall even, by the very force of the motion they are carried far, and where they strike the ice, they are skinned and bruised. Often the one who falls breaks an arm or leg by falling on it; but youth is eager for glory, youth is greedy for victory, and in order to be the braver in real battles, they practise these mock battles.

(Quoted by Rickert, op. cit., p. 227)

Here is a taste of the atmosphere in which Chaucer spent formative years – an atmosphere of energetic and sometimes constricting piety, varied by violent exciting sports and some opportunity for reading.

If Chaucer went to the song-school attached to the grammar school at St Paul's he remembered it in the early parts of *The Prioress's Tale*, where the little boy of seven attends a song-school. The realism and precision of detail, though so brief, are entirely convincing. At St Paul's there were books of exactly the kind that Chaucer's poetry shows him to have read, as we know from a rare piece of documentary evidence, in a will. About the middle of the century the song-school of St Paul's had an unusual schoolmaster, William Ravenstone, who had a large collection of books in Latin. Although he was a chaplain, he seems to have had very few theological books, but a great many other books of various interest, including some practical teaching books and a large number of Latin classics. When he died he left these books to the school, to the number of eighty-four, a chest to keep them in, and provision for an annual gift of money to the boys. There are some 76,000 wills surviving from the fourteenth and fifteenth centuries in England. Of these Miss Deanesly examined 7,568, and found only 388 which bequeath books; yet this was a period when books were valuable and so likely to be mentioned in wills. The wills containing books are far fewer in the fourteenth than in the fifteenth century, and usually only one or two books are mentioned in each will. So Ravenstone's eighty-four are really outstanding. Furthermore, it was extremely difficult to get the use of a library. Most of those that existed were in monasteries, were mainly devotional and theological, and restricted to the use of monks. On the other hand, Chaucer himself from an early period shows a quite unusual knowledge of the classics, while his parents' house was not far from the song-school of St Paul's. So it is possible that Chaucer got his unusual knowledge from Ravenstone's collection, and that the learned and kindly Ravenstone may have been Chaucer's own teacher, either at the song-school, or retained as a private tutor by Chaucer's father.

BOOKS AND LATIN

Books were scarce because they were so toilsome to produce. Paper was slowly coming into use, but the skin of sheep or calf was still the usual material of books. The supply was short and the preparation elaborate. Ink and pens were not easily to be bought: the ink had to be made up, and the quill pens cut from a goose's feather. Scribes sometimes complain about the quality of the pen, or the paper, or the cold of the cloister, in the margins of the books. Serious literature was still almost entirely in Latin, sometimes contained in huge tomes which included many separate items. One book might constitute almost a small library. Other books were small; all without title-pages. Each item was written in folded sheets, like a pamphlet, which were then bound together to form the book. Sometimes discoloured sheets inside a book show that one of the pamphlets which make it up was left for a long time before being bound up with others, and its outer page had become dirty. Scribes wrote on sloping desks, with a stick in one hand to hold the page steady without smudging it, and pen in the other. Much writing was still done in the monasteries, but stationers are recorded in England from the beginning of the century, and by the middle of the century there was probably a commercial bookshop in London, perhaps the only one in England, though Florence had several. The London shop may have employed as many as half a dozen scribes, who busily copied out various items which were then bound together. Professional scriveners, who copied out books for people, are recorded from the middle of the century, and probably existed before. They often made mistakes, and some scribes seem to have left mistakes uncorrected even when they noticed them, because a correction spoiled the look of the page. For this reason a beautiful manuscript may be less reliable in its text than a manuscript untidily written out by a careful amateur. One is bound to make mistakes when copying out by hand. None of Chaucer's own manuscripts survives, but those of his Italian contemporary, Boccaccio, are still preserved, and he made plenty of mistakes when copying out his own poetry. Each copy will have variations, which become complicated when you have copies of copies. All manuscripts are different, and vary from the original copy, though some less so than others. That is why the reconstruction of Chaucer's or Langland's text is a highly technical and laborious job, when, as in the case of *Piers Plowman* or *The Canterbury Tales*, up to eighty manuscripts have to be taken into account and compared.

Most manuscripts, like most books today, had little adornment, and were much less beautiful than most books are today. In the fourteenth century the style of handwriting is what has come to be called Gothic script, which was imitated in type when printing was introduced (the so-called 'blackletter'), and which continued in some books until the seventeenth century in England and the twentieth in Germany. It is markedly mannered and different from modern script and print, and can be very beautiful in its elaborate way. Books were very expensive when professionally produced. The cheapest, of only a few leaves, cost about a shilling (five new pence), which must be multiplied three or four hundred times at least to find its equivalent today. Few good books cost less than ten shillings then, and standard works of philosophy etc., of the kind of which Chaucer's Clerk had twenty by his bed, cost two to three pounds. No wonder his overcoat was threadbare. The book which the Wife of Bath threw into the fire, because her young husband read to her stories unfavourable to women from it, must have cost one to two pounds. Splendidly decorated books cost a very great deal more, since they might mean the employment of several skilled men for several years, although naturally in all these cases the costs varied greatly with the books and the conditions of sale.

All this shows that Ravenstone's bequest of books to his school was generous both in literary riches and in sheer economic value.

It seems likely, from the terms of his will, that whether or not Ravenstone was Chaucer's teacher, he taught more Latin than was usual at a song-school.

Chaucer learnt Latin quite well, and it made him free of a world of great intellectual riches, from poetry to philosophy, via a good deal of humdrum instruction and much moralising. Latin opened up to him the world of science, especially astronomy, in which he became so much interested. Even so, Latin is a hard language, and Chaucer never disdained a French crib when he could find one, as for example in translating Boethius's *Consolation of Philosophy*, which is a difficult text.

Someone must have taught Chaucer French quite formally. There were already phrase books and word lists that would have helped. The reason for supposing this is that Chaucer, as we can judge from his own work, could read Central, Continental French, the French of Paris, very well, for he shows intimate knowledge of *Le Roman de la Rose*, and Machaut's poems. He could also read, if he wanted to, many works written in Anglo-Norman, or Anglo-French, which was the language which had developed from the French conquerors of England, and was now a distinct but dying dialect, of a decidedly provincial kind. Chaucer rarely shows interest in Anglo-Norman though the main source of *The Man of Law's Tale* is in that language. In *The General Prologue* Chaucer gently sneers at the socially pretentious Prioress who speaks the French of 'Stratford-atte-Bowe', a village near London, virtually a suburb. She did not know, says Chaucer, the French of Paris. Since he obviously did, he did not speak French at home, for that would have been Anglo-Norman. Therefore, he spoke English at home and was taught the 'proper' French of the Continental French poets whom he enjoyed so much.

Somebody at some time taught Chaucer arithmetic. A little bit may have been learned at school, but he may have had to have private lessons. Only in Italy in the middle of the fourteenth century was there large scale serious teaching of arithmetic, given in many schools which specialised in secular training for business. Religious people normally distrusted arithmetic, no doubt because it seemed too worldly, too abstract, and morally neutral. The teaching of arithmetic was gaining ground in England. Merchants needed it, and towards the end of the fourteenth century a teacher of arithmetic appears in Oxford. Maybe there was one earlier in the century in London who is not recorded. London, the business centre of the kingdom, would be a natural place for a teacher of the commercial skill of arithmetic. Or perhaps Chaucer's own father taught him, for as a prosperous business man he would both need and be able to carry out arithmetical calculation. He must have set a value on it. Knowledge of arithmetic did not in Chaucer's case lead to trade but to astronomy. When he himself was fifty he started to write a textbook on the astronomical instrument, the astrolabe, for 'little Lewis, my son', who he tells us is ten years old. Perhaps he himself at a similarly tender age had been taught by a similarly enthusiastic father. Knowledge of arithmetic was still relatively rare in the fourteenth century but it was developing and it changed men's mentalities more than we may realise. It was part of the modern, measurable, impersonal, world, promoting habits of accuracy and attention to detail. These habits when transferred to literature lead to the precision, literalism, 'realism', and moral neutrality or relativism which are such notable characteristics, though not the only ones, of Chaucer's later writing.

No one taught Chaucer English. All his poetry shows him to have been a native speaker of English, and as already suggested he must have learnt English naturally, from his parents. He would have learnt his first prayers in English before turning to Latin. Though not part of his formal schooling he would also have heard plenty of songs and stories in his mother tongue. It was upon these that his own later songs and stories were based, though with so much greater richness from his breadth of formal knowledge and of foreign languages.

THE ENGLISH LANGUAGE

There can be no reasonable doubt that both Chaucer and his parents were native English speakers. English has always been the language of the English. The French that was imposed by the Conquest had greater social prestige, and was used for law and administration, but never displaced English as the general spoken vernacular. The question was not, except for the very highest nobility, did a man speak English, but did he speak French as well, or Latin? Many learned men were versed in all three, like Chaucer himself, and his friend Gower, without displacing English as the cradle-tongue of the majority.

Chaucer was probably of long-established English stock. The surname 'Chaucer' (variously spelt, 'Chaucers', 'Chaucier', 'Chaucy', etc.) is indeed French and probably means 'shoemaker', suggesting the level of skilled craftsmen from which the family arose. A great-grandfather was Andrew de Dinnington (the name of an English village from which he must have come), and sometimes known as Andrew le Taverner, 'Andrew-who-keeps-a-pub', who lived in Ipswich. His son Robert acquired the surname 'le Chaucer'. It was a skilled trade, and Robert must have done well from it, but the name has nothing to do with Robert's own family origins, which were probably both humble and totally English from before the Conquest.

In a curious way the recovery of the English language from the heavy blow struck against it by the Conquest is paralleled by the rise of the Chaucer family, as far as we can see it, even to the extent of acquiring a glossy French surname.

As a result of the Conquest, French became by the thirteenth century in England the language of high culture, law and administration, and English lost prestige. It was therefore less used for educated purposes, and lost the standard spelling which had been evolved in late Anglo-Saxon times. It became written more phonetically, according to local dialects. Spelling varied confusingly. The powerful general and abstract words in English, requiring education to acquire, needing to be used at the higher levels of culture, slowly fell into disuse, though many are still to be found in such a text as *The Ancrene Riwle*, written in Herefordshire just after 1200, for three aristocratic young sisters who had become religious recluses. For such English words, French words were usually substituted. Thus the English word for 'peace' was *grith*, but *peace* was one of the earliest French borrowings. The author of *The Ancrene Riwle* refers to *eadmodnesse*, which we now call *humility*. There are many hundreds of examples. On the other hand, these down-to-earth words by which we live and die, eat bread and drink beer, make love, sleep, dream, wake and so forth, are all English. Chaucer's forefathers and he himself spoke them, to the language born.

The language had changed from its Old English form. It had lost most of the endings of words which had shown not only the difference between singular and plural, as still happens, but had served instead of such prepositions as *of, to, for*, etc. (though these are English too) to indicate the meaning of the words and the part they played in the sentence. These endings partly remained in Chaucer's time, but were mostly reduced to an obscure vowel-sound indicated by the letter *-e*. Thus word-order became much more important for establishing meaning. But the ending *-e* often retains meaning in Chaucer's English, for example as the plural of an adjective, and when historically justified (not just added by a scribe) needs to be pronounced for the verse to have the rhythm intended by Chaucer. Most of the vowels remained 'pure', that is, single sounds, not as so often in modern English, dipthongs, that is, double sounds. So 'time' was pronounced not as now, where the *i* represents a dipthong *ah-ee*, but *teem*. Chaucer's English was more beautiful in this respect, and more like modern Italian, French, German, etc. than modern English. Almost all the consonants that were written were pronounced, as for example the *k* in *knight*, or *g* in *gnaw*. The English used by Chaucer is called for scholarly purposes Middle English, to indicate its period. Modern English begins around 1500.

Although these changes in large part came from a lowering of status, a defeat and a deprivation, they can be seen more positively. The basis of the English language remained essentially unaffected. It developed a more advanced word-order because of the decay of word-endings. It absorbed from French and Latin a new vocabulary. It became in general adaptive and flexible and throughout the fourteenth century rose, like the Chaucer family and many other English families, especially in towns, in social status, and in power to deal with varied subject-matter. Its nature was more mixed than either the modern Germanic languages or the modern Romance (i.e. the Roman, i.e. Latin-derived languages). This had some disadvantages; a rather arbitrary spelling, which made learning more difficult; a division in origins of vocabulary which may have promoted class-division; yet it also opened up many linguistic possibilities, and a vast range of meanings which Chaucer and in his time Shakespeare were able to exploit to remarkable effect.

The development of the vocabulary of English and some of the word-order, from Old English to Chaucer's day, can be summed up in one line by Chaucer from *Troilus and Criseyde*, when Criseyde says to Troilus:

> Welcome, my knyght, my pees, my suffisaunce.

III, 1309

Welcome my knyght are all native English words, warm and concrete, though *knight* has developed in meaning to take on all the rich significance of chivalry. *Peace*, more general, was, as already noted, one of the earliest French words to be borrowed and is first recorded in English in the mid-twelfth century. *Suffisaunce* is more general, learned and rare. It means what we now call *sufficiency*. It combines a physical with almost spiritual senses. Chaucer is the first to be recorded using it, and he seems to have been fond of it, using it for a jest as well as perfectly seriously here and elswhere.

Chaucer, native English speaker, had the linguistic flair of major literary genius for picking up words, and he enriched his language with new French words, as well as some Latin and one or two Italian. The deficiencies of English forced him to take up new words, because he wanted to say new things, grafted on to the stock of the old, the basic English tongue. He turned disadvantage to advantage. Yet he was, or more correctly, we are, unlucky, in a sense, with his language. His Middle English is beautiful and interesting. But English has changed more radically in a thousand years than any other European vernacular. Chaucer would not have understood Old English, and modern English people find Middle English more difficult than, say French people find their own language of the corresponding period to be. But let us not exaggerate our difficulties. Chaucer's English is still close to modern English; its differences are intrinsically interesting, and it is much easier for us to learn his language than it was for him to learn Latin or French, without proper dictionaries or grammar books.

THE END OF SCHOOLING AND THE DEVELOPMENT OF THE LITERATE LAYMAN

When a boy went to a grammar school, what was his aim, or his parents' aim for him? That the impassioned pursuit of knowledge for the sake of understanding was as strong then as now we are bound to believe, if only from Chaucer's portrait of the Clerk of Oxford. That is the noblest portrayal of that ideal anywhere in English literature, and wonderfully free from the embarrassment that tinges later attempts by English writers to describe the high calling of teaching and learning that any man might be proud to follow. It is not likely, however, that the pursuit of pure knowledge was any stronger then than now, and the general opinion was perhaps even less in favour of it. All learning, and especially Theology, the Queen of the Sciences, as it was called, was useful learning, to save souls, to administer the law, to cure the sick. And the three professions of the Church, law and medicine were the likely aim of anyone who entered a grammar school at least up to the time of Chaucer. Latin was the foundation of all three. The practitioners of all three professions were usually what it is now convenient to call clerics, that is to say, members of one or other of the official ranks of the Church, though not necessarily all priests.

The reason for this is that when Classical civilisation went under to the barbarians, in the fifth and sixth centuries AD, it was the Christian Church alone which preserved in the West what learning and civilisation there was. In the Dark Ages, with very few exceptions, only churchmen could read or write. The whole story of the European mind from the sixth to the sixteenth centuries may be summed up as the attempt, against appalling difficulties, to preserve, to rediscover, and to extend the almost lost civilisation of the classical world of Greece and Rome. The so-called Renaissance of the fifteenth and sixteenth centuries is really not a rebirth but the most triumphal stage of that process. In Italy, where continuity was strongest (and leaving out of consideration the Arab and Byzantine worlds, which for long preserved more than the West), there may always have been a few laymen who could read and write. But to the barbarian nations of the north of Europe, including the English, it was Christianity itself which brought knowledge of words along with the Word. And both were in Latin. A cleric (the word itself is Latin), or clerk, was a minister of the Church, and so inevitably, because Christianity is the religion of the Book, he was one who could read. And still, at the end of the fourteenth century, to be able to read was in itself regarded as evidence that a man belonged to the official ranks of the Church. This could be an important privilege, for if accused of a serious crime such a man might demand to be tried by canon law rather than by the law of the land, and canon law was often more lenient. If a man were convicted of murder, he would hang by the ordinary law. But if he could claim 'Benefit of Clergy' he received a lighter punishment. And he proved his 'clergy', which meant both his learning and his clerical status, by showing he could read Latin.

Thanks to the Church's own programme of teaching, mainly derived from the Lateran Council of 1215–16, this monopoly of literacy slowly changed and by the middle of the fourteenth century we note in England the coming into existence of literate laymen; men, not in religious orders, who could read both English and Latin, and who could probably write both at a pinch. The prime example of the new literacy is Chaucer himself. Another is Gower, who composed poetry in English, French and Latin. Henry IV knew Latin. None of these could or would claim to be in even minor clerical orders. Most of the knights and ladies of Richard's court could read English. Many of them, at least until right at the end of the century, could read and speak French, though doubtless with a provincial English accent.

It is impossible to know what was the purpose of Chaucer's schooling, whether it was received at school or, less likely, given by private tutor. Maybe his father, the prosperous merchant, proud of his quick, clever, book-learned son, designed for him a university career. On the whole that seems unlikely. The two English universities of Oxford and Cambridge had not then the social prestige they began to acquire in the sixteenth century. They were rather utilitarian in approach, in that they prepared men for the canon law, i.e. church law (not civil law in England), for medicine, and for the church. It is true that mathematics and science, particularly astronomy, were strong at Oxford in the beginning of the century, and in the second half of the century Oxford was riven by theological controversy, especially that initiated by Wycliffe, who inspired the Lollards. There was much here to attract Chaucer. He is notable for his interest in science and astronomy. His sympathies were drawn to the Lollards, as will be shown, and in later life he had a number of connections with Oxford. But the universities were primarily seminaries for priests and theologians. Chaucer was young, secular-minded, realistic, with an eager interest in love and life, inclined to mock fine-drawn theological argumentation ('I cannot bolt it to the bran', that is, 'I can't be bothered to sort it out', he says of theological controversy in *The Nun's Priest's Tale*). Though he was a genuine intellectual (or *because* he was a genuine intellectual), he cannot be imagined as ready to cloister himself in celibate abstract studies. He honoured them in the Clerk of Oxford, but they were not for him.

So what else could he do? He was no doubt quick at figures. Trade gave the impetus for the development of arithmetical skills, which were so important for later science, and indeed, in the background, for Chaucer's own poetry. But Chaucer was a boy too much interested in reading, in poetry, in history, and again, too much of an intellectual, to be a merchant like his father, though his later career drew him at times perilously close to such activities, as he was to complain.

Maybe there was something in him of Perkin Revelour, the charming, idle, lecherous, dancing, gambling, apprentice of the unfinished *The Cook's Tale*; or at least something in him that sympathised with Perkin; but such sympathies would themselves lead him away from trade, not towards it. Perhaps it is symbolic that *The Cook's Tale* of Perkin is unfinished. For such a boy as we might imagine Chaucer to be, of rich parents, immensely talented, eager, intellectual, pleasure loving, the only careers could be either at Court, or in the civil law, for the legal Inns of Court were a kind of secular university. He might even combine both, as some young courtiers did. Whatever Chaucer's father's ambitions were for his son, he must have done as other rich merchants did, and procured him a place as a page in as good a court as he could manage, which was pretty good, even if not the king's. Chaucer must have been about sixteen when he went there, and must have felt joyously in his own element. What a glorious change from school.

Chapter 3

THE COURTLY LIFE

FROISSART'S ACCOUNT

The most glowing description of the world of the English courts comes from Jean Froissart, the man who, of all men, was most enamoured of the brilliance and romance of fourteenth-century chivalry. Unlike Chaucer, he was a professional man-of-letters, rewarded by gifts from patrons and by sinecures in the Church. But his career offers some interesting parallels to that of Chaucer, who must have known him, and who certainly copied his verse. Froissart's early days are even more obscure than Chaucer's. First, we note that in his poetry he makes three references to his age, and thereby gives us the choice of three different birth years – 1333, 1337, 1338. Froissart was a Fleming, and, like Chaucer, seems to have been born to a wealthy middle-class family, and to have early moved in courtly, aristocratic circles. He began Latin at twelve, which was later perhaps than an English boy would have done. But, he says with un-Chaucerian complacence, he was more interested in the little girls, and in fighting the other boys, than in his lessons. In 1362 he came to England, to find as his patron his fellow-countrywoman, Edward's Queen Philippa, whose praises he so warmly tells wherever he finds occasion. The young Froissart, enamoured of chivalry, was enraptured by the English court, then at the height of its glory. London was delightful, with a splendid and honourable court, a king feared by three kingdoms, with a noble queen, whom Froissart served with beautiful songs and treatises of love. This court, with its well-spoken knights, aroused in him a youthful enthusiasm which he never lost. The English knighthood was in the full flush of its early splendid successes in the Hundred Years War. The court was full of the heroes of both sides, including Prince Edward, 'the first knight of the world', whom later ages have called the Black Prince; with his Princess, Joan, the Fair Maid of Kent, 'the most beautiful woman in the whole realm of England' says Froissart, 'and the most loving', with her strange, rich, new fashions of dress which the moralists so condemned. His first visit was the most brilliant moment of Froissart's life, and one he never forgot. 'I could not tell nor recount in a day the noble dinners, the suppers, the festivals, the entertainments, the gifts, the presents, the jewels, which were made, given and presented', he cries. He was astonished and delighted by the courtly manners of the English knights. They had an absolute faith in a knight's word of honour, such as was never found, he says, among the Germans. To the many captured French knights who remained at the English court awaiting their ransoms and passing the time in sports, and feasting with their captors, that court was no place of exile and desolation; it was more like some important town today during an international congress. In this court it was Froissart's delight to collect the materials for his great *Chronicles*, to write fashionable verse, and to talk with gallant lords and ladies of those two 'eternal' themes, Arms and Love.

There was another side to all this. Froissart himself, later in life, said hard things about the English. The Hundred Years War appears to us now as a long-drawn-out horror of desolation and suffering inflicted on the fair land of France and her wretched peasants. Even within the limits of his own chivalric ideal Froissart sees easily enough, and describes clearly enough many instances of bad faith and wanton cruelty. But though much that was said about chivalry in the fourteenth century was lip-service, the ideal itself was a potent and glittering one, and for all its faults it has enriched the human mind. It gave the basic structure of accepted feelings and ideas for courtiers, and for Chaucer, in the secular and even the religious realms of the mind. Its genuine power over the actions of men was limited, and sometimes failed completely, as can be easily seen in Froissart's *Chronicles* themselves. But there are also many examples where the ideal did not fail. Perhaps the most striking brief example of the ideal, because of the person who expresses it, and at such a late date, is the sentence which the unhappy and disastrous King Richard II was said to have uttered, when very near the time of his death: 'Je suis loyal chevalier et oncques ne forfiz chevalerie'. Whatever his faults, the king *believed* in the chivalric ideal.

THE BASIS OF COURT CULTURE

The court was a mixture of ceremony and practical usefulness in which the one often supported the other. The courtesy books with their emphasis on good manners influenced the way the court actually worked, and the way the court worked affected the nature of the ceremonies and amusements which took place. All the same, there was a distinction between ceremony and amusement on the one side, and practical usefulness on the other, and this distinction is reflected in the records we have. The life of leisure, the fine flow of court culture which is the chief subject of this chapter, had roots in utility. But all too often the records show us only roots or flower and, as in the court game of the competing parties of the Flower and of the Leaf, the two often seem in opposition. We cannot see the connections. Our knowledge of Chaucer's life suffers. His poetry is the finest aspect of the flower of court culture, and he was famous as a poet in his day even in France. Yet the records show him only as a minor courtier; a diplomatic envoy; a Comptroller of Customs; Clerk of the Works; member of commissions such as that which inquired into the state of the Thames embankments; subject to writs for small debts. What a portrait of England's famous poet! Yet in such details, interesting enough in themselves, we must ground ourselves, if we are to re-create in imagination that beautiful but transient flower of court culture which in the fifteenth century so quickly faded and fell. Chaucer knew that

> al nis but a faire
> This world, that passeth soone as floures faire.

Troilus V, 1804–1

It is Vanity Fair that we shall be describing.

The King's court was in origin the household of the greatest of the 'magnates' or great lords. There were vast estates to be administered, rents and debts to be collected, justice to be done, a thousand daily decisions large and small to be taken. All magnates had such big households, comprising all ranks from the humblest kitchen-helper to the magnate's personal council, which in John of Gaunt's case was a hundred and fifty strong. But the King's household was now something more than that of the greatest magnate; it was turning into the administrative centre of the kingdom. Originally domestic departments, like that of the wardrobe, were becoming departments of government. The wardrobe became divided into the King's wardrobe, the great wardrobe, and the privy wardrobe. The great wardrobe became as it were the Ministry of Supply. The privy wardrobe became an armaments store, settled in the Tower of London, where it was responsible for stocks of bows and arrows, pikes, lances, equipment for horses, tools, and even that new material which was to destroy knighthood, gunpowder. Departments such as these were becoming detached from the court proper, but their dependence on it was still close. The same is true for other departments of the King's government, such as the law courts. The King had been the chief law-giver, but he no longer sat on the bench of justice. Parliament had grown out of the council of great men who advised the King, though it was also a court of law, but the developments of the century, notably the King's need of money from the nation for the nation's wars, which he could not finance out of his own estates, forced him to make Parliament more representative of the nation at large. Members of Parliament, judges, heads of great departments of state, were many of them courtiers also; so, in his minor way, was Chaucer, Justice of the Peace, and in one Parliament a Knight of the Shire for Kent.

The court itself, and all these various parts or aspects of it, had at the beginning of the century no fixed place of abode. One reason was that such large gatherings of people were difficult to feed for long at a time when communications were slow and almost every household had to be self-sufficient. The court had to move about the country so as to spread the burden of its maintenance. This was the case not only for the King's court but for the court of any magnate, or even sometimes for the abbot of a great monastery. This ceaseless moving about was still characteristic of the King's court right to the end of the century. When Froissart paid his last visit to England, in the mid-1390s, he says he stayed in the King's court as long as he pleased, not always in one place, for the King often moved to Eltham, to Leeds, to Kingston, to Sheen, to Chertsey, or to Windsor, all of them in the surroundings of London.

It had been necessary for the King's court to move not only to find provisions, but to govern the country, and all the departments of state moved with him. Even in the late fourteenth century Parliament met in different places, such as Gloucester and Northampton, as well as Westminster. But the important development of the latter part of the century was the increasing fixity of the departments of state at Westminster, and their consequent detachment from the King and his court. They began to have a life of their own, which increased their efficiency, but which also altered both their character and the character of the court. The court itself became rather more a place of entertainment and less a place of business.

THE COURT AS A PLACE OF LEISURE AND CULTURE

As a result, it was possible to realise the essential courtly life more fully than in any previous English court. From the time at least of Richard's marriage to Anne of Bohemia in 1382 a great court existed for the first time in England, taking much of its inspiration from the papal court of Avignon and the French court at Paris. It was leisured though still basically functional; it had many people (far too many, in the opinion of Parliament); most of these people were on a footing of general equality; there were many ladies, decorative, distracting, and some would say, inspiring; a number of patrons and patronesses of the arts of life and the life of Art.

New demands for luxuries imported from the South, new feelings about the way life should be lived, new feelings about literature, paintings, music, were all seeping in from the southern courts, to settle in the poetry of Chaucer, based so largely on French and Italian poets of the new movements, like Machaut and Boccaccio. If one major influence which Chaucer felt and recorded was the new mixture of devoutness and scepticism, mathematics and morality, deriving from the city, the other major influence was the new decorativeness, the new sensibility, which characterise the court culture of his time.

A suggestion of the elaborate organisation and multifarious activities of a great medieval court can very well be gained from a few extracts from the registers of the Black Prince, who in his day was the flower of princes. These records of payment, administrative decisions and the like, open up many windows on the times. Thus there is a long list of payments made on 5 September 1355. The sums paid are not important, but the totals of which they are part show how a medieval prince valued what he thought important or desirable. An embroiderer of Brussels is owed the almost incredibly vast sum of £1,436 8s.4d.; Martin Parde of Pistoia, a jewel merchant, is owed £3,133 13s.4d.; a London goldsmith £574 3s.8d.; another embroiderer £295 4s.10d.; yet another of Cologne £97 15s.11d.; Hugh le Peyntour of London is paid for painting £82 13s.; Lambkeyn, a saddler of Germany, is given an advance of £1,368 for saddlery for a forthcoming campaign. Various knights also receive payments. Here is evidence, like that of Chaucer's poems, for the international quality of the court culture of the day, as well as its extravagant splendour. Another long list of payments was made on 7 July 1361. Several knights received instalments of sums of £100 or more which the Prince had promised them for their services at the battle of Poitiers. It is easy to see here the 'magnificence' which men expected of a prince; and also the efficient administration which maintained the courts of magnates and the King. Such payments are not quite typical of the register as a whole; the entries are almost daily, and the prince did not spend hundreds of pounds daily on jewellery; the usual run of entries refers to the continual stream of minor decisions, judgements and payments connected with the running of a great estate, and though the Prince himself often ordered them, high officials, trusted knights of his household, did most of the administration, or advised the Prince. Chaucer eventually became a minor figure among such as these, in the King's court.

Idleness, or at any rate leisure, is necessary to the attainment of any way of life that is not governed by mere brute necessity. Yet much of the apparently merely decorative part of court life served practical purposes, even political purposes, while the performance of practical necessities was enlivened by turning them into occasions for ceremony and enjoyment. Some feeling of this underlay the justification of such a life. Why should lords and prelates be allowed more delicate foods, clothes, etc., than ordinary men, asks the monk and scholar, Uthred of Boldon, and immediately proceeds to answer himself: because, according to Aristotle, superiors are occupied with the mental and spiritual work of government, while others are occupied with less demanding bodily work; and superiors are more discreet in avoiding excess, and so may be allowed more subtle food and so on, while subjects are less able to restrain themselves. But illicit self-indulgence is even less lawful for superiors than for inferiors. The working of such feelings of justification in practice are seen in the case of King John who had been captured by the Black Prince at the English victory of Poitiers in 1356. He spent years in England, living in a sumptuously courtly style, waiting for a huge ransom to be collected from his subjects. He was allowed to return to France, leaving hostages, including his son, for his ransom; these hostages broke their parole and returned to France. Deeply humiliated, the King insisted on returning to prison in England, against all the advice of his nobles. Here was a fine sense of that truth and honour which for Chaucer distinguish the Knight, besides the generosity and courtesy which are equally a part of the ideal, and which John had also amply shown. The justification for such a life lies in the ideal of chivalry, an ideal which Richard himself, at the end of his life, claimed he had always followed.

CHIVALRY AND ITS IDEALS

The Golden Age of chivalry was always in the past. The present always sees how miserably the ideal is now betrayed in ordinary daily life. Yet the ideal was real in itself and all knights at least paid it lip-service and often it must have softened and ennobled lives otherwise thoughtless and harsh. And furthermore, though envisaged in the past, it was really creative of the future. Chivalry eventually produced in England one of the most potent ideals of social behaviour that the world has drawn from the West – the ideal of the gentleman. Probably we are seeing, or have already seen, the last age of this ideal, but it still deserves honour. In the fourteenth century it was still

27

maturing, but yet Chaucer conveys much of its essence in his portrait of the Knight in *The General Prologue* to *The Canterbury Tales*.

Chivalry was the code of the knighthood, the armed retainers of great lords, the most important fighting men, who were drawn from the upper classes of society. Since the prime need for any society is to maintain itself, and this can ultimately be done only by force, in the days when force depended largely on personal strength the chief persons in society were those best able to fight by force of arms. In an age of primitive technology the mounted horseman was supreme. Chivalry began in the eleventh century when these rough and violent chieftains and their followers began to be brought to recognise some of the medieval Christian ideals. It developed with the polishing of manners which a slowly improving civilisation made possible, and which borrowed much from the superior civilisation of the Arabs, with whom the West fought so long, especially in Spain. The improvement in manners led to a special conception of love which is the tap-root of our whole idea of romantic love. Personal bravery, Christian faith, polished manners, love: these are the elements of the chivalric ideal – an ideal confined to the knightly class, inappropriate to clerics and peasants.

In the life of the Black Prince, written by his own follower and admirer, Chandos Herald, the two chivalric virtues which are emphasised are bravery and loyalty; and with them go *franchise*, generosity, and pity. In *Sir Gawain and the Green Knight* the virtues of the hero, Gawain, are *franchise*, fellowship, chastity, courtesy and pity. The bravery that men admired was, in our eyes, sometimes a foolhardy recklessness. Sir Ralph Hastings did not value death at two cherries, says Chandos Herald, and Sir William Felton 'the valiant, very boldly and bravely charged among the enemy like a man devoid of sense and discretion'.

The loyalty was usually conceived on an intensely personal level. It might be loyalty to one's lord, though the lower ranks of the people seem to have felt this more than the upper. It might be loyalty to one's friend. We have almost lost the concept of the passionate friendship between men that is part of the basis of *The Knight's Tale*, and which was quite free from perversion. It is said that when Sir John Clanvowe died near Constantinople in 1391, his friend Sir William Neville, another of the Lollard knights, died within two days of grief. Machaut in his *Prise d'Alexandrie* describes how a squire fought over the body of his friend and cousin, for they loved each other and were companions in arms (ll. 5131–3). Even modern war has known such comradeship in plenty. It is curious that the feeling for this kind of attachment has almost completely dropped out of our literature. Another type of loyalty is that of the knight for his lady, which needs fuller discussion later.

Franchise means a manner of well-bred ease and naturalness. It implies self-confidence, and therefore a frank and easy approach to other people. Pity is a virtue obvious in itself; Chandos Herald says that the Black Prince undertook the Spanish campaign out of pity and friendship for the exiled King Peter. One of Chaucer's favourite lines (which he took from Italian poetry) is

> For pitee renneth soone in gentil herte   [*runs*; *noble*
>
> (*The Knight's Tale, CT* I, l. 1761, *The Merchant's Tale, CT* IV, l. 1986,
> *The Squire's Tale; CT* V, l. 479, *Prologue F, The Legend of Good
> Women*, l. 503; cf. *The Man of Law's Tale, CT* II, l. 660)

Pity is the virtuous feeling that Chaucer most often expresses. It had its limitations; Chandos Herald does not tell us, but Froissart does, of the sack of Limoges, when the Black Prince looked on unmoved as men, women, and children were slaughtered on their knees as they besought mercy from the English soldiers. His stern heart was at last melted when he saw three Frenchmen gallantly and desperately defending themselves against a greater number of Englishmen. These fighters he spared.

Generosity again is a self-explanatory virtue, yet even so it had somewhat different aspects. A knight was expected to be without regard for money and possessions:

> Fy on possessioun   [*Fie*
> But if a man be vertuous withal!   [*Unless*
>
> *CT* V, ll. 686–7

says Chaucer's Franklin. Generosity was especially the virtue of a prince, and Edward III and the Black Prince were both models of knighthood in the prodigal way in which they scattered rich gifts among their retainers and friends. Men loved the prince to be magnificent and if he had not been he would have lost their regard. As a result, the treasuries of medieval kings were continually in trouble; Edward bankrupted several great Italian banking houses by not paying what he owed them, and though the Black Prince had enormous revenues he died heavily in debt. (On the other side of the picture it was becoming increasingly possible to make one's fortune at court, and men like Clanvowe, Burley, Sturry, and Chaucer expected personal gain.)

The last virtue was courtesy. In this had once been included all the others, but by the end of the fourteenth century its chief meaning was 'good manners' of the kind that was encouraged by the courtesy books already mentioned. Perhaps the extreme example of the new delicacy of manners that was being slowly developed was Richard's almost unique use of the handkerchief. An earlier example is the Black Prince's insistence on serving King John as a squire after the King had been captured at Poitiers. Courtesy was conceived very much in terms of speech. The knightly and learned educations both emphasised the 'art of speech', which Chaucer refers to, for example, in *The Squire's Tale*. Ability to speak convincingly was continually needed in the courts of law, in diplomacy, in university disputations, in the King's court: but as well as usefulness a grace was sought. Thus when Sir Gawain, hero of the late-fourteenth-century poem, *Sir Gawain and the Green Knight*, reaches a castle, and people learn that he is the Gawain of Arthur's court who is famed for his courtesy – 'Lo, Gawain with his olde courtesie' as Chaucer elsewhere describes him – they rejoice that he will be able to instruct them in the 'stainless terms of noble speech'. Chaucer's perfect knight

> nevere yet no vileynye ne sayde   [*rudeness*
> In all his lyf unto no maner wight.   [*to any kind of person*

And in *The Book of the Duchess* the Black Knight does not fail to praise the *eloquence* of his lady.

The chivalric ideal was not staid. Time and again there is emphasis on joy as one of the supreme qualities or even virtues of courtly knights and ladies. Joy is not so appropriate on the battlefield, though most knights loved fighting. The traditional praise is 'like a lion on the field', but it goes on, 'like a lamb in the hall'. Joy was especially the virtue and the reward of lovers. Chaucer says at the end of the third book of the *Troilus* that he has 'said fully in his song'

> Th'effect and joie of Troilus servise.   [*love*
>
> III, 1815

In the portrait of the lady in *The Book of the Duchess*, which is almost wholly taken from French sources, the lady's gaiety is everywhere praised, and, though care is taken not to make her appear light-minded, 'dulnesse was of hir adrad'. Nothing is more typical of the courtly ideal than the praise of joy; life was so often nasty, brutish and short; youth passed soon; religion was often gloomy and repressive, but even if, as in one of Chaucer's favourite phrases, 'ever the latter end of joy is woe', then at least let joy be gathered while it flowers.

The chivalric and courtly view of life is entirely accepted by Chaucer. He deepens and ennobles the ideal, though he appears not to be much interested in some of the more superficial and popular parts of it, in hunting and sport generally, for example. (In this he shows himself rather similar to Richard, and different from the majority of English people.) But he has no reservations about chivalry. In the *General Prologue* the knightly ideal is split up between two characters, the Knight and the Squire, his son. The Squire represents the more obviously youthful parts of the ideal, the gaiety and fashionableness of courtly life, the bright clothes, the music and poetry, and the interest in love. The Knight represents the deeper moral qualities of the ideal, which the Squire has yet to grow into.

The Knight

> loved chivalrie,
> Trouthe and honour, fredom and curteisie.

'Truth' is one rendering for loyalty, but goes beyond this. It is the supreme virtue of Troilus, Chaucer's own great hero, and implies not only loyalty but a strong personal integrity.

THE LOVE OF LADIES

Romantic love is the abiding interest of medieval secular literature, finding many different forms, and altering the sentiments first of Europe and eventually almost the whole free world down to our own day. In literature a knight is always braver for being in love, though there is very little in the chronicles even of Froissart, and nothing in less gossipy records, to suggest that in actual warfare much account was made of being in love. Yet at least in literature, and eventually perhaps in life, an exalted feminine ideal of the beloved was created, which is beautiful and refreshing. It created the concept of 'the lady', who appears so frequently embodied in Chaucer's heroines, from Blanche the Duchess onwards, and who was surely a potent image in his mind, created by, or for, the ideal of the court. The lady is beautiful, honourable, chaste, educated, eloquent at need, kind, and merciful. She still lives in what is entirely a man's world, and most of her virtues are seen as adaptations of those of the knight. Bravery alone is not required of her. She is passive, not expected to love except after long wooing, and then it is not her love she grants, but her 'pity', her 'mercy'. Rarely is there any sense of equality. The lady is either superior, as in love, or inferior, as in marriage. But her qualified, temporary, and idealised superiority must surely have affected the rough military society and softened and subtilised it. Many of Chaucer's remarks in his poems show that he was conscious of the ladies in his audience, and no doubt their presence encouraged his interest in the personal and private aspects of life, as a female audience always does – witness the history of the novel, which has always relied on women readers for its steady audience. The typically public and impersonal subjects of literature have until recently interested mainly masculine audiences, and where Chaucer deals with such serious subjects directly and explicitly, as in his writings on philosophy, astronomy, and religion, his audience is not essentially courtly.

The ideal of the courtly life was gay, young, passionate, and colourful. Tournaments, dancing, feasts, these are the joys of the court, to which one must add, as is clear from the poetry, hunting, May games, indoor games, and poetry itself.

THE TOURNAMENT

Courtly life achieved its most characteristic expression in the tournament, which lasted until the early seventeenth century as a partly fictional expression of the high ideals of love and bravery, splendour and freedom, untrammelled, though not unconditioned, by utilitarian needs and policies. The tournament was living art, and Chaucer rendered it, as he must have frequently observed it, with keen appreciation. In this respect the often sceptical Chaucer seems to have no reservations. He kept these for the Arthurian myth which Edward III had revived in the middle of the century, and which often underpinned tournaments, as it did the Order of the Garter. Chaucer is sceptical about Arthurian stories, and flippant about the story of Lancelot (which is as true as his own story of cock and fox, he says, *Nun's Priest's Tale, CT*, VII, 3211–13). In this Chaucer is untypical of and in advance of his age.

By the late fourteenth century the tournament had achieved a remarkable balance between 'earnest and game'. It was stylised, usually fought between two knights, though sometimes more, had rules enforced by heralds, and was very much a spectator sport played before huge crowds. It had much of the imitative and fictitious nature of art. Yet it remained dangerous, which kept it thrilling, and it was still quite often used, or attempted to be used, to settle serious issues in a rather archaic way, recalling trial by combat.

The tournament's physical origins were in the twelfth century, as mass mêlées, quite as much practice for war as a sport. The first tournament recorded in England at which ladies were present is one at Staines in 1215, where a lady presented to the winner the prize of a bear. There were literary origins too, in no less a work than Geoffrey of Monmouth's *History of the Kings of Britain* (c. 1135), which so effectively sent the Arthurian story on its way. There ladies are said to reward knights who perform great feats of chivalry for love.

Many examples in the fourteenth century illustrate the mixture of reality and fiction in the tournament. When Edward III began the Hundred Years War in 1337, the French King challenged him to single combat, to decide the issues at stake. It is typical of Edward, and perhaps of the English in general, that although he loved the tournament dearly, and was good at it, he staved off the challenge, and preferred the more realistic methods of pillaging and burning his adversary's lands. During periods of truce in the war the French and English knights sometimes arranged jousts between them. Chaucer's Knight in *The General Prologue* had 'fought for our faith at Tramsyssene three times in the lists, and always killed his foe'. Thus, the so-to-speak practical elements of the tournament still flourished, among all the artificiality and art, as the following examples illustrate.

The tournament could be used to decide an issue of politics or law. An accused knight might appeal to the test of arms to defend his honour. The most celebrated example was when Mowbray accused Hereford (later King Henry IV) of treason. Hereford challenged him, and Richard appointed them to fight it out at a tournament at Conventry, which, as everyone knows from Shakespeare's play, *Richard II*, he cancelled at the very last minute. Sometimes people accused, or accusing others, at Parliament, offered to prove the truth of their assertions with their bodies. When Brembre, the London grocer and capitalist, was accused by the Lords Appellant, he offered to prove his innocence by battle 'as a knight should'. The gages (gauntlets and such) of those who wished to take up his challenge were hurled to the floor like a hail of snow, but politics intervened, and in the end, though the King had spoken for him, he was miserably executed. Sir Simon Burley, in the same crisis, also made the same offer, though just as unsuccessfully. The Savoy knight, Sir Oton de Grandson, 'flower of them that make [i.e. write poetry] in France', as Chaucer calls him, lost his life, when quite an old man, in a tournament that was a judicial duel. In *The Knight's Tale* the tournament seems to be the old fashioned mêlée, but there were plenty of jousts between single knights in Chaucer's day. An adept jouster, like a modern prize-fighter, could make a rich living out of his victories, in which he captured horse and rich armour, as well as valuable prizes. Henry of Lancaster, the foremost baron of his day, and father of Blanche the Duchess whom Gaunt married and Chaucer mourned, wrote a devotional book in French, *Le Livre de Seyntz Medecines*, in which he casually remarks that you can tell a man who has been in tournaments by the way his nose is knocked about. There are plenty of cases of knights being fatally wounded in jousts. In such cases the survivor often thought it best to flee, in case he should be imprisoned for murder. Nevertheless the imaginative power of the joust was great. Chaucer's great contemporary, William Langland, a clerical, non-courtly writer, takes the joust as the imaginative base for the greatest episode in *Piers Plowman*, when Christ comes to the Crucifixion as knight to the tournament, dressed in the armour of human nature, to joust with the devil for Christian souls. Chaucer is more realistic, his imagination less creative of myth. Yet the tournament itself, as Froissart shows, in ordinary life, had much of the nature of art and fiction.

The most famous tournament in England in Chaucer's time was the great jousting held in Smithfield in 1390. Chaucer did not turn his back on this, for he was Clerk of the King's Works at the time, and was responsible for putting up the scaffolding; but he left no description. Froissart tells us about it. Heralds had published the festival throughout England, Scotland, Germany, Flanders, Brabant, Hainault, and France, and a number of foreign knights came. It began about three in the afternoon of Sunday, 2 October, when sixty squires of honour rode sixty war-horses out of the Tower of London. Then followed sixty ladies, richly dressed, riding side-saddle (a fashion said to have been brought to England by Richard's Queen Anne) and each lady leading with a silver chain a knight armed in tilting armour. Accompanied by many trumpeters and minstrels, they rode through the city to Smithfield, where the King and Queen and many ladies waited in richly decorated rooms. The ladies then took their places with the spectators, the knights were mounted and had their helmets laced on, and the jousting began, continuing till it was too dark to see. Prizes were given, and they all had supper at the Bishop of London's palace, where the King and Queen were staying, and the 'goodly dancing' continued till dawn. All this was joyous sport and art, with no need for utilitarian justification.

On the next day, says Froissart, you could see many squires and attendants of the knights going about London with armour, and doing other business. This reminds one of the much more vivid passage in *The Knight's Tale* (ll. 2491–521) about the lords on their coursers, squires nailing the spears, buckling the helms, putting straps on the shields; armourers bustling to and fro with file and hammer; yeomen and common people going about with their thick staves; and everyone speculating on the chances of the champions. In his description of the fighting Chaucer says that when Theseus decides that the tournament shall be fought with blunted weapons, to save the loss of noble life, the people praise him (a detail which Chaucer took from Boccaccio) but it seems more likely that the usual sentiments of the crowd were more bloodthirsty. Thus fiction and reality overlap in that act of imagination which is the attraction of all sport.

MUSIC IN COURT

The court was a place of music and Chaucer's poetry is not just musical in itself but full of references to music. From the time that Chaucer became a page he would have had occasion to hear, and probably sing, certainly to write, songs to entertain the company.

Music for Chaucer is 'heavenly'.

All educated people seem to have had some ability at music, though medieval music was so difficult to read that they must always have played and sung by ear alone. There are frequent references in Chaucer's poetry to ladies playing music, while the Squire was singing or playing the flute all day. Not only was the Squire a beautifully dressed young man, and a good soldier and jouster; not only could he write and draw; he could also compose poetry and write the music to it. This was the normal courtly ideal, as we see from several knights and squires in Chaucer's poetry, and also from what we know of such a man as the third Earl of Salisbury. Richard II himself wrote songs, though none of them has survived. That great soldier and courtier, Henry of Lancaster, says that from his lips have come many love-songs which have often drawn him and others to sin. Chaucer makes the same confession at the end of *The Canterbury Tales*. One of the noticeable things about *The General Prologue* is the number of times music and especially singing are mentioned.

In Chaucer's works, as we may suppose was largely true of the court, music is mainly festive and social, associated with warm feelings, especially love and joy. The great music of the time was religious, and the greatest European musician was none other than Machaut, but the English court seems not much interested in religious music and no great musicians are found in England until the fifteenth century.

FEASTING

The glamour of courtly life was embodied in many other forms. Feasting in company often provided the focus, because food and drink may not only be delicious in themselves but also symbolise loving fellowship, common interests, stability. Feasts at great religious festivals emphasise spiritual truths. Feasts mark the passage of the seasons. By ingesting food and drink we symbolically absorb and control the world. Order and happiness are seen and felt to prevail.

Feasts were accompanied by music from minstrel bands, playing wind and stringed instruments and various kinds of drums. Entertainments like masques (sometimes called 'mummings' or 'interludes') were played, with fancy dress and sometimes with very elaborate scenery. The food was in vast quantities and very elaborately dressed, often with ornate if ephemeral table decorations made of paper painted by talented artists and adorned with verses, called 'subtleties'. After the feasts came more music and much dancing, where saucy or loving looks were interchanged between knights and ladies.

LITERATURE

Somewhere among all this, or more likely scattered everywhere, was what we call 'literature'. The word perhaps gives too formal a notion. There were songs in plenty on all sorts of occasions as already noted. The 'interludes' and 'mummings' had speeches (Chaucer's follower, the monk and author Lydgate, wrote a 'Mumming'). Minstrels may have told romances to small groups, for some romances represent themselves, truly or not, as being told by a minstrel to a listening group. As will be noted later, squires were expected to 'occupy the court' with stories or readings from chronicles. Small groups of ladies were probably read to as they sewed, and in *Troilus* Book II Chaucer shows Criseyde and her ladies being read to in her parlour. The famous frontispiece to the Corpus Christi Manuscript of *Troilus* shows Chaucer himself reading from a pulpit in a garden to the young king and queen and a group of brightly clad courtiers. This is probably an idealised view of the past, since it was painted about 1415, thirty years after the poem was written, but it gives something that is genuinely in the 'feel' of the poem as written for and perhaps delivered to an interested group of courtiers, young knights and ladies, including the young king and queen, older men, scholars and lawyers, representing many different kinds of interests but united in loyalty to courtly ideals.

OUT-OF-DOORS

Most courtiers probably spent much of their time out-of-doors. Although the tournament represents the out-of-doors quintessence of the courtly life, an even more frequent activity, passionately pursued by most men, was hunting. Even ladies might go hunting with hawks. For men were reserved the even more exhilarating joys of the chase after fox and deer, and after the more dangerous boar, which had to be killed by the thrust of a spear at close quarters. Beyond the intrinsic physical pleasure of exercise, hunting, like eating, is a way of symbolically and actually controlling the world while being a part of it. The royal passion for hunting caused great forests to be turned into game reserves. The laws protecting the king's forests inflicted cruel punishments on those who infringed them. The paradoxical sympathy between hunter and hunted has often been noted – they share the same carnal nature. The delights of the hunt are vividly portrayed in the contemporary poem *Sir Gawain and the Green Knight*, but Chaucer himself shows little interest in the hunt. In his first poem,

The Book of the Duchess, he represents himself going off to join the hunt, but he soon wanders away on his own, eventually to find the Man in Black in the depths of the forest lamenting the death of his beloved.

CHAUCER'S REPRESENTATION OF COURTLY LIFE

Though Chaucer vividly represents the lively surface of life, he soon turns, especially in his earlier poems, to the inner life of feeling and personal relationships. He was not entirely typical – what great poet could be? – of the general traits and interests of the ordinary run of people, for all his capacity for sympathising with them. Nevertheless, since he was orthodox rather than rebellious, wise as well as cynical, he makes an extraordinarily good spokesman for the court culture of Richard's reign, and for chivalry as it was then understood. To anticipate for a moment his later life, we may say that the whole body of his work, but above all *The Knight's Tale*, is the greatest document of courtly and knightly values in this period. In *The Knight's Tale* we find the court as the centre of the kingdom, with its concerns for war and justice, but also its leisure, its delight in hunting and tournament. The younger people are chiefly concerned with love and war, but Theseus, the wise king, and his father, can make a sober assessment of the whole of life. Religion, philosophy and science find a place in controlling and interpreting the harsh chances of life. For all the splendours of the court, the raptures of love, and the glories of martial success, much, perhaps most of life, is hard, and there is plenty of suffering. *The Knight's Tale* is a sympathetic poem, but it contains also a note of stern resignation, and a resolute will 'to make a virtue of necessity' as Theseus says. It also occasionally sounds a note of flippant hardness which is one of Chaucer's most constant though intermittent features, and which is very difficult to describe in modern terms, because it lies alongside, yet does not, as one might have thought, cancel out, the positive ideals, values and sympathies. Even when we have made allowance for Chaucer's remarkable genius, we must agree that the court culture which could help to produce such a body of writings which so variously blend love and loyalty and gaiety, bravery and pity, *franchise*, generosity, and courtesy, philosophical and worldly wit and wisdom, was one of the great achievements in the history of English culture.

CHAUCER'S EXPERIENCE OF WAR

The sober hardness and stoic acceptance of pain that underlie *The Knight's Tale* also recall us to the facts of Chaucer's own experience of courtly life. We see him as a page in 1357. In 1359–60 he was taking part in a military campaign. Men usually 'took arms' about the age of twenty or twenty-one, and Chaucer in later life gave evidence in the Scrope-Grosvenor lawsuit that it was in this campaign that he himself took arms, so we may suppose him to have been about twenty in 1359–60. He went as a *valettus* or 'yeoman', probably in the contingent led by Lionel, husband of Chaucer's 'lady', the Countess Elizabeth of Ulster, and was paid sixpence a day.

The campaign was rather miserable. It began in autumn 1359, and various delays caused trouble with mercenaries over rations. The vast army moved slowly, and the rain was almost continuous. The army reached Rheims by 4 December and besieged but could not take the town. At some stage after 11 January Chaucer was captured by the enemy. In the negotiations after the end of the campaign, in March 1360, Chaucer was ransomed by the king – in actual fact, of course, through the office of the king's court, not by personal intervention – for £16. Various other *valetti* were ransomed for £10, a chaplain for £8. John de Burley received for his horse £20, and Robert de Clynton £16 14s. for his. Later in the year Chaucer was still in Duke Lionel's service, as can be told from the Duke's expense book; and during the peace negotiations he went back to France, on his return carrying letters from Calais to England. This was perhaps the first of his many journeys in a position of trust, or he may simply have acted as a courier.

1360 marks a stage in Chaucer's career. He had entered the court and seen something of its glamour. He had been blooded and seen something of the splendour and horror and boredom of war. He was about to become a working courtier, and he was surely known as a promising poet. Before turning to his more specifically literary background we may well sum up what sort of person he was by quoting his own description of the Squire in *The Canterbury Tales*. Of course, Chaucer was not the son of a knight. But he was certainly page and perhaps squire in one of the greatest households of England. He had been in 'chivachye' in Flanders, Artois and Picardy; he certainly was a rhymer; and many young men of his age have been in love. Chaucer's picture of the Squire is an idealised one, and not consciously a self-portrait. But it describes the type of young man superbly well, and Chaucer must have been such another. We are hardly likely to get nearer to a description of the young Chaucer than this:

a yong Squier,

A lovyere and a lusty bacheler,	[*young knight*
With lokkes crulle as they were leyd in presse.	[*curled*
Of twenty yeer of age he was, I gesse.	
Of his stature he was of evene lengthe,	
And wonderly delyvere, and of greet strengthe.	[*nimble*
And he hadde been somtyme in chyvachie	
In Flaundres, in Artoys, and Pycardie,	
And born hym weel, as of so litel space,	
In hope to stonden in his lady grace.	
Embrouded was he, as it were a meede	[*embroidered*; *meadow*
Al ful of fresshe floures, whyte and reede.	
Syngynge he was, or floytynge, al the day;	
He was as fressh as is the month of May.	
Short was his gowne, with sleves longe and wyde.	
Wel koude he sitte on hors and faire ryde.	
He koude songes make and wel endite,	[*write*
Juste and eek daunce, and weel purtreye and write.	[*joust*; *draw*
So hoote he lovede that by nyghtertale	[*night-time*
He sleep namoore than dooth a nyghtyngale.	
Curteis he was, lowely, and servysable,	
And carf biforn his fader at the table.	

General Prologue, 79–100

Chapter 4

THE ENGLISH AND EUROPEAN LITERARY TRADITIONS

EARLY READING

What had Chaucer been reading as a boy and young man? Youthful reading is the seedsowing time of the mind, and Chaucer was obviously an avid reader. The reading which made the deepest impression on him, most attracted his imagination, and formed his intellectual habits, can be traced partly from its effects, and partly from his own references.

THE ENGLISH ROMANCES

The earliest impression was that made by English romances. We can detect their influence in Chaucer's earliest poem, *The Book of the Duchess*, at the least conscious level, the minor points of style. The first fifteen lines of that poem are translated from a poem by Froissart. But the translation is full of the tags of the fourteenth-century English rhyming romances; *be this lyght, day ne nyght, wel nygh noght, by my trouthe, cometh or gooth, leef nor looth, joye or sorowe*. The phrases make the style lively, emphatic, dramatic, with doublets and alternatives, mild oaths, expletives. In other words, the style is that of oral delivery, real or imitated. It buttonholes the reader with its direct, informal intimacy, its conversational, personal ease. At once a relationship is created between poet and audience or reader. It is in one sense a climax of the earlier minstrel style, but here the minstrel is the poet himself.

We may imagine him listening when younger to narrative poems, perhaps read to the family at home from such a book as the large Auchinleck manuscript, (now in the National Library of Scotland), which among over fifty separate items, almost all in English, contains eighteen romances. These account for three-quarters of the surviving bulk of the manuscript (and what has been lost is mostly texts of romance). This big book, produced around 1330–40 by a London bookshop, for just such an audience as wealthy merchants, contains many other items which would have influenced Chaucer; the four saints' lives, the fifteen varied religious and didactic pieces, and the five humorous or satiric pieces. It has been argued that Chaucer knew this very volume. Whether he did or not, it is a true 'Gothic' miscellany of the very type of *The Canterbury Tales*.

The English romances are usually written in tail-rhyme, that is, of stanzas of around twelve four-stress, eight-syllabled lines, rhyming, and each stanza concluding with a two-syllable, one-stress phrase, the tail-ryhme itself. They tell stirring stories of virtuous, often patriotic, heroes who fight evil and win a bride and a kingdom. The stories are essentially folktales, to be associated with fairytales, or the cinema's early Westerns. The clear favourite is *Guy of Warwick*, which has versions in short couplets (like *The Book of the Duchess*) as well as in tail-rhyme. A very typical shorter example is the tale of *Sir Degaré*, where the hero, abandoned in childhood, almost marries his unknown mother, and has to discover his father. Romances such as these were popular until the seventeenth century.

These archetypal stories, often slackly written, came to seem as ridiculous to Chaucer as they do to most moderns. As usual he was *avant-garde* for his age, and untypical in some of his tastes. He mocked them cruelly in *The Canterbury Tales* by the comic parody *Sir Thopas*, but it is quite significant that he attributes this tale to himself as one of the pilgrims. The self-mockery has a real basis in his actual origins, as well as in his character.

FRENCH POETRY

Chaucer grew and developed from the English romances under powerful influences of a very different kind. At some depth was the complex of underlying new sensibilities like those related to the study of arithmetic, as already described, but more obvious, and more immediately useful, was his knowledge of French poetry – poetry of Paris.

There are two main sources which strike us particularly when considering Chaucer's early reading. The first is *Le Roman de la Rose*, and the second is the poems by Machaut. Other poems and poets there were, like the love-visions which derive from *Le Roman de la Rose*, and the poems of his contemporaries Froissart and

Deschamps, who followed Machaut. There were manuscript anthologies of French poetry which must have been known to him. It has been argued that his own earliest poems were written in French, and there is a collection of poems in French by 'Ch' which could be attributed to him. Other English courtiers and Gower, as already noted, wrote poetry in French. But the only early poems which are certainly by Chaucer are imitations of the French, like *The Complaint unto Pity*, and such translations as *The Romaunt of the Rose* and *An ABC*.

LE ROMAN DE LA ROSE

The English *Romaunt of the Rose*, which survives in only one manuscript, is a fragment of some 7,500 octosyllabic lines, of which probably only the first 1,705 lines are Chaucer's. This English *Romaunt* is a translation of parts of the French *Le Roman de la Rose*, one of the great formative books of the Middle Ages. More than 200 French manuscripts of the *Roman*, besides translations into other European languages, and twenty-one early printed editions, bear witness to its enormous popularity. It was at the well-head of the tradition in which Machaut, Deschamps and Froissart wrote. And although Chaucer actually translated very little of its more than 20,000 lines, he knew the whole poem extremely well. It permeated his thought so deeply that his later works reveal its influence even more profoundly than his early poems.

The *Roman* was written by two authors as different as chalk from cheese. Guillaume de Lorris wrote the delightful first part of some 4,000 lines, about the year 1225. The poem tells how the narrator fell asleep and dreamt it was the sweetest of May mornings. Wandering by a clear river, he came to a beautiful Garden 'from whose walls sorrow flies far', whose gate was kept by Idleness, and whose lord was Mirth, and from which everything old, ugly, poor and vicious was excluded. Within this garden of youthful delights the Dreamer eventually saw the Rose, and as he looked, the arrows of Cupid, the god of love, struck him again and again. But the Rose (a lady's love) was defended by thorns, by guardians such as Modesty and Rebuff (*Daunger*). Furthermore, the Lady Reason, who had been created in Paradise by God himself, attempted to dissuade the Dreamer from trying to win the Rose at all.

Guillaume did not finish his poem. It was finished some fifty years later by Jean de Meung, whose nickname, 'Le Clopinel', the Hobbler, not unaptly suggests his difference from Guillaume. Jean took over the machinery of the poem to convey a great quantity of very various matter; philosophy, science, nature poetry, controversy and satire of all kinds, but especially of women. It was this huge addition of Jean's that caused the *Roman* to be sometimes cited in the fourteenth century as a satire against love, notwithstanding its beginning.

The whole poem is a Gothic poetic encyclopaedia. It set or reinforced the fashion for several important literary traditions. The device of the dream, the artificially bright May morning, the lovely Garden representing the youthful view of the joyous world, the allegorical framework, as well as many individual types and comments, from Guillaume's first part, all appear again and again in later poetry. Guillaume's poem sets out the 'law of love'. His god of love is the medieval Cupid, no fat, blind, naked infant, but a princely youth who hunts men. The lover receives his code from the god, and learns that nobility must derive from virtue, not from lineage; that he must always be faithful; always fashionable though not extravagant in dress; accomplished in both manly and artistic exercises. In a word, he must be a gentleman in every respect, with his teeth as unstained as his honour. For the practice of these virtues the lover is promised the highest joys and bitterest sorrows that life can offer.

Even in Guillaume, however, love has an antagonist, the Lady Reason, who descends from her tower to defend Chastity and to argue against the dictates of Cupid. Guillaume makes her arguments seem cold and merely prudential, and we sympathise with the lover's rejection of them. But the conflict is deep at the heart of love as seen by the medieval poets, and it is by no means certain that Guillaume himself would have been finally on Cupid's side. The antithesis between the service of love and the service of God was clear, and always profoundly felt. There is no doubt that Chaucer also felt it.

Jean de Meung's addition, swollen and inconsistent as it is, contributed as much or more to the poem's reputation as Guillaume's beginning. In both parts the ideal of love is less intense than the feudal aristocratic tradition of Provence from which it derives, in which the lady was worshipped almost as a goddess. But it was perhaps largely due to Jean that later poets felt there was nothing strange in using the device of a love story to treat all kinds of philosophical and scientific matter in poetry. The habit of mind by which all subjects may be gathered in under one heading of love is aptly summed up in the words of Thomas Middleton as late as 1623:

> Love has an intellect that runs through all
> The scrutinous sciences, and like a cunning poet
> Catches a quantity of every knowledge
> Yet brings all home into one mystery,
> Into one secret, that he proceeds in.

The Changeling, Act III, Sc. 3

43

The scientific and philosophical aspects of Jean's addition were well calculated to stimulate Chaucer's already awakened interest and new sensibility towards intellectual questions. The new urban spirit breathes through this work from Paris.

Jean's work includes much more in its Gothic miscellaneity, some of it highly traditional. There is the clerical satire of women, which goes back for many centuries, and also the more rollicking rough derision of women found in popular folktale, which probably goes back to the beginning of the human race.

Parts of Boethius's *Consolation of Philosophy*, and Ovid's story of Pygmalion, are translated in the *Roman*. Jean also partly translates the twelfth-century Latin *Complaint of Nature* to create an image of fecund Nature, a goddess who urges both sexes to vigorous promiscuity in order to people the world. She has something of the power of myth. Jean's bold sophistry brings the whole poem to a remarkable ending in which he allegorically portrays, with a touch of humour, and without much concealment, the climax of sexual intercourse.

MACHAUT

The tradition of European love-poetry became exceedingly rich and varied by the fourteenth century. It was not so much a river as a whole series of rivers flowing in the same direction but each with a somewhat different course and character. Medieval romantic love certainly cannot be summed up as always adulterous, courteous, parodic of religion, joyous. It was all these things at times. It was also tender, pious, violent, tragic. Much of its charm lies in the different forms of story and song that it takes at different periods with different authors. It is less often nowadays called 'courtly love', a term invented by nineteenth-century scholars. We should rather call it romantic love, or use the term often mentioned in its own day, *fine amour*, 'refined love', which hits off its essential element and distinguishes it from simple sexual passion.

Machaut (*c*. 1300–77) who was the leading musician of his day was also the leading poet of France (which was at that time made up of several kingdoms) and a major influence on Chaucer. He was nominally a cleric, yet he led the adventurous, amorous, much-travelled life of a courtier, indebted to various kings for patronage and for the conferment of well-paid benefices of which he was an absentee incumbent. He wrote many poems developing the tradition of love, and two debate-poems, the *Jugement du Roi de Behaigne* and the *Jugement du Roi de Navarre* which much influenced Chaucer. *Behaigne* presents a debate between a sorrowful knight and an equally sorrowful lady, who meet by accident in a forest. The lady's own knight is dead; while the lady of the knight in the forest has betrayed him. They debate as to whose plight is worse, and go to Jean of Luxembourg, King of Bohemia (Machaut's current patron) for a decision. He decides that the knight suffers more. Although the situation is set up artificially, the human problems are real and painful. The artificiality distances but does not trivialise them. Machaut has some delicacy of perception and an extraordinarily copious style. This may make him seem tedious now; it must have been a wonderful stimulus to the imagination of one brought up on the much barer style of English lyrics, or the colloquial clichés of the English romances. Close but not slavish imitation of *Behaigne* gave Chaucer the basic structure and much of the very phraseology for his much subtler *Book of the Duchess*. Both poems indicate by their fictional characters real people without being allegorical in any strict sense.

The other poem by Machaut, *Le Jugement du Roi de Navarre*, is notable for its prologue of 458 lines in which the poet tells of the horror he felt, shut up for safety in his own room, during the plague at Rheims, where he was a canon, and where he resided during Edward III's siege of 1359–60, when Chaucer was outside the walls. Most fourteenth-century European poets introduce themselves into some of their own poems. Guillaume virtually does so in *Le Roman de la Rose*; Dante is the most famous example; Machaut, Deschamps, Froissart follow suit, and all the major English poets, Langland, Gower, the *Pearl*-poet, and some minor poets, like Lydgate and Hoccleve, do the same. The poet-in-the-poem may be said to be a characteristically Gothic frame-breaking device, for he is both in and out of the picture. In the poem he is not quite literally his entire 'real' self, yet he is not entirely fictional. Such a personage is sometimes called the 'Narrator', and so he is, but the term is misleading if it implies a character entirely 'inside' the poem, unrelated to a genuine autobiographical 'outside' reality. Machaut illustrates this in *Navarre*. He was really in Rheims, as he writes in the poem, but when he describes himself going into the forest and having a dispute with a lady called 'Happiness' (*Bonneurté*), he slides into fiction. Yet the fiction was probably based on real situations and debates, for the lady in the poem accuses the judgement in the previous poem, *Behaigne*, of being unfair to woman. She probably represents actual criticisms made to Machaut in real life. Chaucer was influenced by this characteristically Gothic shifting point-of-view created by the poet's variable *persona* in the poem. He developed the device of the *persona* in his own way very elaborately and fluidly.

OTHER READING AND INFLUENCES

Chaucer's earliest work might almost be described in horse-breeding terms as by Machaut out of the English romances, but that would weaken the sense of other greatly varied resources acquired and poured into the prepared mould of English language and literature. We have so far concentrated on those literary influences which came to him through living how and when he did, in an English upper-class family and in an Anglo-French court culture. Not to be forgotten are the formally learnt Latin school-texts, which made him not only an educated man but a poet. Virgil may have given him some sense of the dignity and gravity which great poetry could aspire to, and which he mentions at the end of *Troilus*, where he places himself quite consciously in the great line of

Virgile, Ovide, Omer, Lucan and Stace

V, 1792

Of the poets mentioned besides Virgil, he could only have read Homer in a brief poor Latin summary, and he was relying rather on his great reputation, than on direct knowledge. Lucan and Statius were well-known Silver Latin poets of elaborately rich style with valuable material. Ovid was the favourite, as he was of almost everybody, read at school and cherished throughout life. Ovid, though a classical writer, enshrines a very medieval ideal of writing. He is full of matter, mythological, historical, amorous, personal, comic, pathetic. His style is richly rhetorical. He can be ironical, and in his *Ars Amatoria* is sexually very explicit. He also condemns love in his *Remedia Amoris*. Lively and various, he provides something for everyone. In his *Heroides*, a series of poems purporting to be letters from ladies betrayed by their lovers, wittily written but full of genuine pathos and sympathy for women, he touched a note which Chaucer responded to in various ways from *The Book of the Duchess* through *Troilus* to *The Legend of Good Women*, many of whose heroines are based on Ovid's poems. The sadness of betrayal in personal relationships, and of death, which is the greatest betrayal, imaged in these stories, corresponds to some deep sense of loss in Chaucer himself, which he managed finally to express and purge only in middle life.

Finally, one must recall the devotionally religious element in the early influences on Chaucer. On the basis of all those prayers learnt at school and home was built a series of devotional works, saint's lives and sermons, which found incidental expression in many poems, and more explicitly in such major Canterbury tales as *The Man of Law's Tale* of Constance, *The Clerk's Tale* of Patient Griselda, *The Second Nun's Tale* of Cecilia, *The Prioress's Tale*, and the moralising prose tracts *Melibeus* and *The Parson's Tale*. At this early stage in

Chaucer's life the vein of devotion is represented by the translation from French, *An ABC*, a devout poem to the Virgin Mary, elaborate, pious, sentimental, metrically very adept. Probably he also tried his hand at prose, but no early prose survives. It would have been practical utilitarian devotional or scientific prose. English prose was becoming an instrument for fictional entertainment during Chaucer's own lifetime in the *Travels* of Sir John Mandeville, but this was an historical spoof of a kind which somehow seems quite alien to Chaucer.

Chapter 5

A WORKING COURTIER AND
THE BOOK OF THE DUCHESS

A SIX-YEAR GAP IN THE RECORDS

In October 1360 Chaucer had been paid by Lionel, Earl of Ulster, for bringing letters from Calais to England. The next record is for 22 February 1366. It is a safe-conduct for Chaucer and three companions to travel in the kingdom of Navarre, the Basque country, which lay over the Pyrenees between Aquitaine, held by the English, and the Spanish kingdoms of Castile and Aragon. During these six years Chaucer presumably continued at least at first at Lionel's court. He was reading widely, and probably writing. At some time he started translating *Le Roman de la Rose*, and may have written a number of lyrics of the type he could have learnt from Machaut. What else did he do?

WAS CHAUCER AT THE INNER TEMPLE?

A comment by Thomas Speght in his edition of Chaucer published in 1598, gives us a clue. Speght says that Master Buckley, who was probably the same Buckley whose duty it was at that time to preserve the records of the law school called the Inner Temple, 'did see a Record in the same house (i.e. the Inner Temple) where Geoffrey Chaucer was fined two shillings for beating a Fransiscane fryer in Fleetstreete'. There seems no particular reason for disbelieving the record, though all the actual documents for that period have been lost and one cannot be certain.

It is likely enough that Chaucer was a lively even passionate young man, and his works bear no signs of love for friars, Franciscan or otherwise. The incident suggests the vitality and assertiveness which the poetry demonstrates, but which Chaucer's mocking presentation of himself in later life as plump and easily put down may make us forget.

The suggestion that he attended the Inner Temple is most attractive. It provides another instalment of the secular, liberal, intellectual education that his works at their best illustrate. His presence at the Inner Temple would also at least in part account for his absence from court records, though as these are also incomplete the argument is not conclusive.

In the administration of the country men trained in law were beginning to compete with the clerics, and several of Chaucer's companions had had this training. A young man ambitious of distinction in civil life would find a desirable and usual education in one of the Inns of Court, for Oxford and Cambridge prepared a man mainly for holy orders. The account nearest to the Temple training of Chaucer's own day is given by Sir John Fortescue, whose own legal training began in 1414 in Lincoln's Inn. If a training similar to this was not actually Chaucer's, it was at least that of many men known to him. Students first entered an Inn of Chancery, about the age of sixteen. Here they studied the first principles of law, and after two years entered an Inn of Court. Fortescue writes:

> Of these greater inns there are four in number, and some two hundred students belong in the aforementioned form to the least of them. In these greater inns, no student could be maintained on less expense than £13 6s.8d a year, and if he had servants to himself alone, as the majority have, then he will by so much the more bear expenses. Because of this costliness, there are not many who learn the laws in the inns except the sons of nobles. For poor and common people cannot bear so much cost for the maintenance of their sons. And merchants rarely desire to reduce their stock by such annual burdens. Hence it comes about that there is scarcely a man learned in the laws to be found in the realm, who is not noble or sprung of noble lineage. ... In these greater inns, indeed, and also in the lesser, there is, besides a school of law, a kind of academy of all the manners that the nobles learn. There they learn to sing and to exercise themselves in every kind of harmonics. They are also taught there to practise dancing and all games proper for nobles, as those brought up in the king's household are accustomed to practise. In the vacations most of them apply themselves to the study of legal science, and at festivals to the reading, after the divine services, of Holy Scripture and of chronicles. This is indeed a cultivation of virtues and a banishment of all vice.

(Sir John Fortescue, *De Laudibus Legum Anglie*, edited and translated by S.B. Chrimes, 1942, pp. 117–19)

This is an idealised account, but it shows what was expected of an upper-class legal education. There is a good deal in Chaucer's career to accord with it. His family were well-to-do, and their connection with the court may have made them ambitious for their son, as is suggested by his position as page to the Countess Elizabeth. John Chaucer, as one of the leading merchants in the City, could afford to give his son this expensive education. A legal training would have been exceedingly valuable to Chaucer in the many official positions he filled later in life.

Training in law was also training for a court career. The king's court itself, as already noted, was producing administrative departments for the whole kingdom, unconsciously breaking away from feudalism. A great historian of the fourteenth century has summed up Chaucer's position in this development:

> There was an increasing tendency towards the building up of a homogeneous civil service within which circulation was unrestricted, and whereby a permanent career was more easily obtainable in the service of the state. Particularly noticeable was the tendency towards making the posts of the [royal] household the training ground of professional politicians. Even when dwelling in the king's court, these men were more than courtiers, and, on obtaining political charges, they showed that it was possible to combine their duty to the crown with general sympathy with the episcopal and baronial tradition of independent watchfulness of royal action. When the court officers did not rise to this higher level, they remained personally insignificant, and left little mark on history. Though anti-clericalism as a principle was no longer prominent, there remained a career for lay as well as for clerical talent. This was the inevitable result of the extension of education to circles outside the clerical sphere. There was the education of the court, which made the *miles literatus*, the knight who knew Latin, no longer a rare or an extraordinary phenomenon, as he had been in the reign of Henry III. How far a court training could under Edward III give a thorough culture to men, originating in the middle class of townsmen, and so remote from the clerical profession that the university had nothing to say to them, can well be illustrated by the career of that eminent civil servant, Geoffrey Chaucer. But a highly educated layman, like Chaucer, was still the exception in courtly circles. The real source of the destruction of the clerical monopoly of office was to be found in the excellent education which the law schools of London now gave to the common lawyers.

(T.F. Tout, *Chapters in the Administrative History of Medieval England*, Longmans, 1928, vol. iii, pp. 201–2)

It is quite likely that Chaucer was both a lawyer and a *miles literatus*, a 'literate knight', though he never, unlike many of his friends, took knighthood.

WAS CHAUCER IN AQUITAINE?

The safe-conduct through the kingdom of Navarre in 1366 does nevertheless raise most interesting possibilities of experience for Chaucer much closer to knighthood than any legal Inn of Court. The reason why he was travelling through Navarre is not given. That he had three unnamed companions suggests that he was the senior. Such a group was more likely to be on some diplomatic mission than on a pilgrimage. There is no record of his being sent from any English court, but there was no need for him to be, since there was a major and magnificent English court at Bordeaux, that of the Black Prince, no less. The Prince was continuously in Aquitaine in the 1360s, conducting intermittent warfare with the French, who claimed the sovereignty of Aquitaine. The English had a particular interest in the kingdom of Castile, which bordered Navarre. If Castile were allied with France it could send its highly efficient navy to harry English shipping in the Channel and attack English south-coast towns. The king of Castile from 1350 to 1369 was Don Pedro. He was known to his enemies as Pedro the Cruel, but Chaucer calls him the noble, worthy Pedro, glory of Spain (*Monk's Tale, CT* VII, 2375). He favoured the English, so they supported him. In 1367 he was dethroned by his half-brother Henry of Trastamara, supported by the French. The Black Prince therefore in the same year invaded Spain with a large army and won the great battle of Najera, which enabled Pedro to regain his throne. He was murdered two years later.

Chaucer would have missed Najera because by 1367 he had become a *valectus* of King Edward III in London, but he could well have been previously a member of the Black Prince's household in Bordeaux, for his earlier lady, the Countess of Ulster, had died in 1363. Several of Chaucer's later friends and associates, especially among the Lollard knights (to be mentioned later) had been knights of the Black Prince and had seen action in Aquitaine and Spain. Most prominent of these was Sir Lewis Clifford, a very distinguished man, a friend of Chaucer's, who once carried a poem from the French poet Deschamps to Chaucer complimenting him on being noble, learned, wise and a great translator. Another was Sir Thomas Latimer, and another was Sir William Beauchamp who became Captain of Calais. Chaucer may have first come across these men when serving with them in Aquitaine. Moreover, Chaucer was married by 1366 to Philippa, who was the daughter of Sir Giles (otherwise Payne) Roet, who was a herald and King of Arms for Aquitaine.

It would seem a fair guess, therefore, that between 1360 and 1366 Chaucer passed a year or years, in Aquitaine, associated with the Black Prince's household, and that in February 1366, when he was certainly in Navarre, he was engaged in some diplomatic mission, probably between the courts of the Black Prince and Pedro of Castile. He made many such diplomatic journeys in later life.

CHAUCER'S WIFE PHILIPPA

Philippa Chaucer is first recorded as receiving an annual salary of ten marks (£6 13s.4d.), for being one of the Queen's ladies-in-waiting, on 12 September 1366. The date of Chaucer's marriage to Philippa is not known. She was herself a working court-lady. When Edward III's Queen Philippa died in 1369 Chaucer's wife became lady-in-waiting to John of Gaunt's second wife Constance, who was daughter of Pedro of Castile, and who after his death claimed his throne. Philippa's younger sister Katharine, widow of Sir Hugh Swynford since 1372, was also a lady-in-waiting to Constance, and became John of Gaunt's acknowledged mistress, for his second marriage was purely political. She bore him several children and on Constance's death in 1396 married him, thus scandalising the great ladies of court. They did not object to his having a mistress, but they did object to the social implications of his marrying his concubine, daughter of a plain knight. These subtleties of conventional morality are worth bearing in mind when we read the love-affairs in Chaucer's poems. The poems' own morality is not simple.

Philippa besides her salary received various gifts from Gaunt, such as his New Year gifts in 1380, 1381, 1382, of a silver cup. She received her last payment on 18 June 1387 and probably died soon after this. Nothing is known of the family life of Geoffrey and Philippa, except that they were often necessarily separated by their work. Chaucer tends to make jokes about marriage and in the late poem to Bukton refers jestingly to his own freedom – his wife being dead. He may well have been a trying husband, with his love-poetry and all. We do not know. His marriage was long-lasting, and jokes at the expense of wives and marriage are traditional and popular among men. Thomas Chaucer, who became wealthy and distinguished in the fifteenth century, was one of their sons. 'Little Lewis' for whom Chaucer wrote his *Treatise on the Astrolabe* was presumably another, but has left no further trace. No other children are known. The gifts received by Philippa, and others that Chaucer received from Gaunt either jointly with her, or separately, are no evidence of special favour from him. They were part of the general system of normal remuneration, where wages were still partly in kind, in the form of food, drink, clothes and valuables.

WORKING IN THE KING'S COURT

From 1367 to 1369 both Chaucer and his wife were occupied in the royal household, with a modest but sufficient income. By 1368

Chaucer had become an Esquire of the King's Household. It was an age before personal service had come to be thought degrading, and his occupations varied between making beds and going on important ambassadorial messages. He remained an esquire at least till 1378, perhaps later, and doubtless there was more bedmaking in the first year of his appointment than in the last. But it was not a job which the well-born despised. We get most of our information about it from Edward IV's fifteenth-century Household Book which was based on earlier ordinances. There were four 'valecti' or 'Yeoman of Chambre', and they had to

> make beddis, to beare or hold torches, to sett boardis, to apparell all Chambers, and such othir seruices as the Chamberlaine, or Vshers of Chambre, comaunde or assigne; to attend the Chambre; to watche the King by course; to goe in messages, etc.

They were to eat in the king's chamber, or in the hall.

Of Squires of the Household there were to be forty, or more if the king so pleased, with the advice of his high council,

> chosen men in worship & of great worth: Also to be of sundry shires, to knowe the disposicion of the Cuntries; & of these, to be continually in Court; XX squiers attendantes vppon the Kinges person, in Riding and going (i.e. walking), & to serue his table from serveyeng bourd & other places, as the Kinges Sewer will assigne them. Alsoe by assent amongst them all, some to serue the Chamber at one tyme, some the Hall at another tyme, of every messe that commeth from the dressing bourd to their handes for such seruice, Soe that thereof be nothing with-drawen by them, vppon such paine as the Steward, Tresorer, comptroller, or the Judges at the Compting bourd in their absence, after their demerites, will award; They eating in the Hall, sitting togither at both meales after, as they serue, by assent. This was the old manner, both for honour & profett of the King & his Court, euery each of them taketh for his livery at night, dimidium (i.e. a half) gallon ale; And for winter season, each of them ij Candles parice, j faggot or els dimidium tallwood. And when any of them is presente in Court, him is allowed for wages daily in the Checkroll vijd ob. (i.e. sevenpence halfpenny); and clothing winter and sommer, of the Compting-house, or els xls (i.e. forty shillings), it hath euer bine in speciall Charge to squiers in this Court to weare the Coulour of the Kinges liuery Customably, for the more glory, & in worshippinge this honourable houshold.

The account goes on to regulate further details: They shall keep one servant each, sleep two to a bed, pay for the carriage of their bedding, not depart without leave, keep no dogs in court, etc. This is the tradition of efficient organisation which occasionally drew down the scorn of the captive French knights, but which nevertheless must have been enormously important in making Edward III's Court so brilliant. And so here we find Chaucer, expected to keep up a handsome appearance as a personal servant and aide to the king, taking his part in a well-run (for the times) administrative machine. With twenty squires on duty and twenty off, his tasks cannot have been heavy. The Household Book notes that:

> These Esquires of household of old be accustomed, winter and summer, in afternoones and in eueninges, to drawe to Lordes Chambres within Court, there to keep honest company after there Cunninge, in talking of Cronicles of Kinges, and of others Pollicies, or in pipeing or harpeing, synginges, or other actes marcealls, to help to occupie the Court, and accompanie estraingers, till the time require of departing.

We may imagine these gatherings, splendid as the frontispiece to the copy of *Troilus*, in Corpus Christi College Library, Cambridge, when the great lords and ladies, as well as the less noble ranks, talked of arms and love, gossiped about the political news, heard songs and stories. Here the youthful Chaucer, in splendid livery, perhaps sang those lyrics, now lost, which caused Venus in Gower's poem to say:

> And gret wel Chaucer when ye mete   [greet
> As mi disciple and mi poete:
> For in the floures of his youthe
> In sondri wise, as he well couthe   [knew
> Of Dities and of Songes Glade
> The whiche he for mi sake made,
> The lond fulfild is oueral.

Confessio Amantis (first version) VIII, 2941–7

At the end of his life, Chaucer asked for Christ's mercy for 'many a song and many a leccherous lay'. These splendid, sophisticated courtly gatherings were perhaps the primary audience Chaucer had in mind for his love-poems, his popular comic tales, his sermons.

Chaucer was now at the centre of the mainstream of English culture. In himself he seems to draw almost all the multiple threads of the secular culture of the nation together – the English, the popular, the learned and intellectual, the pious and devout, the chivalric and military, the administrative, the courtly. Some of these strands did not easily interweave with others, but the acceptance of this mixture of partly incompatible elements is very characteristic of the medieval Gothic amalgam.

Not even Chaucer could bring everything together. His two great contemporary poets, Langland and the *Gawain*-poet, though not quite so inclusive, have a broad range which includes other elements. Langland represents the more anguished depth of religious feeling as it contemplates suffering and evil. The *Gawain*-poet moves in a world of romance and myth, of public cataclysm and personal grief, of resolute endurance. Langland sees the countryside's labour and poverty, the London of low-class pubs. The *Gawain*-poet sees the world of the Northern hills and moorlands and the jewelled brightness of the Heavenly Jerusalem. These are areas which Chaucer only glimpses. But no man can do, or see, everything, and the inclusiveness of Chaucer still exceeds that of any other writer of his time or later, including Shakespeare. The centrality of the king's court, with all its multiple relationships with and travelling about in England gave him a position unique for an English poet. His own responsibilities were serious and they forced upon him travel, knowledge of men and affairs, a sense of the world.

KING EDWARD III AND THE HUNDRED YEARS WAR

King Edward III, who dominated his court, came to the throne in 1327 at the age of fourteen, when his father, Edward II, was foully murdered at the instance of Mortimer, who then ruled with Edward's mother Isabella. At fifteen Edward was married to Philippa of Hainault. At seventeen he displaced Mortimer, and in spite of Isabella's pleading, had him hanged. Almost immediately he was engaged in an ill-advised war with the Scots, as he was frequently to be throughout his reign. While he was engaged in winning fruitless victories in Scotland, the French king, Scotland's ally, was stirring up trouble in Aquitaine, the great area in south-western France of which Bordeaux was the chief town, and which at that time owed obedience to the English king. There were also conflicts of trading interests between France and England in the Low Countries, and English and French traders were killing each other on the seas. But, with all the other reasons for English enmity to France, no doubt Froissart has much of the truth of it when he says,

> The English will never love or honour their king, unless he be victorious and a lover of arms and war against their neighbours and especially such as are greater and richer than themselves. Their land is more fulfilled of riches and all manner of goods when they are at war than in times of peace. They take delight and solace in battles and slaughter: covetous and envious are they above measure of other men's wealth. ... The King of England must needs obey his people and do their will.

Edward was warlike and successful. In 1337, two or three years before Chaucer's birth, he declared war on France and began the so-called Hundred Years War, an intermittent affair which lasted throughout Chaucer's life. Apart from raids on English south-coast towns the fighting was in France, a dismal record of pillage and plunder. The great English victories against superior numbers and old-fashioned tactics at Crècy (1346) and Poitiers (1356) could not offset the long English retreat from their French possessions, but made the war in its earlier stages appear profitable and glorious. Edward celebrated the victory of Crècy and the capture of Calais by instituting in 1347 the Order of the Garter, based on the idea of King Arthur and the Knights of the Round Table. The institution of such orders was popular with the nobility of the time, but few such orders have lasted, like the Garter, to the present day. Several of Chaucer's friends, for example Sir Lewis Clifford, were Knights of the Garter.

THE BLACK DEATH

The second half of the fourteenth century, covering the whole of Chaucer's lifetime, was a period of great stress and rapid development, including the great calamity of the Black Death, 1348–9, and what seemed to some at the time the equally great calamity of the Peasants' Revolt of 1381. It may be useful to remember these as a backdrop to our view of Chaucer's own life, especially as we come to 1368, which is now known to be the date of *The Book of the Duchess*. The poem is an elegy for John of Gaunt's first wife Blanche, daughter of Henry of Lancaster, through whom Gaunt inherited the vast Lancastrian estates. The marriage had been a political match for this second of Edward III's sons, but there is little doubt that it was also a love-match. The death of Blanche reminds us of the death and grief which always threatens the pride of life.

The first of the great national calamities of Chaucer's lifetime was the great visitation of the plague which swept Europe, and which devastated England in 1348–9. Known as the Black Death, it is thought that about a third of the population died. Apart from the terror of such widespread death, the disease was in itself horrible. Hard lumps arose in the groin and armpit which were exceptionally painful and could not be lanced. Swellings, carbuncles, vomiting, spitting blood, were among the other symptoms. Sometimes the victims flung themselves out of their beds from pain and delirium. The mortality was so great that in some places whole villages and tracts of land lay waste and uninhabited; but the towns suffered most with their crowded and insanitary conditions.

The fearful mortality hastened many changes which were bringing a new world with so many birth-pangs out of the old, but the immediate results were misery, derangement and loss. The progress of the arts and sciences was hindered. The University of Oxford almost ceased to function for two or three years after the Black Death. The economic results were a great rise in prices and a great shortage of labour. Since special statutes were enacted to keep wages down the strain on the poor became heavier, and the potential value of their labour quite disproportionate to its legal reward. Parliament tried to enforce the Statutes of Labourers, to keep wages down. The great nobles who paid lip-service and more to the ideal of chivalry were the actual leaders of the country, and their government in this long crisis was bad. The Black Prince, the embodiment of fourteenth-century chivalry, great in tournaments, great in war, devout in religion, was also selfishly extravagant, and coldly indifferent to the sufferings of his people.

Yet the pessimism caused by the Black Death in England can be exaggerated. Certainly the chroniclers express their horror, and there was great dislocation and social discontent. But the plague was a dreadful intensification of the normally difficult conditions of life rather than a total change in the quality of disaster. Perhaps the morbidity and sentimentality of much specifically religious writing, such as sermons, in the fifteenth century, were an indirect result of continuous later visitations of plague, which if not as bad as the Black Death were bad enough. But fourteenth-century English literature, which expresses something of the mind of the national culture, is by no means mainly pessimistic. It may be stoically grim, but it has none of the nihilism, *ennui, angst*, and horror of life often found in late twentieth-century literature.

THE BOOK OF THE DUCHESS

No other poem by Chaucer is so clearly tied to a person, place and time as *The Book of the Duchess*. Its subject is an elegy for John of Gaunt's beloved first wife, Blanche, daughter of Henry of Lancaster, mother of his five children, who died aged twenty-eight on 12 September 1368. Although she brought the huge estates of Lancaster to the relatively landless son of the king, it seems also to have been a love-match, and in his will at the end of his life Gaunt asked to be buried beside her, in Old St Paul's.

'Blanche' is French for 'white', the name given to the lady in the poem (l.948). At the end of the poem there is reference to

> A long castel with walles white
> Be seynt Johan, on a ryche hil
>
> ll. 1318–19

which is a series of non-comic puns on the names of *John* of Gaunt, otherwise *Lancaster* (= long castle), and his castle at *Richmond*, then called Rychemont, or 'rich hill', in Yorkshire. The centre of the poem is the long account by a man in black, met by the poet in a forest, of how he met and loved his lady, how beautiful and good she was, and how great is his grief now that she is dead. The man in black must represent Gaunt. Although all this is clear, the indirectness of the reference shows what a delicate, courteous, almost tentative, poem it is. Such consolation as it offers is totally unobtrusive, for the praise of the lady is put in the mourner's own mouth, and the only consolation comes from the memory of a joy once possessed, and its recollection in words. It is a poem whose deepest feeling is wonderfully subtle. The poem is also completely secular. There is not the slightest glimpse of religious hope. There are even touches of that flippancy which Chaucer was never able to suppress, especially in relation to death.

It is permissible to imagine the poem being first 'published' on an occasion at court (which, because of the various comings and goings of Gaunt and Chaucer, must have been between late September and late October, 1368), at which Chaucer read aloud his poem to John of Gaunt and an assembled company, as an offering of sympathy. Such a personal presentation would allow many subtle yet clear indications by tone and gesture of the living meaning, which we can only guess at. There are only three manuscripts of the poem, so it never had wide written circulation.

The poem is written in the traditional four-stress, roughly eight-syllable metre which though learnt from French had long been naturalised in English. Its 1,334 lines might have taken three-quarters of an hour to read aloud.

The poet begins tactfully by recounting his inability to sleep because of his own sorrow at his eight-year-old sickness. Here we have the poet as minstrel, even actor, but acting himself. It both is and is not the real-life man. The opening lines are translated from Froissart. Their oblique reference would seem most likely to refer to an uncured, incurable, love-sickness. It is highly conventional, and to that extent fictional (and Chaucer had been married for at least two years). Yet to refer to the 'Narrator' as if he were a purely dramatic figure *within* the poem, bearing no relationship to the real-life man outside, deprives our reading of a richness, a tang, a stimulating obscurity or puzzle about the relationship between the real poet and his presentation of himself. To think of a purely dramatic Narrator cuts the poem off from actual life in the fourteenth century and thus from us, while as we have seen, there is no doubt that the poem arises immediately out of a real grief, only a few weeks old.

The poet presents himself as another mourner, sleepless from sorrow, as if to remind John of Gaunt that there are other griefs, and that grief if persisted in will lead to death, as lack of sleep would. Yet the conventional pose of the sleepless lover distances the poet from the real grief in his audience and removes any ponderous intrusiveness. The poet tells how, to relieve his sleeplessness, he read the story from Ovid of King Seys and his wife Alcyone. Seys on a journey is drowned, and his wife dies of mourning. Again the tactfully indirect relevance. The pathos of the story is genuine, but in the account of how the pagan goddess Juno instructs a messenger to get Morpheus, the god of sleep, to bring a sight of the dead body of Seys to Alcyone there is, strangely enough, a brisk humour. Chaucer leaves out Ovid's ending, in which the dead husband and wife are changed into sea-birds and live again in loving happiness. There is no easy consolation.

With a change of mood the poet then presents himself as having made a comic vow to Morpheus for the sake of sleep, and then as falling immediately asleep. This is all preliminary, we now discover, to a dream.

Dream-poetry is whole genre, or collection of genres, in medieval European poetry, of great wealth, as A.C. Spearing has shown. It was the essential vehicle of the love-vision, and *Le Roman de la Rose* had set the fashion. A dream is so internal and unverifiable, yet so authentically personal; so vivid, yet so free from everyday limitations of cause and effect; obviously symbolic, yet obviously attached to life. All this makes it the perfect vehicle for poetry like Chaucer's which has one foot in the real world, one foot in fantasy. It has the necessary non-responsibility of art, yet dreams from Biblical times onwards have been claimed to reveal religious and other truth. By Chaucer's time an elaborate classification of dreams had developed with its roots in late-Classical Latin literature. Chaucer fully avails himself of the charm, touches of realism, apparently arbitrary sequences of event, and symbolic possibilities of the form.

He dreams he awakes on a bright morning in a beautifully painted chamber, and hears outside the noise of the beginning of a hunt. At once he is out of his room on a horse to follow them. The huntsmen lose the scent and, the horse forgotten, the poet is then walking in the wood, led away by a little dog, in its turn immediately forgotten. In the flowery ways of this great wood, full of wild creatures, he comes upon a man in black, who speaks aloud a poem which laments the death of his lady. There follows a beautifully courteous exchange, in which it is clear that the man in black is the superior, because the poet speaks to him so deferentially, using the polite second-person plural form 'you', while the man in black uses the more condescending second person singular 'Thou'. The poet, disregarding or forgetting the earlier poetic complaint about death, gently asks the man in black the cause of his sorrow. Although this has already been stated, Chaucer has to make clear to his audience without question what the true issue is. In this kind of poetry the audience, as in Shakespeare, is always put in possession of all the knowledge it needs, which normally exceeds that of any of the characters within the poem. The dream-like atmosphere, and the poet's deferential presentation of himself as a simple, literalistic, but sympathetic person, allow us to accept the situation without question, and though we realise the essence of the matter we are eager to follow the poet's gentle questioning in order to hear the account of the man in black, and how he came to this plight. He describes himself metaphorically as in conflict with Fortune. He had fallen in love with a bright lady, described as all medieval heroines are, with golden hair, fair face, long slender neck and arms, joyous of speech, good and gentle of nature. The poet's simple questioning prompts an account of how eventually the lady came to love the man in black after his long and faithful service. The poet represents himself as unable to understand metaphors of death, and the man in black is forced to undertake his own self-expressive therapy, to accept cruel reality for himself, by saying literally, 'She is dead'. The poet utters a brief exclamation of pity and the poem, its work done, abruptly concludes.

So Chaucer from the very first confronts death and suffering at the heart of courtly glamour and joy. The only consolation offered is to have known beauty and joy in a beloved person. Symbolically, in the heart of the wood, Chaucer goes to the heart of the matter, leaving aside the pleasant superficial bustle of the world, yet returning to it with resolution and relief.

The centrality of Chaucer's position in life mentioned earlier is complemented by the urgent necessity he obviously feels also to go to the depths and margins of experience, to the extremes, for it is there, paradoxically, that the central issues of life and death show most clearly. Margins and borders of experience, and transitions, the crossing over from one sort of life to another, of which the most startling example is death, continually draw his attention. His mind was as continually voyaging into strange lands and seas of thought as his body was of the world. A restless curiosity possesses him, to find the hunt, to wander in the wood, to ask the man the cause of his grief; all his life he seeks, through philosophy and science and religion, through love and marriage, through the texture of ordinary life, for further meanings, as he explores further into experience from the new reading of both familiar and unfamiliar texts. He has a restlessly creative mind, not disdaining the old, but feeding on it and continuously transforming it.

The Book of the Duchess is an exciting point in the history of English poetry, which here comes of age in its new form after the Conquest. The poem is organically English, but flowers with the riches of the whole European tradition, the Bible, Ovid, *Le Roman de la Rose*, Machaut. The immediate model is provided by Machaut, and much is translated direct from *Behaigne* and other poems of his, which must have helped Chaucer to write it as fast as he did. But all is absorbed into a characteristically Chaucerian form, a narrative with philosophic undertones yet rising to lyric tenderness; stoically accepting sorrow but celebrating joy; pathetic, but lightened with flippant and comic notes. The style is sometimes diffuse and not always firmly controlled but nevertheless the poem is a fully Chaucerian masterpiece.

Chapter 6

DIPLOMAT AND CIVIL SERVANT

Chaucer wrote *The Book of the Duchess* only just in time, for by November 1368 John of Gaunt's mother, Queen Philippa, was already suggesting that he should marry the daughter of Louis de Male, Countess of Flanders, though this came to nothing. Politics cannot wait on personal feelings and the marriages of the great have always been a matter of public policy. Nor can death of individuals interrupt the public flow of event, of fast and festival. Christmas was celebrated in 1368 with accustomed splendour, and cloth and robes were duly issued to all at court, including Geoffrey and Philippa Chaucer, whose work was often thus paid in kind. From now on there is a steady flow of documents recording such issues, other gifts, and the payments of annuities, to both Geoffrey and Philippa. Through them we are able to trace the outline of their lives.

THE ITALIAN JOURNEY

For several years Chaucer remained with the Court, though he made a short trip abroad in the summer and autumn of 1370. Then on 1 December 1372 he left London on his first visit to Italy.

This Italian journey was of the utmost significance to Chaucer's imaginative life, comparable to the flowering such an Italian journey brought to Goethe. Unfortunately, European culture had not by Chaucer's time developed to the extent of keeping individual personal diaries, and we have no such personal knowledge of Chaucer's responses as we have of Goethe's – perhaps fortunately, considering what Goethe got up to. One reason why Chaucer was chosen to go was perhaps that he already knew some Italian. He could have picked it up from Italian merchants whom his father dealt with in London. If he knew Italian already, there is no evidence from his poetry that he yet knew Italian literature. Dante and Petrarch were already famous in Italy but there is no sign that knowledge of them had reached England.

Chaucer was one of three commissioners who were sent to negotiate a trade agreement with Genoa. Often one of such a group of commissioners was legally trained, and it may be that Chaucer also owed his appointment to such a training. At any rate a special position of trust and responsibility seems to have been his, for he was detached on a secret mission to Florence, perhaps to negotiate a private loan for the king. He was back in London by 23 May 1373, so that, allowing for travelling time, he spent two or three months in Italy, in winter and early spring. A few years later, in 1378, he spent July in Milan, on another diplomatic mission. His first visit in particular was of the greatest importance for the development of his poetry.

FOURTEENTH-CENTURY ITALIAN CULTURE

Italy was already rich in the visual arts, though the contrast with England in the fourteenth century was not so great as might be thought. England was almost as rich as Italy in decorated churches, in coloured statues plated with gold and silver, in tapestried and frescoed chambers. The great efflorescence of Italian Renaissance art had barely begun.

But Italian towns were much richer. Even small towns had from the thirteenth century been built in stone and contained magnificent public buildings and private palaces. There were far more schools, far better shops. Science was more advanced. Modern arithmetic at the service not only of merchants but of painters was well advanced, with all that that implies. Clockwork, the associated science, that measures time neutrally and regularly, was well developed. The best medicine, the best architecture, much of the best metalwork, in the fourteenth century, were all Italian.

Chaucer would have had a Londoner's kinship with the city of Florence, and would have been able to appreciate Florence's more advanced civilisation. Florence was the chief industrial and financial city of Europe, holding a position comparable with London's in the early twentieth century. It was at least twice the size of the London of Chaucer. Florentines were the principal bankers of Europe (Edward III had borrowed very much money from them), and they had agents and correspondents everywhere. A relic of their importance in London still survives in the name Lombard Street. Florence was far ahead of London in the production of books. In the manufacture of paper, slowly beginning to supplement and eventually to supplant parchment, Italy had almost a monopoly. England had not one paper mill until 1490. And in Florence Dante was venerated, and Petrarch and Boccaccio were still alive. A few months after Chaucer's first visit, Boccaccio was lecturing on Dante. In Italy certainly, and Florence probably, Chaucer first became acquainted with some of the Latin and Italian works of these great writers. It is probable that here too he extended his own library. Chaucer seems to have had an astonishing number of books for a private Englishman of his time. He must have greatly extended his reading and bought copies of the Italian works of Dante and Boccaccio, something of Petrarch, an Italian translation of Ovid, etc. Even here, however, the limited currency of all books must have made his acquisitions to some extent casual and fortuitous. Manuscripts have no title-pages, and rarely tell the authors' names. Many miscellaneous items might be bound up in one volume, and it was next to impossible to collect an author's works, because the author himself was largely ignored. One of the curiosities of literary history which illustrates these matters is Petrarch's ignorance of the *Decameron* until a year or two before his death, although he and Boccaccio had been intimate for many years, and the *Decameron* a popular work. But Boccaccio in his later life was prouder of his Latin works, and even after Dante's great example Latin had in general more prestige than the vernacular.

There is no evidence that Chaucer met Petrarch or Boccaccio and he apparently remained in ignorance of the latter's very name, but he read some of their Italian works with the greatest eagerness. These and Dante he read and re-read, and the result was a continual enrichment and strengthening of his poetic powers throughout the rest of his life. It was not a case of the 'French influence' being changed for an 'Italian influence'. No new channel of development was created by his Italian reading; rather, fresh and more fertile waters poured down the earlier stream of his French manner, following the same direction, nourishing the same interests, but deepening and broadening the flow.

WHAT CHAUCER LEARNT FROM ITALIAN LITERATURE

Chaucer learnt from the Italians new subjects, a new magnificence and control of diction, a new clarity, a new sense of the dignity of poetry. More profoundly, he seems to have responded to the new sense of the world found in Italian city culture and reflected in the poetry of Dante and even that of Boccaccio. In these writers there seems a stronger rendering of mass, space and perspective, which contrasts with the elaborately decorative but less powerfully structured French writing, and which reveals the naivety of most secular English rhyming romances and lyrics. The same kind of difference can be seen between the massive simple figures of Giotto, and the wonderfully elaborate prettiness of so much late Gothic decorative art. 'Realism' is too trivial a word for this new capacity to render a sense of modern secular actuality, which however is not 'naturalism' in the modern materialistic, atheistic sense. Yet a new sense of ordinary everyday reality comes through, even when Dante is reporting on Hell and Heaven, and Boccaccio is trying to write (with modern notes) an ancient epic.

One must not make too much of this. Chaucer did not become a Dante. He retained much that is Gothic, and he was firmly set in a rather different popular and even humorous tradition. His Italian experience broadened his perspectives, warmed his imagination, enriched his knowledge, increasing the effectiveness of what was already present in actuality or potentiality.

COMPTROLLER OF CUSTOMS

Chaucer returned from Italy in May 1373, and probably his wife had to go almost immediately to Tutbury Castle in Staffordshire with Gaunt's second wife, Queen Constance of Castile, to whom she was lady-in-waiting. Since Chaucer personally received payments at Westminster in the following November and February, they were presumably separated a good deal. If they were a devoted couple they were unlucky, though many other esquires and ladies-in-waiting were in a similar position.

In the spring things improved rapidly. On 23 April 1374, during the Garter feast of St George, Chaucer was granted a pitcher of wine daily (later commuted to an annual grant of 20 marks – £13 6s.8d., a considerable sum). A fortnight later (10 May 1374) he obtained the dwelling-house, or what we would now call a flat or apartment, above the city gate of Aldgate, for no rent, though he had to keep it in repair. Such a dwelling was pleasant and convenient and Chaucer was lucky to get it. It must have been obtained by influence with the City, though we do not know whose. The house was obviously taken to prepare for his new appointment, which came four weeks later. On 8 June 1374, Chaucer was appointed Comptroller of the Customs and Subsidy of wools, skins, and tanned hides in the Port of London, with the usual fees. His place of business was about ten minutes' walk from his new house. Five days later (13 June) he and his wife received an annuity of £10 for life from Gaunt, which was presumably a recognition of Philippa's services now that she was leaving to set up house for the first time.

Chaucer's new appointment was not completely a sinecure. He was to write out the rolls of his office with his own hand, and perform his duties personally. These were mainly to act as check on the two collectors, who were such men of substance as Nicholas Brembre, William Walworth (the lord mayor who struck down Wat Tyler), and John Philipot. They were important businessmen in the City. Chaucer's income was £10 a year, probably a good deal increased by fees, and once at least, by £71 4s.6d., being the fine of a merchant whom Chaucer detected shipping wool without paying duty. The house at Aldgate and his work at the Customs were Chaucer's main concerns until 1385 or 1386. During his time here at least two sons, Lewis and Thomas, were born, and he composed *The House of Fame*, *The Parliament of Fowls*, *Troilus and Criseyde*, and several minor poems, besides translating Boethius's *Consolation of Philosophy*. He may have thought of *The Canterbury Tales* here, and even written some of them. It is an astonishingly productive period. There is an amusing and interesting passage in *The House of Fame* referring to this time where he represents himself as being reproached (by an Eagle) for his dullness, because being chained to the office desk all day, and reading half the night, he sees nothing of his very neighbours. There is surely an underlying suggestion here (not necessarily conscious) both of his impatience at his office drudgery, and his escape from it into imaginative flights of the mind, into the imaginative world of books, as symbolised by his flight with the Eagle. Jupiter has considered, the Eagle says, how dutifully Chaucer has laboured in writing songs of love, without any reward, and also,

> beau sir, other thynges; [*good sir*
> That is, that thou hast no tydynges
> Of Loves folk yf they be glade,
> Ne of noght elles that God made;
> And noght oonly fro fer contree
> That ther no tydynge cometh to thee,
> But of thy verray neyghebores,
> That duellen almost at thy dores, [*dwell*
> Thou herist neyther that ne this;
> For when thy labour doon al ys,
> And hast mad alle thy rekenynges,
> In stede of reste and newe thynges,
> Thou goost hom to thy hous anoon;
> And, alos domb as any stoon,
> Thou sittest at another book
> Tyl fully daswed ys thy look, [*dazed*
> And lyvest thus as an heremyte,
> Although thyn abstynence ys lyte. [*little*

And therfore Joves, thorgh hys grace,
Wol that I bere the to a place   [*thee*
Which that hight the Hous of Fame,   [*was called*
To do the som disport and game.

HF, 643–64

It was remarkable at that time for a man to read silently, and that Chaucer could shows the advanced state of his literacy. Most people in reading murmured the words to themselves, as inexpert readers still do. Chaucer had much internalised the reading process.

The reference to his 'reckonings', his arithmetical calculations, his lists of tariffs and customs duties, indicates his arithmetical training, and also suggests that though it was influential it was in tension with the desire for personal and imaginative experience, the longing to meet people, to know love, to hear stories, to know what is going on in the world.

Chaucer's daily duties cannot have been too rigidly enforced, notwithstanding his complaints, for he was sent abroad several times on commissions handling delicate negotiations to stop the war with France, and trying to arrange the marriage of the ten-year-old Prince Richard with Marie of France. (Neither object was achieved.) In December 1376 he was associated with Sir John Burley, Captain of Calais, on a secret mission: from February to March 1377, he went on a mission to Paris, Montreuil and elsewhere, with Sir Thomas Percy (later Earl of Worcester). He was away again 30 April to 26 June 1377. He seems to have been associated with Sir Guiscard d'Angle (one of Richard's tutors) and Sir Richard Sturry, in the marriage negotiations. Sturry was another Lollard knight. There is every reason to suppose him high in favour at court, and regarded as an accomplished courtier, diplomat and administrator.

On 26 June 1377 Edward III, for some years in his dotage, at last died, and the child Richard succeeded to the throne. All Chaucer's posts and emoluments were formally renewed, and in January 1378 he was again abroad negotiating on the same delicate matters. From 28 May to 19 September 1378 he was again in Italy, in Milan, negotiating with Bernabò Visconti, and the famous English *condottiere*, Sir John Hawkwood. During this latter absence he granted the poet John Gower powers of attorney to act for him, so they were evidently good friends. This was the last time Chaucer went abroad on the king's business.

CHAUCER'S RELEASE FROM ACCUSATION OF RAPE: HIS FRIENDS

It was a period of continuing prosperity for him. He and his wife received a steady flow of payments and gifts. There was the fine mentioned earlier, and in November and December 1378 he was granted two lucrative wardships. However, the smooth progress was marred by two incidents, one private, one public. The first is suggested by the deed, dated 1 May 1380, whereby one Cecily Chaumpaigne released Geoffrey Chaucer Esquire of every sort of action 'both of my rape (*meo raptu*), and of any other matter or cause'. Since it was a release it might seem that Chaucer was not guilty, but many critics have held that there is no smoke without fire. *Raptus* may mean abduction of the kind of which Chaucer's father was the victim, or it may mean rape in the modern sense. Chaucer may have been guilty of either or both, though the latter seems unimaginable. All we can say is that whatever tangled story lies behind this curious document it impeded neither Chaucer's career nor the regard of his friends. The names of witnesses and friends of Chaucer appearing in the document are those of distinguished men: Sir William Beauchamp, Chamberlain of the King, and for long one of Chaucer's circle; John de Clanvowe and William de Neville, two of those serious-minded Lollard knights; John Philipot, grocer, Collector of Customs, and later a lord mayor of London. These were all men of the 'king's party' at court (as were the lawyer Strode, and Gower, to whom *Troilus* is dedicated) and with the two latter give an execellent cross-section of the friends who made up Chaucer's more intimate circle of acquaintances – solid men, courtiers, merchants, men of learning, all closely associated.

THE PEASANTS' REVOLT

The other incident which must have disturbed Chaucer was a disaster of national dimensions – the Peasants' Revolt, when in June 1381 a wild mob stormed the City, and for three days held it under a reign of terror, the objects of their particular hostility being lawyers, collectors of the king's taxes, John of Gaunt and his followers, and the wretched immigrant Flemish weavers. There was some incendiarism and Gaunt's splendid house, the Savoy, in the Strand, was totally destroyed. There were many killings; the aged and gentle Archbishop Sudbury, regarded as the representative of oppressive government, being Chancellor, was haled out of the Tower and beheaded; and many Flemish weavers suffered. The rebels were, however, pathetically loyal to the person of the king, and the Revolt was calmed down, as is well known, by Richard's bold meeting with the peasants. He made a promise of general pardon and though the ringleaders were punished this was generally adhered to. There was no cruel aftermath of punishment of the rebels, though Chaucer's friend Gower (a small landowner in Kent) represents a more hysterical attitude when in his poem *Vox Clamantis* he describes the peasants as domestic beasts gone suddenly and outrageously mad.

CHAUCER'S POLITICAL ATTITUDE

Chaucer kept his views to himself; he was not a man fanatically to espouse one party or another. The orthodoxy, the idealism, the conviction of the world's sinfulness which are the ground-bass of his poetry, lead us to expect nothing else. His summing-up of experience which is the nearest thing we have to a personal expression of emotion about the world may well have been written within a few years of these events. It is to be found in the Balades, *Gentilesse* and *Lak of Stedfastnesse*.

> Trouthe is put doun, resoun is holden fable;
> Vertu hath now no dominacioun;
> Pitee exyled, no man is merciable;
> Through covetyse is blent discrecioun.   [*blinded; moderation*
> The world hath mad a permutacioun
> Fro right to wrong, fro trouthe to fikelnesse,
> That al is lost for lak of stedfastnesse.

Lak of Stedfastnesse, 15–21

Wickedness and misery are seen as springing from 'instability', that is, from lack of loyalty, and the consequent upsetting of the proper order of society. The *envoy* to King Richard in the same poem aligns Chaucer with the usual political theories of his day, in both their punitive and idealistic forms:

> O prince, desyre to be honourable,
> Cherish thy folk and hate extorcioun!
> Suffre nothing that may be reprevable
> To thyn estat don in thy regioun.
> Shew forth thy swerd of castigacioun,   [*punishment*
> Dred God, do law, love trouthe and worthinesse,
> And wed thy folk agein to stedfastnesse.

Lak of Stedfastnesse, 22–28

Behind and beneath this is the even more fundamental Christian and Boethian combination of resignation to fortune, and contempt of the world. Such an attitude is most clearly found in *Truth*, written when Chaucer was a good deal older. At this earlier and most successful period of his life Chaucer was less inclined to deny the world; nevertheless the doctrine of rejection was at all times an important element in his thought, and it may well be mentioned in connection with this crisis ('trouthe' here means also God):

> That thee is sent, receyve in buxumnesse;   [*obedience*
> The wrastling for this world axeth a fal.   [*wrestling*; *asks for*
> Her is non hoom, her nis but wildernesse: [*is not*
> Forth, pilgrim, forth! Forth, beste, out of thy stal!
> Know thy contree, look up, thank God of al;
> Hold the heye wey, and lat thy gost thee lede;   [*high*
> And trouthe thee shal delivere, it is no drede.   [*doubt*

Truth, 15–21

Chaucer continued at the Customs House until 1386, apparently with success. In November 1381 he received ten marks as a reward for diligence, and in 1382 he was appointed controller of the petty customs in the port of London. This latter was also probably a reward, as he was allowed to appoint a permanent deputy.

WITHDRAWAL TO KENT

In February 1385 he applied to exercise his main controllership also by permanent deputy. Since in each of the two preceding years he had been allowed to be away from his post for a month or so to attend to his private affairs, it seems he was breaking away from his administrative duties. He was appointed a Justice of the Peace for Kent in October 1385, and in August 1386 became Knight of the Shire to attend the Parliament of October, and he probably went to live in Kent some time in 1385. His house over Aldgate was leased to another man in October 1386, and in December his two controllerships were granted to two other men. It is possible that he voluntarily resigned, but he may have lost them for political reasons. There were three main factions, a 'court' or 'kings' party', led by Sir Simon Burley; a Lancastrian faction, grouped round John of Gaunt; and a baronial opposition led by the Duke of Gloucester and the Earl of Warwick, which hated the Lancastrians and was largely contemptuous of the court. In 1386 the barons, called the Lords Appellant, struck first at the Lancastrians, who were in uneasy alliance with the court party, and then, even more devastatingly, at the court party.

The barons succeeded, temporarily, in 'capturing' the king's authority and the royal administration. Chaucer seems to have been associated principally with the court party, as were most of his circle. There was a purge of the king's men from administrative posts. This is perhaps why Chaucer lost his controllerships. It was an uneasy and dangerous time, and he may have felt himself well out of it down in Kent.

Chapter 7

FROM *HOUSE OF FAME* TO *PARLIAMENT OF FOWLS*

The years of business at the Customs House were thus extraordinarily full of literary activity, both reading and writing. Chaucer's intellectual interests led him to delight in knowledge for its own sake, and for the sake of understanding the full spectacle of life. In this period he translated the great work of Boethius, *The Consolation of Philosophy*. His interest in astronomy and astrology (the two were almost indistinguishable in his day), based on his command of arithmetic, now clearly appears as an important element in his thought. His interest in the psychology of dreams and in physics is shown in *The House of Fame*. The many references to the natural sciences and to medicine in *The Canterbury Tales* reflect reading of which at least part was done at this period. None of these many subjects can be considered as diverging from, or hostile to, his poetry. They were in part the very material of his poetry; and they helped to focus his view of the world, of human character, of the course of good and ill in human life. The desire for a total view, a *Summa*, of earthly knowledge and experience, is a characteristic of the men of the High and Late Middle Ages, whether they wrote in prose or verse. They are such encyclopaedists as Vincent of Beauvais and the Englishmen Alexander Neckham and Bartholomew; the great theologians, St Albertus Magnus and St Thomas Aquinas; and chief among poets, Dante. Chaucer's contemporary Langland and his friend Gower each attempted similar syntheses, and *The Canterbury Tales* is partly to be understood in this light. *The House of Fame* and the *Parliament* are also probably attempts at synthesis, for when a learned and courtly poet wished to gather in the whole created universe, he bound it together with 'the fayre chain of love'.

THE HOUSE OF FAME

The House of Fame must have been written after the Italian journey, because it is threaded with reminiscences of Dante and Boccaccio. On the other hand, it is still written in the old short four-stress English couplets and in the French manner. It must have been written some time in the mid–1370s. Chaucer has still not read the book by Macrobius on Cicero's *Dream of Scipio* because he still thinks, as he did in *The Book of the Duchess*, that Scipio was a king (*HF* II, l. 916). The poem is very mixed in tone. There is even an extravagant facetiousness at times. There is an attempt to evoke deep pathos. The poem is unfinished and of the three books into which it is divided the third has a disproportionate number of the total 2,158 lines. The form got out of hand. At the same time it evokes some powerful symbols, has much fascinating description, and, in Book II, for the first time we experience the fully ripe and controlled Chaucerian humour, both intellectual and self-mocking. The poet seems to be trying to put new wine into an old bottle.

The old bottle is the French love-vision, or dream-poem, deriving ultimately from *Le Roman de la Rose*, as developed in Machaut and *The Book of the Duchess*. Chaucer begins with personal reflections in that Cockney chirpiness of style of the English romances:

> God turne us every drem to goode!
> For hyt is wonder, be the roode   [*cross*
> To my wyt, what causeth swevenes ...   [*dreams*

House of Fame, 1–3

But no English romance had then discussed the nature and classification of dreams, using many learned ideas and words – *gendres*, *dysordynaunce*, *acustumaunce*, *melancolyous*, all recorded here in English for the first time.

The poet proceeds to an invocation of the god of sleep in the same light-hearted manner and tells how he fell asleep on the night of 10 December. Why so precise a date, and what meaning to attach to the tiring two miles pilgrimage to the holy body of St Leonard which is then referred to, remain unknown. There is a strong sense of a private joke to an inner circle.

The poet dreams he is in the Temple of Venus, made of glass, full of tabernacles and richly adorned images, like a fourteenth-century Gothic church. The portrait of Venus is there, shown naked, floating in the sea, with a rose garland on her head, carrying a comb, accompanied by doves, her son Cupid, and her husband Vulcan, the lame god of smiths, with his brown face. There is a long literary history behind this description, to be described later (p. 102). Here it is enough to say that such a picture of Venus shows her as the goddess of sexual lust and unfaithful love. Doves were thought to be specially amorous birds; red and white roses illustrated sexual passion; Vulcan had caught Venus naked in bed with Mars.

The poet sees written on the walls the story of Virgil's *Aeneid*, ambiguously conveyed both as writing and a series of pictures. Virgil's *gravitas* is abandoned in favour of Ovid's pathos, for the story is mainly focused on the seduction and betrayal of Dido by Aeneas, the son of Venus. The plight of Dido is emphasised by a speech from her after the manner of Ovid's *Heroides*, and reinforced by reference to other deserted heroines.

The poet leaves the temple and finds himself in a barren sandy desert, which is a surprising image for a man who presumably had never seen such a sight. It symbolises, consciously or unconsciously, a spiritual barrenness and uncertainty where to go, what to do. But a shining golden eagle descends and so this first book concludes.

The poem of the Second Book returns to the sportive tone of the Introduction to the First. Chaucer makes a playfully exaggerated claim for the outstanding worth of his dream, and comprehensively invokes Cipris, the Muses, and his own Thought. Throughout this passage there are reminiscences of Dante and Boccaccio, sometimes close, but Chaucer has not yet caught their larger manner.

The story of the dream is then lightheartedly continued. The poet dreams he is swept up into the heavens by the eagle. He is stunned with fear and astonishment, for which the Eagle admonishes him pretty sharply, softening enough, however, to explain to him that Jupiter has taken pity on him because he has served blind Cupid and fair Venus so 'ententyfly', 'withoute guerdon ever yit' – in other words, because he has been unrewarded (whether by love or royal gift is deliberately ambiguous). Then follows the famous passage already quoted, describing how he studies far into the night because he must work during the day, and so knows nothing of how the world goes. As a reward he is to be taken to the House of Fame, where he will find news of love, and all the variety of love's experience. The poet, whom the Eagle clearly identifies by calling him Geoffrey (l. 729), refuses to believe that this is possible; whence follows the Eagle's brilliant exposition of the properties of sound. It finishes with the Eagle's amusing crow of self-satisfied triumph, after which he shows the poet the heavens, 'gladding' him with his explanations. It is characteristic of Chaucer that as he looks about and sees the 'airish beasts' and the way the clouds, rains and winds are made, he breaks out

> 'O God', quod y, 'that made Adam,　　　　　　　　　　[*I*
> Moche ys thy myght and thy noblesse!'

HF, 970–1

It is equally characteristic that when the Eagle is anxious to inform him about the names of the stars, the poet says he is too old to learn. The Eagle points out how useful such knowledge will be 'when thou redest poetrie', but Chaucer says he will rely on the writer's words, and that anyway he is so near the stars that they will blind him if he looks at them. Then he is landed at Fame's 'place', so concluding Book II.

WHAT IS FAME?

The Third Book also begins with an invocation, an interestingly modest disclaimer of 'art poetical', and a comment on how the metre of the lines may sometimes lack a syllable. Both remarks indicate an increasing awareness of the craft of poetry. The poet dreams he comes to a mountain of ice, with many half-melted names written on it. On this uncertain foundation is perched a castle wonderfully adorned, bustling with all kinds of people, including heralds, jugglers, classical heroes and heroines, all dancing and springing about. Within is the magnificent Hall of Fame, and Fame herself, sitting on a ruby throne, varying in height from human size to one reaching the heavens, reminiscent in appearance of some of the creatures described in Revelation, the last book of the Bible. The hall is upheld by pillars carved in human form (like Gothic cathedrals, such as the porches at Chartres). These figures, upholding the Hall of Fame, are the great writers of the past.

Groups of people come up to the Goddess Fame. She grants or withholds worldly honour quite without regard to desert. The poet himself is asked if he is seeking fame. He replies

'Nay, for sothe, frend,' quod y;   [*I*
'I cam noght hyder, graunt mercy,   [*many thanks*
For no such cause, by my hed!
Sufficeth me, as I were ded,
That no wight have my name in honde.
I wot myself best how y stonde;
For what I drye, or what I thynke,   [*endure*
I wil myselven al hyt drynke,
Certeyn, for the more part,
As fer forth as I kan myn art.'

HF, 1873–82

One can hardly doubt that this modest, sober independence does indeed represent Chaucer's own attitude. But what *is* he doing, someone asks him? 'That will I tell thee', he says. It is to learn some new tidings, *he does not know what*, either of love or similar glad things. What he has seen so far he already knew and is nothing to the point. His unnamed questioner replies with another question – 'What are the tidings that you have thus brought here, which you have heard? But no matter, I see what you desire to hear.' This is the sort of mysterious inconsequentiality which makes the poem so exasperating, and suggests either 'private jokes in panelled rooms', or that Chaucer never really worked out what he wanted to say. He is taken to the House of Twigs, a vast hall built of wickerwork, continually going round – another extraordinary image. In it is a tumultuous crowd of people exchanging whispers, rumours, stories, which themselves take on a kind of corporality. This is the House of Fame in the world's Latinate sense of Rumour, where he is to see such strange sights and hear such new things as will console him for the distress he has endured so cheerfully, having been so empty of all bliss since Fortune destroyed his heart's rest. It is the Eagle who tells him all this, thus harking back to the earlier passage where the poet was told of Jupiter's pity. His sadness may be due to the frustration of his poetry caused by the pressure of business which ties him to his office accounts all day when he would prefer to be reading. At least, strange sights and 'tidings', whether these be 'news' or 'stories', would seem to be a rather more satisfactory reward for one who was denied freedom and learning, than for one who was unlucky in love. The poet goes about inquiring eagerly for certain news – which he hints is now known pretty widely (another puzzle) – when there is suddenly a rush to one corner of the hall. A man of great authority steps forth ... and the poem breaks off. What message the man of authority could have delivered is unknown. It seems quite possible that it eluded Chaucer. The poem must have been very near its end; it has suddenly risen to a climax, demanding a really striking announcement, yet there seems nothing that could have been a satisfactory literary climax. The notion that the poem is written as a deliberate prelude to some *real* announcement seems wildly impractical. We cannot tie the poem to any external event, as we can *The Book of the Duchess*.

The poem is an exploration of love and fame, and for all the frequent lightness of tone, and confidence of manner, the darker side of both is prominent. The poet is eager for stories about people, but the disorderliness of humanity is distressing, and the ambivalence of worldly values is painful.

The flight into the skies is an ancient religious and literary motif, an image of aspiration, of desire for higher experience, for a larger point-of-view, greater knowledge, for paradise, where men are free and spontaneous and good, out of time. Yet Chaucer also mocks this; treats it with scientific realism; rejects the sublimity which he is offered and perhaps yearns for, refuses to be 'stellified' (ll. 584–92). Knowledge of the stars he will have, but as an earthly astronomer, not as religious prophet or classical god. To use the anthropological terms of Mircea Eliade, Chaucer refuses the role of *shaman*, priest, magician, prophet, with access to other-worldly experience: he chooses this life, this earth, these people. Whatever the difficulties or the sorrows, he chooses with self-deprecatory humour the actually human. The reason, we may guess, why the man of authority has nothing to say is because Chaucer cannot bring himself to put authoritative words into his mouth. What could be important enough? To some readers, coming to *The House of Fame* for the first time, it is a tiresome poem, and the first book is indeed now rather faded. But the more one thinks about the whole in the context of Chaucer's life, the more interesting and ambiguous this extraordinary poem becomes. Its wealth of detail has hardly been touched on here, and its suggestive final silence teases us out of thought.

THE 'COMPLAINT': *ANELIDA AND ARCITE*

A good many poems about love are poems of discontent. Love itself is so often unreciprocated or betrayed, and the lover has time on his hands to write about it. Such discontent may also reflect other forms of discontent or sorrow in life. There was a tradition of sorrowful poems of love which was as powerful, and as natural, as the equally noticeable number of modern pop-songs of various kinds about unsatisfied love. In the fourteenth century the poems were more formal, and called 'complaints', like the words first spoken by the man in black in *The Book of the Duchess*. Chaucer had written such poems early: *A Complaint unto Pity*, and *A Complaint to his Lady*. They have something of the feeling, for us, of 'periphrastic studies in a worn-out poetical fashion', to quote T.S. Eliot. *The House of Fame* is one attempt to escape, by going back to the love-vision again, and looking at it in the light of Dante's and Boccaccio's poetry. Another attempt is the poem *Anelida and Arcite*. It starts off splendidly, modelled on Boccaccio's epic, *Teseida*:

> Thou ferse god of armes, Mars the rede ...

We immediately notice the more powerful, expansive five-stress line, forming the seven-line rhyming stanza which came to be called rhyme royal, and which Chaucer probably based on the model of Boccaccio. It is the first example in English of this splendid metre, which combines the spaciousness needed for storytelling with the capacity to rise to lyric intensity. The influence of Boccaccio's *Teseida* is plainly apparent, for there is to be a story attached to Theseus, who is the principal person in and gives his name to *Teseida*. But Chaucer's story here rapidly dwindles into one about the love of Queen Anelida betrayed by the false Arcite, and concludes with a 138–line 'Complaint' spoken to her, whose content is entirely in the old-fashioned French manner, though it is a miracle of verbal dexterity in the new stanza form. Here again Chaucer has tried and failed to assimilate Italian content and style.

THE LIFE OF SAINT CECILIA

A similar difficulty occurs in a different way with another poem written about this time, or rather, with its Introduction and Invocation, opening devices encouraged by the example of Boccaccio's poems. Chaucer's poem is *The Life of Saint Cecilia*, which might have been written at any time after he had developed the rhyme royal stanza, and could even have preceded *Anelida and Arcite*. It was later put among *The Canterbury Tales* as *The Second Nun's Tale*, awaiting a revision it never received. The poem is a fairly close translation from Latin, in a style at once better and worse than that of his previous secular poems – less diffuse and pretentious, but also less rich, vivid and musical. It has a genuine warmth of devotion, the quiet certitude of piety, an occasional pleasant freshness and prettiness of detail. The most striking things in it come in the Introduction, and Invocation to Mary. There is a clumsy first stanza about the wickedness of Idleness – the Devil finds work for idle hands to do. This is a conventional opening, and obviously aims at the *Roman* where the lovely portress of the Rose-garden is named Idleness, but the arrangement of ideas seems to be Chaucer's own. The serious religious message is quite the opposite to courtly frivolity, and recalls again that profound duality in Chaucer's mind which derives from the clash between his religious convictions and his worldliness; a clash of which these pros and cons about Idleness are a superficial, though genuine, manifestation. The passage owes nothing to Italian influence.

On the other hand, the Invocation to the Blessed Virgin is a translation from Dante, where Dante's art shines through, clear, direct, elevated. It is an astonishing contrast in poetic merit to Chaucer's own unaided labourings with the commonplace thought on idleness in the first stanza. The difference gives us some measure of the lesson the great Italian was able to teach Chaucer. Henceforward there is something of Dante in nearly everything that Chaucer writes – a measure of the eagerness with which he learnt, though the differences between their two poetic characters are immense.

THE PARLIAMENT OF FOWLS

The struggle to assimilate Italian influence and achieve a larger perspective reaches a triumphant stage in *The Parliament of Fowls*. The underlying mood of questioning discontent and uncertainty is the same, but it is more focused:

> For bothe I hadde thyng which that I nolde,   [*did not want*
> And ek I nadde that thyng that I wolde   [*also had not what I wanted*
>
> *PF*, 90–1

This expresses a feeling most people have had at some time and might apply to a thousand things, from a wife to a job to some particular object. But the discontent is nobly and entertainingly framed and expressed. Chaucer uses a pattern similar to that of *The Book of the Duchess* and *The House of Fame*. The poet is inside as well as outside the poem. He is progressively less active a participant – a discreet but persistent questioner in *The Book of the Duchess*; somewhat ostentatiously standing aside, yet invited to take part, in *The House of Fame*; hardly more than a pair of eyes and ears in *The Parliament*; yet as a poet a subtle manipulator.

The Parliament shows full control of the splendid Italianate rhyme royal stanza. Again he begins with a comment on art, again gives an account of a book he has read, again sleeps and tells us his dream.

The impulse seems to arise from the genuine discovery of a book, old but new to him. It is the substantial Commentary by Macrobius on the text which it preserves, Cicero's *Dream of Scipio*. Chaucer now discovers that Scipio was not a king, but a noble Roman, and the whole book excited him, in that it seemed to offer some sort of answer to his perennial question.

A modern reader may well not share Chaucer's apparent concern to discover the secret of life, for it is no less. But most sensitive people are at times discontented, and share at least occasionally some such anxiety about what is the right thing to do, what is the sense of life. Modern concerns may still be the same; how to find or retain a lover, for example; or may differ; how to avoid nuclear war, achieve a just society, or conquer poverty. Underlying all such concerns is the deeper question, *why* should we be upset by the evil of the world? What impels us to expect, or work for, the common good? Why should we or others be loyal to old promises when the urge has departed? Above all, when we have so many intimations of goodness, beauty and joy in life, why should there be so much incompatibility and disharmony, unfairness, even apart from downright evil? When joy is offered, why so much pain? There are many aspects of life in which such questions arise, but personal relationships are the most immediate and the most poignant. The most urgent personal relationship for many people is sexual love, and this for Chaucer is the endlessly interesting centre of joy and sorrow, as it was for so many of the French poets, and for so much of the leisured aspects of the courtly life.

We have followed Chaucer's poetry already far enough to learn from the poems themselves something of the way he, and most courtiers, conceived of the nature of love, as it had developed from earlier poems like *Le Roman de la Rose*. To understand his idea of love an open-minded reading of the poems themselves, without thrusting modern assumptions in too crudely, will be the best guide.

Chaucer begins *The Parliament*, as already remarked, with exclamations on the nature of art, but he deliberately and jestingly misleads us in the first line or two, and soon deflects well-established comments on the nature of art to say that it is the art of love *he* is talking about. Then he switches us again to the old book he had discovered, in which he read so eagerly 'a certeyn thing to lerne', for the whole day (his duties at the Customs laid aside or neglected). What was the certain thing? We are never told. There is a recurring sense of enigma at the heart of the poem. *The Dream of Scipio* itself is summarised in the poem. Scipio is carried in a dream to a point in the heavens from where he can see the utter triviality of the whole earth and its concerns. But a man may win to the bliss of heaven. How to get there? 'Know thyself first immortal', and work for the common good (ll. 73–5). It is a secularised version of religious truth.

Macrobius wrote in Latin about 400 AD, and like Boethius preserved in relatively elementary form something of the science and art of Classical Antiquity on which men could build after the collapse of Roman civilisation under barbarian attack. His commentary is concerned with the scientific concepts that might be educed from Cicero's *The Dream of Scipio*, such as the roundness of the world, of which he preserved the knowledge, and the importance of certain numbers. Chaucer read the Commentary with interest and makes incidental use of some parts, but for his poem he takes the core of it, *The Dream of Scipio*, as the centre of his eager search. But he finished the book anxious and worried, with the couplet already quoted, that he had what he did not want, and lacked what he did want.

Why was he disappointed? Partly perhaps at the banality of the message, for we all know what we ought to do, most of the time, and that we ought to be good. It may be true, but it rarely illuminates, consoles or compensates us. More specifically, there is no word about love, and love is the subject of major interest.

The poet falls asleep and dreams, and as he writes 'now' of the dream he had 'then', he invokes 'Cytherea', the name he uses when he wants to indicate the planet Venus, who, he says, made him dream this dream, and whom he asks to give him strength to write. Astronomy and astrology were seriously studied together in the fourteenth century, as will be shown further in the next chapter, and Venus is both a mythological personification to adorn the poetry and a genuine almost personal planetary force. According to astrology Venus the planet influenced love, friendship, affection, company, domesticity, sexual intercourse, pleasure, as well also, if unpropitious, as the miseries of love. The planet Venus now becomes the poem's guiding star, and though the invocation is light-hearted, it is not ironical. Chaucer has achieved at last an appropriate lightness of tone that is not merely flippant or, as in the *The House of Fame*, verging on the extravagantly facetious, but is still strong and fresh.

In the poet's dream Scipio, who gave such worthy but perhaps unattractive advice in Cicero's book, comes to show the poet not heaven nor hell, but a wondrous park, with a twofold promise on its gates; first that

> This is the wey to al good aventure, [*events*
>
> *PF*, 131

but also, just opposite,

> Th' eschewing is only the remedye! [*avoiding*
>
> *PF*, 140

A clear reminiscence of the words on the gates of Hell in Dante's *Divine Comedy* is included. The park is delightfully described. This section is largely translated from Boccaccio's *Teseida*. Chaucer improves on his original, making Boccaccio's abstract words flower into colourful, lively images. The lovely garden is refreshed by light sweet breezes and the ravishing melodies of birds; it is adorned with blossomy boughs, green meadows, flowers white, blue, yellow and red – an Earthly Paradise. It symbolises the bright expectant springtime of young life and love; clearly, also, it stands for the whole created world, and the birds which later appear symbolise both human society and all created beings.

After describing the temperate freshness of the whole park, where there is no 'grievance of hot nor cold', no night nor bitter weather, and no man is old or sick, the dreamer sees Cupid with his followers, Pleasance, Aray, Lust, disfigured Craft, and so forth. Behind these is the temple of Venus, the mother of hot desire. Her temple, in contrast to the freshness outside, is filled with sighs and rich with a thousand sweet odours. Priapus, the lustful god, stands 'in sovereyn place', shameful, ludicrous, obscene, with a *double-entendre* on 'sceptre':

> In swich aray as whan the asse hym shente
> With cri by nighte, and with hys sceptre in honde.
>
> *PF*, 255–6

Venus lies in a 'private corner', all but naked. She disports herself with Richesse who, according to the English *Romaunt* (5993 ff.), will have nothing to do with poor young men, who are the stable and steadfast lovers whom Cupid is really lord of. On the walls of the temple are painted stories of those who have suffered bitterly for love. Infatuated and betrayed love, sometimes illicit, is portrayed everywhere – though as a misfortune, not as a crime. Chaucer adds to *Teseida*'s list of lovers some of those placed by Dante in Hell in the Circle of the Lustful – Dido, Cleopatra, Helen, Achilles, Paris, Tristram. Troilus is also added to these sufferers, without a hint from Dante or Boccaccio.

The temple of Venus therefore shows love only as infatuation, lust, shame, misery, betrayal – indeed, as a justification of Scipio's condemnation of the world. Should any doubt of this exist in the mind of a modern reader, we may refer to Boccaccio's own *Chiose* or notes, issued with *Teseida*. It does not seem likely that Chaucer's copy of *Teseida* contained these notes, but a later age may be grateful for the guidance they give to the general effect Boccaccio aimed at. The *Chiose* devote pages to the significance of the Cupid and Venus passage, attributing allegorical meaning to every detail. It may be doubted whether Chaucer would have been much interested in this excessive allegory, but there is no doubt about the general implications of the Temple of Venus. Boccaccio says

> Venus is twofold; by the first can be and should be understood every honest and legitimate desire, such as to desire a wife in order to have children, and desires similar to this; and this Venus is not meant here. The second Venus is she through whom all lasciviousness is desired, and who is commonly called the goddess of love; and *she it is* whose temple and other qualities belonging to it are described here by the author, as appears in the text.

(G. Boccaccio, *Teseida*, a cura di A. Roncaglia, Bari, 1941, pp. 417 ff. (*My translation*))

The dreamer makes no overt comment on this ill-omened temple, but walks out to comfort himself. One imagines the pleasure of the fresh air again, after the scented warmth inside. So far he has seen little to assuage his discontent. However, he now sees the goddess Nature,

> a queene
> That, as of lyght the somer sonne shene
> Passeth the sterre, right so over mesure
> She fayrer was than any creature.

PF, 298–301

This is St Valentine's day, when every bird must choose his mate at the council held by the great queen, Nature. All the birds are present.

So many are they that the dreamer has scarcely space to stand and they are all in their proper degree, from the noble hawks to the plebeian cuckoo and goose. Nature, the 'vicar', or deputy, of almighty God, commands them to begin to choose their mates, and he that is most worthy shall begin. There is only one condition – that whoever is chosen is not to be constrained against her will. Then the famous debate begins, for the three noblest birds who speak first all love the same formel eagle. They speak in the high-flown language of love. They address the beloved not as a mate, but as a 'sovereign lady'. They humble themselves to the dust before her, claiming rather her pity than her love, though they are fierce enough towards each other. They all claim the reward of the lady's love, one in particular for his truth, one for the length of time of his service, one for the intensity of his devotion. But their argument goes on for so long that the lower orders, who cannot choose before their natural lords have done so, become impatient. Eventually certain birds are chosen to give their opinion as to who should have the formel: the spokesmen are the noble falcon, the 'unnatural' cuckoo, the turtle-dove loyal in love till death, the vulgar and stupid goose. Their speeches are masterpieces of dramatic truth and variety – noble, selfish, loving, foolish, according to the speaker, and tinglingly alive. But their speeches are no help, and Nature gives it to the formel eagle to decide for herself – though Nature's advice is that she should choose the royal tercel, as the noblest. The formel, however, asks for a year's grace, and so the solution is postponed. The other birds then choose their mates, and fly happily away after singing in honour of Nature the lovely roundel:

> Now welcome, somer, with thy sonne softe.

The poet awakes, and betakes himself to other books, always hoping that some day he will meet something by which he will 'fare the better'. He makes no other comment, and it seems unlikely that he himself has resolved the problem which haunted him at the beginning.

We can now, however, at least see something of its terms. Just as the Temple of Venus represents lascivious love, so Nature represents legitimate love. The figure of Nature, developed from the Latin poem *The Complaint of Nature* by the twelfth-century theologian Alanus de Insulis, is the key to the latter part of the poem. She is God's deputy

> That hot, cold, hevy, lyght, moyst and dreye   [*dry*
> Hath knyt by evene noumbres of acord.

PF, 380–1

She knits together the diverse elements of the world by the bond of Love, as Boethius explains in the *Consolation*. Nature here is the expression of God's creative activity. Whatever she ordains is good.

And love, pleasant love, is what she ordains when she tells the birds how,

> Ye knowe wel how, seynt Valentynes day,
> By my statut and thorgh my governaunce,
> Ye come for to cheese – and fle youre wey –   [*choose*
> Youre makes, as I prike yow with plesaunce.   [*mates*

PF, 386–9

Yet Africanus (and a good many others including Boethius) had commanded medieval man 'That he ne shulde hym in the world delyte'. Here is an important contrast of authorities in the poem. Another important contrast lies within the garden of love itself, between good love and corrupted love; Nature and Venus.

The poem thus presents first the major problem of the dualism of the world, then the subsidiary comment on the two kinds of love. We see these not in terms of logical conflict, but rather as masses of light and shade are balanced against each other in a picture.

The love debate itself has its conflicts and contrasts, too, some of them set within each other. There is a social conflict – easily enough appreciated in the turbulent years before and after the Peasants' Revolt. We cannot doubt here where the poet's convictions lie, for it is Nature (i.e. by implication, God) who ordains the ranks of society. There is also, on the most obvious level, the fashionable *demande d'amour*, the question of love; who should win the formel? There is yet another question, inherent in the contest between the suitors – the paradox of love itself as set forth on the gates of the park. Love causes both happiness and unhappiness. In large part, the unhappiness of love is caused by the lascivious Venus – love unrestrained by modesty. But even under Nature there is unhappiness. She is good, and gives us instincts which it is both our pleasure and our duty to satisfy. Yet even in following Nature there is frustration and unhappiness, as there must be for the unsuccessful suitors. The irony is that this afflicts pre-eminently the noblest and worthiest. The lower orders, with their coarse lack of sensibility, their desire primarily for a mate, find no such frustration, and depart happily. Chaucer puts the problem even more plainly in another Valentine poem of the same period – that witty, astrological poem, *The Complaint of Mars*.

> To what fyn made the God that sit so hye,   [*end*
> Benethen him love other companye,
> And streyneth folk to love, malgre her hed?...   [*constrains against
>   their will*
>
> Hit semeth he hath to lovers enmyte,
> And lyk a fissher, as men alday may se,
> Baiteth hys angle-hok with som plesaunce,
> Til many a fissh ys wod til that he be   [*mad*

Sesed therwith; and then at erst hath he
Al his desir, and therwith all myschaunce.

CM, 218...41

What is the total effect in *The Parliament*? Chaucer, like other medieval writers of debates, deliberately leaves the problem open. The satirical humour of parts of the debate does not detract from the genuine seriousness beneath. The strain between the two ways of life, the way of Acceptance, the way of Denial, he does not finally resolve till the end of his life, when, old and tired, he takes the way of Denial and condemns his non-religious writings. But in this fruitful period of mature manhood, conscious of and delighting in his powers and the richness of the world, he very strongly leans towards the way of Acceptance. Nature is good, and genuine love is good, since ordained by her – that is the overwhelming impression left by *The Parliament*.

Chaucer himself called the poem *The Parliament of Fowls* and the debate has always and rightly been considered the heart of the poem. The whole poem is itself a debate about the nature of love, though the movement of thought is by association and contrast, rather than by direct logic. *The Dream of Scipio* gives a world picture in which the world is despised – a view of great authority in Chaucer's day. By contrast, the park of Nature represents the world as God's own lovable creation, and under his law, which has Biblical warrant and was increasingly felt in the fourteenth century. Within the park the pictorial or dramatic descriptions of Venus and the noble and common birds all show contrasting aspects of or attitudes to love. It is typical of Chaucer's method of writing poetry that he presents these contrasts in the form of descriptions with a high degree of surface decoration, and that he leaves an appreciation of them and of the underlying principles of connection and contrast to the reader's wit and imagination. He creates a set of 'states of feeling' which interact and come to fruition in the reader's own mind. He does not argue a case – it is no lecture on love's philosophy. The birds' arguments are more dramatic than logical; they are contrasts in attitudes. Although the ostensible subject of debate is who should marry the formel, the actual subject of what the common birds say is the nature and value of love. And the delightful comedy of their argument only enhances the genuine seriousness of the fundamental issues. *The Parliament* is one of the richest and most remarkable poems of its length in the English language.

Just as *The Book of the Duchess* marks a new start for English poetry, *The Parliament* represents the point of take-off. It blends together without strain a great amount of learning, gathering up the whole European tradition. Its tighter form is attained by returning to the shape of the thirteenth-century French love-visions, much shorter than the thin volubility of Machaut, and by employing the device of the 'question of love'. Yet this is done under the powerful Italian influence, which gives a far stronger stride to the verse. Even so, Chaucer has achieved his own independence of form and content. His self-mocking manner disguises a tremendous absorptive power and an extraordinary mastery. This mastery of compression of many materials without any congestion in a short poem of 699 lines was now ready to be deployed over a much greater length.

Chaucer's reference to Venus allows us to date the poem around 1382. Many scholars have in addition tried to tie the poem to some courtly occasion, such as the betrothal or marriage of Richard II to Anne of Bohemia, but there is no evidence to justify that. The poem is a St Valentine's Day poem. There may well have been annual celebrations of St Valentine's Day in the court, for there are a number of other Valentine Day poems, like *The Complaint of Mars*, and several in French by Oton de Grandson, a Frenchman often at Richard's court.

The poem attracts us particularly by the comic dramatic realism of the debate, and its wonderful sense of daylight and open parkland. We rejoice in the feeling of heightened yet ordinary life. This like a beautiful landscape rests on the massive structures below the surface. Before seeing how Chaucer further deploys his mastery in a great long narrative we need to survey the geology of this poetic country, the underlying intellectual structures which sustain so fertile and colourful a surface. We need to turn to the philosophy, science and mythology, deeply interesting in themselves, which so greatly contribute to the interest and the human warmth of the poetry.

Chapter 8

FROM BOETHIUS TO VENUS

THE DESIRE FOR KNOWLEDGE

Chaucer's interest in the world extended from the appearances of people and love and ordinary life to the underlying difficult intellectual theorising. His interest was secular. He had not been to the university, and he was not interested in the high-powered theology that developed in Italy, Germany, France and Oxford in the thirteenth and fourteenth centuries. On the other hand, science interested him greatly, especially astronomy, of which some kinds of astrology were part. He was interested in dreams and their classification, as well as in other scientific knowledge which he picked up from Macrobius. Medical, historical, grammatical knowledge he picked up from such encyclopaedias as those by Vincent of Beauvais, the *Speculum Historiale, Speculum Morale* (Mirror of History, of Morality), or from Bartholomew the Englishman's *De Proprietatibus Rerum* (On the Properties of Things). He had an unappeasable appetite for knowledge and thought. But like a concerned scientist today he was driven further, to attempt to understand something of the nature of the world. His sceptical, questioning, yet constructive mind needed more than emotional religious devotion could offer him. There were problems that needed to be solved. In the same spirit nowadays an educated man or woman of the world, interested in the developments of the arts and sciences, dissatisfied with the apparently baseless speculations of theology, not concerned with the professional philosophy of the universities, will read difficult though non-specialist books and articles on general questions about life.

There was a fair amount of choice of such books open to Chaucer, some of which he made use of in *The Canterbury Tales*. He tells us in *The Prologue* to *The Legend of Good Women* (F version, written about 1386) that he had translated 'Boece' and also a devout work by the ancient Church Father Origen on Mary Magdalene, as well as *The*

87

Life of Saint Cecilia. In the 'G' version of *The Prologue*, written about 1395, he adds that he had translated the gloomily entitled *Wreched Engendrynge of Mankynde*, otherwise entitled *De Contemptu Mundi* ('Of Contempt for the World'), by Pope Innocent III of the twelfth century. These are works, like the *Tale of Melibeus*, of morality, and indicate not only a continuing but a deepening concern. The 'Boece' is far the most massive influence on his poetry. This is not surprising, for it had been a work of major European importance ever since written in the sixth century. Manuscripts, printed versions, and translations are numerous. In England it held sway until the end of the seventeenth century and Milton was influenced by it. King Alfred in Anglo-Saxon times, and Queen Elizabeth I both translated it.

BOETHIUS

The Consolation of Philosophy builds into its own text something of the circumstances in which it was written, and the work is a classic example both of how much we gain from knowing something about the circumstances of an author and the conditions in which his book was written, and of how much of such essential real information could be written into the text itself in earlier literature, mingling fact and fiction.

Boethius was from an old Roman family, and after the conquest of Rome by the barbarians he served the Emperor Theodoric. He was exceptionally well read in Greek philosophy and his translations of some elementary treatises formed the basis of the later medieval developments in philosophy and logic. He was a Christian and wrote several influential theological tracts. He also had an exceptionally fortunate political career and the joy of seeing his two sons made joint consuls. Then, when he was at the height of Fortune's wheel – an image he himself invented – disaster came. He fell from the Emperor's favour, and after a period of imprisonment in Pavia he was cruelly put to death in 524, still only forty-four years old. While in prison he wrote his greatest work. It draws much of its force from the tremendous reversal of fortune that had overtaken him in his own life. The point of writing it was precisely to 'console' himself, to come to terms with the nature of existence, to make sense of an apparently senseless world, to account for suffering and evil, and to see how to overcome them. There is a moving partial parallel in the twentieth century with the situation and writings of the great German theologian Bonhoeffer, imprisoned and savagely put to death by the Nazis in 1945.

Boethius, though no doubt sustained by his Christian faith, which underpins his work with the belief in a benevolent Creator-God, attempted to meet the problems through the exercise of natural reason, which for him meant relying mainly on the classical pagan philosophers Plato and Seneca. Consolations had been written in classical times, but the elaboration and power of Boethius's work is unique, as at first was its dialogue form addressed to himself.

THE FORM OF *THE CONSOLATION OF PHILOSOPHY*

The *Consolation* is written in elaborate and quite difficult late-classical Latin. It is divided into five books, and each book is divided into alternating sections of prose and verse, called 'proses' and 'metres', though Chaucer translates all into prose. This form, in conjunction with analytical content, is sometimes called Menippean satire, or an anatomy: it was very influential, especially in the twelfth century, and the work of the twelfth-century theologian and satirist, Alanus de Insulis, already referred to, follows it carefully. In a sense *The Canterbury Tales* also may be thought of as a Menippean satire, or anatomy, both analytical and creative, in verse and prose.

A striking feature of the *Consolation* is that the author presents himself as a character within it. It begins with a metre; in Chaucer's translation, 'Allas, I wepynge, am constreyned to bygynnen vers of sorwful matere, that whilom in florysschyng studie made delitable ditees ...' He reproaches Fortune. All this refers to his situation in prison. The following prose then describes how he then sees 'a womman of ful greet reverence', of great beauty, sometimes of human size, sometimes seeming to reach to Heaven. Her beautiful dress bears two Greek letters which signify both active and contemplative life. But part of her dress has been torn by men. The lady sees the poetical Muses approach the bed of Boethius to help him write his complaint, but she drives forth their flatteries with scorn. She is the Lady Philosophy. Her dialogue with Boethius is conveyed in the successive proses, punctuated by beautifully meditative metres.

This opening is peculiarly effective and influential. The author is shown as an inferior character within his own work, a Narrator of what happened and what was said to him; and yet he is also the real person who is outside the whole work and is writing the words attributed to the superior character as well as those attributed to his lesser self of the past within the book. We have here the ambiguity of author/*persona* which was developed into a characteristic Gothic device by so many European poets in the thirteenth and fourteenth centuries.

The device is very effective because it creates, in the *Consolation* as in so many later poems, a complex instrument of meaning and audience control. Because the 'mask' of the writer, the *persona*, is inside the poem, the audience is enabled more easily to identify with him, his sorrow and ignorance. In so far as they do so, their feelings can be worked on, and they can be instructed. They also identify with the superior person in the work, adopting his or her superior knowledge and greater power. The result is that readers or audience both dominate the writer (in the work) and are dominated by him (from outside). There is also a progression. The *persona* begins as inferior to the writer *now* because he was *then*, in the past, ignorant and stupid. The work charts the progress of the *persona*, or rather the progressive narrowing of the gap between *persona* and writer, and consequently, the removal of the initial inferiority of the *persona*. At the end *persona* and writer are united in understanding. In identifying with and following the progress of the *persona*, the audience also repairs its inferiority, is agreeably instructed, and finally becomes at one with the writer. A satisfying unity of feeling and idea is achieved at the end. The work is never totally self-enclosed, like a printed book, of whose author we are as entirely ignorant, as you, dear reader, are of me, except in so far as you can guess about me from my manner of writing. (If you consult the blurb you are going outside the text, into the context, and you almost certainly have done this if you are sensible, because all books need to be read in personal and historical context if the author's full meaning is to be understood.) With as much knowledge of context as possible, the creative, sympathetic participation of the audience or reader in the text is then necessary for full understanding. The initial presence of the modest, suffering, ignorant *persona* is an encouragement to participate. The duality of the author/*persona* creates an attractive blend of realism and fiction.

A GREAT LADY INSTRUCTS THE AUTHOR

The situation in which, in the work, a great, superior lady instructs the inferior author became a favourite literary device in medieval literature. The Lady is a sort of Jungian Anima, or mother-figure within the mind of the author, in the *Consolation*. She is a similar personage in the very Boethian *Complaint of Nature* by Alanus de Insulis. In Langland she is Mother-church. Mutations are possible and fruitful. In Dante's *Divine Comedy* the beloved lady Beatrice is the equivalent. In *Pearl* the lady who instructs the author is his own transformed dead daughter. Chaucer borrows Nature from Alanus in *The Parliament*. His Alcestis in *The Prologue* to *The Legend of Good Women* is a distant relative. Chaucer's imagination does not much lend itself to archetypal, mythic forms. In particular he does not easily conceive of figures, especially female figures, of authority. The man in black's 'instruction' in *The Book of the Duchess* has some relationship to the device. It is at bottom a device for presenting an argument within the writer's own mind, in his divided spirit, between two aspects of the self, in which he attempts to adjust himself to the reality which the later 'higher', more philosophical part of him perceives, to win over his recalcitrant, earlier, lesser physical self, and to achieve a wholeness within which he will overcome sorrow with reconciliation. Chaucer sees this very well, even if he makes little use of the figure of authority, and his *Troilus* in particular is influenced by the attempt to reconcile oneself to painful reality portrayed by the *Consolation*.

THE CONTENT OF THE *CONSOLATION*

The *Consolation* is a complex work, proceeding by question, argument and answer, and only its main themes and questions can be summarised here. Book I centres on the essential question, if God exists and is good, where does evil come from? Book II is concerned with Fortune, a concept which Boethius did much to elaborate, and concludes with the remarkable poem, metre 8, which Chaucer also translated into verse and incorporated as the climax at the end of Book III of the *Troilus*, celebrating the bond of love which holds all things in the world in harmonious unity. Book III of the *Consolation* discusses what goods bring true, as opposed to uncertain, happiness. Books IV and V deal with the problems of free will and destiny.

The subject matter of the *Consolation* may be summed up in Milton's description of the Fallen Angels, who reasoned high

> Of Providence, Foreknowledge, Will and Fate –
> Fixed fate, free will, foreknowledge absolute –
> And found no end, in wandering mazes lost.
> Of good and evil much they argued then,
> Of happiness and final misery,
> Passion and apathy, and glory and shame –
>
> *Paradise Lost*, 559–64

though Boethius did not lose himself in the labyrinth. Boethius's first and undisputed premise is belief in a good and all-powerful God, who can do no evil, and who has created the world. This granted, he is obviously faced with two great difficulties. First, how can a good God have allowed so much misery and evil to enter the world? Secondly, since such a God must know *everything*, he knows the future. If God knows now what is going to happen in the future, then the future must be fixed, and nothing we can do can alter it. (This connects with the first problem, since it ultimately implies that God makes us do evil as well as good, whether we will or no.) The horror of this predestination, this determinism, appals Boethius, and he spends much time confuting it. Indeed, a great deal of the philosophy of the Middle Ages was concerned with it, and the philosophical poets, Dante and Jean de Meun, write about it. It is one of the dominant themes of learned controversy in England in the fourteenth century, and Chaucer often refers to it.

Boethius solves the problem of pain and evil by saying that although we all rightly and naturally desire happiness, we seek it under the wrong forms (as in the love of wife and family, of wealth and power, of natural scenery, of the arts). True happiness is the Good, which is God, who only is permanence. We should therefore love God alone; and to do this we must master ourselves and our natural passions. If we master our passions, we shall be free from the trammels of the world, and so shall find true happiness and freedom in God. The ultimate lesson is one that many modern scientists would accept, namely that 'reality' is essentially 'mind-stuff', and that mind is superior to matter.

He solves the problem of predestination by first pointing out that eternity is quite different from time-going-on-for-ever. It is outside time. Everything on earth, past, present and future, is in God's eternal Now. Secondly, he says that it is a man's passions only which are part of the normal chain of inevitable cause and effect. Once his soul has freed itself from the domination of the passions by loving the divine, man's will is free.

This bleak summary of the central thought of the *Consolation* conveys nothing of its delight – the noble conception of an all-wise, loving Creator, of the loveliness of the world as created by God, and as continually maintained by him. There is an inevitable dualism in the *Consolation* which is of extreme importance in appreciating both Chaucer's thought, and that of the Middle Ages as a whole. God is good, and therefore His creation must be good: yet we know that so much is bad. Should we, therefore, in loving God, despise His world? It seems wrong to undervalue the world, since God made it 'and saw that it was good', but if we love the world, do we not inevitably forget God, loving his gifts instead of Him?

Most thinkers in the Middle Ages tended to emphasise the need to be on the safe side, and to despise mundane affairs. The dualism of medieval Christian teaching could provide an agonising problem for an intelligent, sensuous and pious man – especially in matters of love.

However, at this full flowering period of his life, Chaucer was most attracted by the possibility of synthesis. The possibility of reconciliation is inherent in the *Consolation* itself, as may be seen from two important passages which Chaucer later put into poems. One of these, already referred to, is praise of 'the bond of love' (II, metre 8). The other is praise of God's creative activity. Boethius in *Consolation* III, metre 9, says that the world is perfectly made, and is governed and controlled by God's everlasting Reason, which binds the elements in harmony in 'the fayre cheyne of love'. This is the basis of Theseus's great speech in *The Knight's Tale* (*CT* I, 2987 ff.).

These and similar passages emphasise the goodness of creation and the divine source of love. Human love and marriage appear as part of the divinely maintained order of things. Love and reason here spring from the same source. The possibility of reconciling the inherent tension between them was further improved by the teaching of astrology.

DATE AND QUALITY OF THE TRANSLATION

The precise date of Chaucer's translation of Boethius's *Consolation of Philosophy* is uncertain. It was probably done some time about 1380, although it is likely he knew the book some years before that, and much of its substance had been conveyed in the *Roman*. The translation was written with scholarly care, and he consulted a French translation and commentary, and perhaps other commentaries, for many existed in Latin.

Chaucer's care is such that at times he is awkwardly literal, but the work is in general, though difficult, a masterpiece of English prose. His task was the more difficult in that there were virtually no precedents in English for this kind of prose. He was not content only with a literal translation, important though that was to him. Professor Margaret Schlauch has shown that he deliberately used rythmical devices based on the patterns of the *cursus* (or rhythmic ending) of Latin prose, and other rhetorical adornments like alliteration and word-echo, to dignify the style.

OXFORD INTELLECTUAL SCEPTICISM AND EMPIRICISM

The *Consolation* was simple and unprofessional compared with the power of thirteenth- and fourteenth-century scholasticism, but that in itself made it available to Chaucer, a courtier and a literary man, not a professional philosopher and theologian. Yet Chaucer, with his remarkable intellectual sensibility used the *Consolation* in a way that echoes some of the main prepossessions of fourteenth-century thought, which centred on problems of determinism and free will, and which were notable for the beginnings of English empiricism. His Oxford connections may have helped him here. In the early fourteenth century Oxford was the dominant centre of European thought. Ockham, who may be said to have represented both a sceptical rationalism and a passionate fideism (two sides of the same coin) was an Oxford man. A number of fellows of Merton did important scientific and theological work, and Bradwardine, who was one of them, and died as Archbishop of Canterbury in the Black Death, wrote a vast tome on free will and predestination, though of this Chaucer in *The Nun's Priest's Tale* says he cannot 'bulte it to the bren'. What does seem clear is that Chaucer caught something of the new spirit of rational enquiry without needing deep professional acquaintance with its detail. And he eventually shared the fideism, the faith without reason, that inevitably accompanies rationalism even today, though the terms are different.

OTHER INTELLECTUAL INTERESTS AND CHAUCER'S ATTITUDE

Chaucer's other general intellectual interests also reflected the advanced movements of the age. He could have acquired his alchemical and medical, even his ornithological, knowledge from Vincent of Beauvais's encyclopaedia. In so far as interest in religion is intellectual Chaucer had a characteristic sympathy with Lollardy. Lollardy was a major growth-point of the spirit of the fourteenth century. It was extremely literalistic, therefore radical, and anti-ecclesiastical, anti-traditional. It was also passionately simple-minded, and Chaucer's association and sympathy stop far short of commitment. He had other secular interests of a different kind. He was astonishingly well read in secular literature, and in secular history, in Latin (though mostly in Ovid apart from anthology pieces), and in French and Italian. He might almost be thought of as our first professional literary intellectual, except that he was not paid for being so. His intellectual imagination is classicising and historical rather than romantic and mythopoeic. He is an important example of the development of the lay spirit in the fourteenth century.

ASTRONOMY

As already noted, another deep interest was in astronomy, where though he was amateur he was far from superficial. Astronomy was scientific, but in so far as astronomy was inextricably entangled with astrology, which had close connections with classical mythology, Chaucer's scientific interest also very obviously fed his philosophical and poetical interests.

One of the constant notes of the *Consolation* which must have especially appealed to Chaucer is the praise of the beauty of the starry heavens, which are the perfect example of the beauty of the natural world when it obeys God's laws. They are the embodiment of the serenity and radiance and perfect order – those brave translunary things – which are so notably lacking in our sphere beneath the moon.

By Chaucer's day there was a very considerable accumulation of astronomical knowledge. The movement of the stars was very well recognised and plotted out; prediction was possible; tables for calculating stellar movements, and such instruments for observing the height of the stars as the astrolabe – though not yet the telescope – were all in relatively common use. Chaucer's ability in arithmetic would have made calculations easy for him.

As it happens, the model of the universe then formed by astronomers was wrong. It was the model going by the name of Ptolemy, an astronomer of the second century AD. In the Ptolemaic universe the earth is the centre, tiny, relatively dull, subject to change, decay and death. Around this centre were thought to be a series of rotating concentric transparent spheres, in which were successively fixed the planets and the sun. These are the 'heavens', which for example Dante moves through on his way to Paradise. The nearest sphere and planet is that of the moon, which provided the limit of corruptibility. Outside the moon and successively outside each other are the spheres of Mercury, Venus, the Sun, Mars, Jupiter, Saturn. Then comes the sphere of the fixed stars, which is the general scattering of stars about the sky in their slow-moving constellations. Outside these eight spheres is a ninth, the *Primum Mobile* or First Mover, whose function is to transform the love of God into the energy which moves the stars, whose movement produces the harmony of the spheres.

Within the fixed stars is a particularly noticeable band of constellations which go all round the sphere like the seam on a cricket ball. This band is called the Zodiac. When one looks up from earth one can see various planets at different times against a different background of Zodiacal stars, for they all travel roughly the same path round the Earth, at slightly different speeds. When planets could be seen against a particular constellation, or sign, of the Zodiac, they were thought to have a particular relation to it, and to have a special effect on events on earth.

Although we know that the Ptolemaic model is wrong, most of us know that only because books tell us so. If we cannot work great telescopes, etc. we are happy to take the modern picture of the universe on trust, on the authority of scientists, incomprehensible though space must be. Medieval men did the same, and accepted the authority of experts. With the instruments at their disposal the Ptolemaic model in fact better explained the observable movements of the stars than did the new Copernican model of the sixteenth century. Only further theoretical refinements, and the invention of the telescope in the early seventeenth century justified the later model.

Chaucer would have loved the telescope. His technical and practical interest in the mechanics of astronomy is illustrated in his *Treatise on the Astrolabe*, which was the principal instrument, with some resemblance to a quadrant or sextant, used by medieval astronomers for measuring the height of the stars. It is an elementary treatise, mainly translated, but with some attractive personal notes, which Chaucer wrote for his 'little son Lewis'. It is unfinished. Perhaps the boy died. It was written about 1392, when Chaucer was at the height of his poetic powers, and shows how seriously he took both the astronomy and his fatherly obligations and interests. He modestly comments in his prefatory remarks to Lewis that 'I n'am but a lewd compilator of the labour of olde astrolgiens, and have it translatyd in myn Englissh oonly for thy doctrine. And with this swerd shal I sleen envie.' All the same, the very idea of undertaking such a work was original, and the work is a milestone in the history of English scientific prose.

There is also in existence a similarly technical treatise, finished, called *The Equatorie of the Planetis* (edited by Dr Derek Price in 1955). Only one manuscript exists, and in a margin of one page seems to be written the name 'Chaucer'. It has been suggested that the manuscript is in Chaucer's very own hand. The language would correspond to his period and dialect, and the spelling seems quite likely to be his. The work is quite impersonal but an important part of a notable movement of scientific English prose of which Chaucer was in the forefront.

Astronomy is scientific, specialist, non-evaluative, based on calculation, in a word, 'modern'. It was however inextricably interwoven, as Chaucer knew, and illustrates by his abrupt withdrawal in the *Astrolabe*, with astrology, which is a quite different matter. Astrology is concerned with evaluation, it has a moral quality, it affects the whole of life, it is in a word 'archaic', not only in being ancient but in representing our timeless hopes and fears which are always part of the human condition. We must now turn to a brief consideration of astrology in the fourteenth century.

ASTROLOGY

The Moon unquestionably influences the tides, and the Sun controls our seasons on earth. It was inevitable that from earliest times other stars too should have been thought to control events on earth, and the fortunes of men. This is astrology. The power of astrology to meet some requirement of the mind and imagination is witnessed today, when so many popular newspapers and magazines in advanced industrial societies publish horoscopes and astrological predictions, which many people believe. Astrology is demonstrably rubbish, but its modern prevalence may help us sympathetically to imagine the situation in the fourteenth century when, in the conditions of the time, it could not be seen to be rubbish, but was regarded as a master-science. All men accepted it. The more learned the scientist or theologian (they were often combined in the same person) the more firmly he believed that the weather, the crops, the very stones of the earth, and all animal life including the animal part of human beings, were governed in their properties by the stars. The theory of astrological influences was the fourteenth-century scientific theory of the normal working of cause and effect now explained in terms of Newton's and Einstein's laws of dynamics and so forth. Medical men, scientists, politicians, merchants would have been incompetent if they did not either know some astrology or (in the two latter classes) consult the experts.

The troubled and harassed years of the fourteenth century gave a great impetus to men's desire to know the future, and so perhaps to be able to control their fates. But the possibility of knowing the future immediately raised the problems of predestination faced by Boethius, while orthodox Christian doctrine was irrevocably committed to belief in free will. Furthermore, the aim of controlling man's outer environment, rather than his inner spiritual state, is one which any religion must regard with misgiving. Hence there was a good deal of religious writing against science, in particular against astrology, not so much because it was thought to be untrue, as because it was thought that it might lead men on the wrong track. Those parts of the science which tended to destroy belief in freedom of the will (judicial astrology) or which appeared to truckle with supernatural (and probably evil) agents were especially condemned as magic. Professor Thorndyke has amply proved that science and magic spring from the same impulse of the mind to control the external rather than the internal world, and it often seems that what men call magic is really faulty science. Astrology, to fourteenth-century minds, merged imperceptibly into magic, but it was difficult to draw the dividing line. This explains the many contradictions and confusions in writers on the subject, and Chaucer's own *volte-face* in the *Astrolabe* (II, 4), where after he has gone on from astronomical information to the discussion of fortunate and unfortunate aspects of the stars, he suddenly says, 'Natheles these ben observaunces of judicial matere and rytes of payens, in whiche my spirit hath no feith'. The crux of the problem lay in questions of morals and ethics. Philosophical and religious problems were not so obvious in the case of, say, weather predictions. The orthodox view with regard to men's actions may be summed up in the words of St Thomas Aquinas:

> The majority of men, in fact, are governed by their passions, which are dependent on bodily appetites; in these the influence of the stars is clearly felt. Few indeed are the wise who are capable of resisting their animal instincts. Astrologers, consequently, are able to foretell the truth in the majority of cases, especially when they undertake general predictions. In particular predictions they do not attain certainty, for nothing prevents a man from resisting the dictates of his lower faculties. Wherefore the astrologers themselves are wont to say 'that the wise man rules the stars', forasmuch, namely, as he rules his own passions.
>
> (*Summa Theologica*, I.I. 115.4 Ad Tertium (5.544). Quoted by T.O. Wedel, 'The medieval attitude toward astrology', *Yale Studies in English*, lx, Yale, 1920).

Chaucer does not make his heroes 'wise men'.

The stars, therefore, are thought to form a person's character and often to motivate his desires and actions. In Chaucer's work at this period there is little emphasis on *resisting* the course guided by the stars. The reason is that God's Providence – or as he puts it in *The Knight's Tale*,

> The destinee, ministre general,
> That executeth in the world over al   [*carries out*
> The purveiaunce that God hath seyn biforn –   [*providence*
>
> *CT* I, 1663 – 5

which controls the whole world with the 'chain of love', must intend all for the best. There is a strong streak of optimistic determinism in Chaucer's thought at this time. Since Love is what guides the world and maintains its order, as both Boethius and the Gospel of St John say, the planet of love – Venus – assumes particular importance. Venus the planet was regarded as the scientific or immediate 'cause' of love not only between human beings, but of the 'love' which guides the mating of animals, and even the attraction asserted by the force of gravity (for to the fourteenth century the whole material universe was in a sense 'alive', almost sentient). Moreover, Venus was the Goddess of Love in much of the classical literature which Chaucer knew so well.

MYTHOLOGY AND MYTHOGRAPHY

By mythology here is meant stories about the gods. Every age has them. By the time they come to be thought of as 'mythology', rather than as sacred stories, scepticism has crept in. A further stage is reached when men collect and compare stories about the gods, make dictionaries of attributes, analyse their meaning. This further stage is called mythography.

THE CLASSICAL HERITAGE

For the Middle Ages the Biblical stories which make the foundation of Christianity were literally true and sacred, although they could be allegorised, interpreted and retold. The classical heritage was different. There were many pagan gods, and in the first few centuries of the Christian era many people still took them seriously, and even invented new ones, like the goddess Fortune. The ancient gods and goddesses, Jupiter, Mars, Venus, Mercury, etc. were still strong enough to be violently attacked by St Augustine in his *The City of God* (413–27 AD). The attacks by him and others were successful, and by the sixth century they were finished as sacred powers. This released them for other valuable purposes in the Christian Middle Ages.

The gods were also characters in stories. Originally these were presumably sacred, but even by the Greek Homer's time, the seventh century BC, in his *Iliad* and *Odyssey*, the gods are portrayed in a fascinatingly human style, even if regarded as divine. By the time of the Latin classical writers, Virgil and Ovid (with many others), stories of the gods could present them in many different ways, from serious to comic. The earliest comic story on record is about them, and is found in Homer. The goddess of love, Aphrodite (in Latin, Venus) was married to the ugly, lame god of smiths, Hephaistos (in Latin, Vulcan). She had an affair with Ares (Latin, Mars), god of war. The jealous husband by his art wove a metal net so fine it could not be seen and hung it over the bed. Then he trapped Aphrodite and Ares together and displayed them naked to the other gods. They laughed as much at the jealous husband making public his shame as at the lovers, while Hermes (Latin, Mercury) said that he would not mind being in Ares' position. This story as told by Ovid became the most famous story about Venus. On the other hand, in Virgil's *Aeneid*, Venus is rather the beautiful, tender, anxious mother of both Cupid and Aeneas. Aeneas had a mortal father. Stories varied as to who Cupid's father was. The stories of the gods, like all myths and folktales, existed in numerous different forms. They are traditional stories, and the very act of retelling a traditional story both repeats the old and introduces something new. The Christian church was the great educational force in the Middle Ages, and it had no choice but to use pagan Latin texts, as already noted, as the most refined instruments of education. Hence the use of Virgil and Ovid. In the early centuries there was continuous unease about this, arising from the intrinsically non-Christian nature of the texts, and also from the nature of the subject matter of many of the stories, such as the one just quoted about Venus. By Chaucer's time this unease had largely though not entirely disappeared. Reference to pagan gods was commonplace, and it was well understood that they were either fictional characters, or allegories, or planets, or in some cases poetical references to God himself. Thus Jupiter (Jove) might be either a fictional character, an allegory, a planet, or an educated way of referring to God in a story. (In the nineteenth century Englishmen might still use the mild oath 'By Jove', instead of the less polite 'By God'.) Superficial inconsistencies might arise, but they puzzle no one except unduly literalistic twentieth-century readers.

THE SCIENTIFIC ASSOCIATION

There were two general reasons why names of some of the pagan gods should have become Christian commonplaces. One will already have been realised by the reader. The names of a number of them had been given to certain stars to identify them, especially the planets. In origin perhaps the influences attributed to planets had been taken over from the gods with whom they had been associated, as Venus planet of love, and Mars of war. By the fourteenth century the actual planet was thought to be the source of the influence, which might be strong or weak according to the planet's apparent relationship in the sky to other planets and stars. Chaucer's *Complaint of Mars* is a witty conflation of planetary movements and influences with the love-story. The poem has a basis of astronomical truth, and is adorned with humanising mythological fantasy. Though non-religious, there is nothing anti-Christian or particularly pagan about it, except in its remote origins, and these would not have occurred to fourteenth-century readers.

THE MYTHOGRAPHERS

Besides astronomy and astrology, the other main reason for the Christianisation or, at any rate, for the sterilisation of pagan qualities in classical mythology, was the work of the mythographers. Mythographers, that is scholars, had begun to analyse myths long before the birth of Christ. The stories are often so strange that they need interpreting. One favourite way of interpreting was attributed to a scholar called Euhemerus, whose work, now lost, argued that the so-called gods were really supremely successful mortals whom others had by mistake come to consider divine. Euhemerism is still used occasionally by some as an explanation for myths. Another line of interpretation was to consider the stories as allegories of various kinds. Commentators on classical texts developed many theories. Cicero in *De Nature Deorum* (On the Nature of the Gods) wrote an influential book incorporating different points of view. The schoolbook *De Nuptiis Philologiae et Mercurii* (On the Marriage of Philosophy and Mercury) by Martianus Capella in the fifth century uses mythology to attempt to enliven a dry description of the Seven Liberal Arts. There were many others.

FULGENTIUS TO BOCCACCIO

From the point of view of the Middle Ages the basic mythographer was Fulgentius, whose *Mitologiarum Libri Tres* (Three Books of Mythologies) appeared in the sixth century, and whose remarks were endlessly repeated by later writers. He takes the stories and allegorises them to show that they 'really' mean quite different physical or historical events, or moral concepts. A good example of the method of Fulgentius is given by his interpretation of the famous mythological episode of the Judgement of Paris. Paris was a Trojan prince. Some time after his judgement, to be described in a moment, he eloped to Troy with the beautiful Helen, wife of the Greek king Menelaus, whom Paris had been visiting. Menelaus in order to reclaim Helen started the Trojan war, in which the Greeks after ten years' fighting utterly destroyed Troy. The judgement of Paris which preceded all this was made when this princely shepherd was visited on his lonely hillside by three beautiful naked goddesses, Minerva, Juno and Venus (to give them their Latin names), and told to decide who was supreme. He chose Venus, goddess of love. Fulgentius interprets this as an allegory of the soul's need to choose between the contemplative life (Minerva), the active life (Juno), and the voluptuous life (Venus). He then Christianises the story by interpreting it as an allegory of the Fall of Adam (because of his love of Eve) as told in *Genesis* II, with Jupiter signifying God.

Fulgentius is remarkable for describing for the first time the appearance of the gods, and indicating the significance of their characteristics. They paint Venus naked, he writes, either because she sends away naked those who are addicted to her, or because the crime of lust cannot be concealed, or because it is only suitable to the naked. She has roses because they are red, and sting, like lust, the red coming from shame, the sting from sin. As roses please for a while then fade, so lust pleases for a moment then always departs. She has doves with her because they are notoriously lecherous. They paint her floating in the sea because lust in the end suffers shipwreck. She carries a conch-shell because this creature is totally immersed in copulation. Fulgentius also tells and allegorises the story of Venus and Mars.

Just as Augustine's powerful attack made it impossible to take Venus seriously as divine, and thus paradoxically made it theologically safe to read about her, so Fulgentius's condemnatory allegory made her morally respectable because she showed up how bad lust is. Theologically and morally safe, scientifically acceptable, the later career of Venus was highly successful, so that she could in the end represent God's own love, and be presented by Boccaccio and Chaucer as a classical representation of the Blessed Virgin Mary, Empress of Heaven and Earth and Hell.

It is impossible to follow here all the mythographers and poets who wrote about Venus in the Middle Ages. One Albricus Phiosophicus, probably a Canon of St Paul's in London in the twelfth century, wrote an account limited mainly to descriptions, leaving out allegorisation, which may be the source of Chaucer's description in *The House of Fame*, ll. 130 ff. Chaucer is rarely interested in allegory: he prefers the historical or scientific fact 'without glose' (commentary).

To conclude this account of mythography we may take as an example Boccaccio, a little older than Chaucer, so rich a source for him, yet such a contrast. Boccaccio, like Chaucer, but earlier in life, turned away from the vernacular poems and stories at which he was such a genius, and devoted the rest of his life to religion and scholarship. In particular he collected up all the stories of the gods, and tried to classify and interpret them, like a fourteenth-century version of the immensely influential modern French scholar, Professor C. Lévi-Strauss. So contemporary at all times is mythography. Boccaccio wrote a vast compendium in Latin, *De Genealogia Deorum*, 'Concerning the Genealogy of the Gods', which was copied, reprinted and translated frequently during the next four centuries in Europe. Chaucer either did not know it, or was not interested in it. But though Chaucer was antipathetic to allegory, he could not avoid being susceptible to the kind of meanings that might be implicit in traditional figures in literature. And he would have relished the ambiguities.

Boccaccio's discussion of Venus in the *De Genealogia Deorum* is typical of his method and material. He is not quite clear how many Venuses there are, but it is vital to realise that there are more than one. The first is the greater Venus, sixth daughter of the Sky and the Day. Boccaccio comments on the many confused stories about her, but as they have been deduced from the properties of the planet, he says, he will first describe what the astrologers say. The core of the matter is this. Since as a planet she appears fixed in the sky and moving with it, she seems to be produced by it, hence her father is the Sky. She is called daughter of the Day because of her brightness. Since God made nothing in vain, he made the stars 'in order that by their movement and influence, the seasons of the passing year should be varied, mortal things generated, what generated should be born, what born fostered, and in time should come to an end'. The effects of Venus are those of 'love, friendship, affection, company, domesticity, union between animals, and especially the begetting of children. ... Whence it may be admitted that by her are caused the pleasures of men.' When she attends marriages she wears the girdle called the Ceston, signifying love, friendship, eloquence and caresses. 'This bond is not carried if not in honest marriage, and therefore all other coupling is called incest.' At times the astrologers say she is associated with the Furies, and this is especially liable to happen in spring when 'not only brute animals, but also women, whose complexion is for the most part warm and moist when spring comes, incline more strongly towards heat and wantonness. Which inclination, if modesty does not restrain it, may be converted into fury.' The Furies may also be said to come when there is bitterness or deceit or desertion in love. Venus can also indicate mere sexuality, and the lustful are born under her domination.

The second Venus is the seventh daughter of the Sky, and mother of Cupid. By her Boccaccio understands the *lascivious* life, as referred to above. She signifies sexual intercourse. He then quotes *verbatim* the condemnatory passage from Fulgentius about Venus just summarised above.

The third Venus, eleventh daughter of Jove, was wife of Vulcan, mistress of Mars, mother of Aeneas. Some think she was the same as that lady of Cyprus who was wife of Adonis. But Boccaccio thinks not. It was this latter lady, a yet different one, who invented prostitution in order to cover her own promiscuity, and was thus a fourth Venus.

Chaucer must have known from various writings these and similar stories about the gods. Although such explicit allegories were not for him, their general interest is that they help to reveal many symbolic or potential meanings in ancient stories.

THE ATTRACTION OF STORIES

We have now seen examples of Chaucer's intellectual interests and of the influences under which he worked. Their range is astonishing. The 'shape' of Chaucer's mind is becoming clearer: the world as it is forms his dominating concern, and within that personal relationships, especially love, are dominant. The setting of life is important, whether present or historical. Yet the realistic surface, though fascinating, is not enough. The depths and direction of the river of life are probed. Chaucer is empirical, yet reflective; speculative, but in a scientific and practical way, not in abstract metaphysics or improbable allegories; his mind is always in movement and he is attracted to movement, to exploration of event. He turned more and more towards stories as a way of satisfying those desires. Stories have a surface of event, character and description which are intrinsically interesting, as in lively daily life. They also have depths. One way of registering the feeling that a story has greater significance than mere reportage is by allegorising it, as Fulgentius allegorises the Judgement of Paris, or theologians allegorised Biblical stories. Chaucer's feeling for material reality normally rejected such allegorising, with few exceptions. But stories have significances other than allegorical. One sort is simply the actual significances that events and people have in ordinary life, and on which the writer may comment, seriously, flippantly or ironically, within the work, as if the story had actually happened. Chaucer enjoyed doing that. He likes to comment, meditate, or respond in feeling to the story as it goes along. Such a method is familiar with such a novelist as Scott, who has much in common with Chaucer. So it is that stories became increasingly attractive to him as pleasurable in themselves, and also as providing opportunities for reflecting on life, and conveying his feelings about life, its comedy or pathos, its sheer interest.

Stories also have other kinds of significance, deriving from the patterns of events and people. Usually a story-teller by the very fact of telling the story does not draw attention to, and may not even be conscious of, such deeper or more general implications, but they have their effect on the reader who also may respond only subconsciously. Chaucer on the whole likes to comment on the course of the story in a conscious way, arousing the reader's conscious responses. That is particularly so in the two philosophical romances we now consider.

Chapter 9

A PHILOSOPHICAL ROMANCE:
THE KNIGHT'S TALE

TWO ITALIAN STORIES

The two major poems that Chaucer now turned to write were stories whose plot, mythological apparatus and historical perspective come from Boccaccio, but for which Boethius supplies the substance for philosophical commentary. The characters, setting, style and general verve are Chaucer's own. Each is a story of love. They are the stories of *Palamon and Arcite* and of *Troilus and Criseyde*, each referred to in the early, F *Prologue* to *The Legend of Good Women*, and therefore certainly composed before 1386, and before *The Canterbury Tales*.

Chaucer had bought at least three books in Florence in 1374. One was Dante's *Divine Comedy*; the second was Boccaccio's *Teseida*; the third was Boccaccio's *Il Filostrato*. *The Divine Comedy* he used in detail but it was an end in itself, not raw material he could work on. Boccaccio's more human less perfect narratives were more malleable. *Teseida* offered some brilliant passages, an interesting story, and a tantalising challenge in form. Chaucer had tried to use something of *Teseida*'s splendid diction and expansive narrative in *Anelida and Arcite* and had fallen back defeated on his earlier French manner. He tried again in *Palamon and Arcite* and got it right. *Palamon and Arcite* is very different from his earlier work and he tells us in *The Prologue* to *The Legend of Good Women* that 'the story is little known'. Perhaps the novelty of the poem made it at first unpopular. But Chaucer knew it was very good and used it later, probably unaltered, in *The Canterbury Tales* as *The Knight's Tale*, which for convenience we continue to call it.

THE KNIGHT'S TALE OF PALAMON AND ARCITE

The Knight's Tale is almost the most splendid of Chaucer's poems. It has everything: a firm plot, rich descriptions, clear characters, comedy, pathos, philosophical depth, a mature detachment. Young readers may find it slow, but the mature can savour every detail, from the extravagant behaviour of the young men, and idealised beauty of the girl, to the sententious sensible grim wisdom of the old. The poem illustrates Chaucer's full mastery over his source, Boccaccio's *Teseida*, his full assimilation of Italian vigour in the light of Boethian philosophy.

TESEIDA

Teseida is the first 'modern' epic, that is, one that copies Virgil's *Aeneid*. It is a work of genuine Humanism, that is, Neoclassicism, going back to the Latin classics and imitating them closely, though in the vernacular. *Teseida* is modelled on Virgil's *Aeneid*, with twelve books, historical introduction, journey to the underworld, funeral games, etc. Boccaccio even wrote copious notes, the *Chiose* already mentioned, so that his new epic was as learnedly presented as Virgil's now was in learned medieval editions. But its essential plot is a slender medieval romance. Boccaccio was still medieval under the Humanist cloak. Chaucer was, from this point of view, fully medieval. He threw away the cloak, ruthlessly cutting out excess material. All the same, he was inspired by Boccaccio's example to give the story elaborate decoration selectively borrowed and improved.

METRE

Chaucer was also inspired by Boccaccio's and Dante's eleven-syllable metre to use for the first time in English the five-stress, ten- or eleven-syllable line in couplets. With the independence and originality of genius he broke away from the stanza to the larger unit of the paragraph. The new rhythm has a longer, firmer, stride and pace, modulating to the syntax of the spoken word, but continuously sustained by the underlying regularity of the beat and the rhyme. There is nothing as good as this again after Chaucer till the mid-sixteenth century. (In reading the verse final –*e* or other similar endings, such as –*es* should be sounded as required for the regularity of the metre.)

THE STORY OF *THE KNIGHT'S TALE*

The story goes straight to the point, summarising many hundreds of Boccaccio's lines in a few dozen. 'As olde stories tellen us', it begins in the traditional way – once upon a time – there was a duke called Theseus, lord of Athens. He has conquered the Amazons, married their queen Hippolyta, and brought back her and her young sister Emily. Just as he arrives home a band of ladies, widowed in war at Thebes, ask him to avenge them on the tyrant Creon. Immediately, as true knight, he swears to do so, and turns for Thebes. We see the magnificence of a great king off to war, such as Edward III must have appeared.

> The rede statue of Mars, with spere and targe   [*shield*
> So shyneth in his white baner large
> That alle the feeldes glyteren up and doun   [*fields*
> And by his baner born is his penoun
> Of gold ful riche, in which ther was ybete   [*embroidered*
> The Mynotaur which that he slough in Crete.   [*slew*
> Thus rit this duc, thus rit this conqerour,   [*rides*
> And in his hoost of chivalrie the flour   [*army*
> Til that he cam to Thebes and alighte
> Faire in a field, ther as he thoughte to fighte.

CT I, 975–84

In his victorious battle two young Theban knights are captured, all but dead, and Theseus imprisons them for ever in Athens in a tower. They are two cousins and dear friends, Palamon and Arcite (the latter pronounced and sometimes spelt Arcita).

One day in May they see from their prison the beautiful golden-haired Emily at dawn gathering white and red flowers and singing. Palamon is the first to see her and is as it were stung to the heart. Palamon hardly knows if he has seen a woman or a goddess. Arcite then sees her and is equally affected. Alas they then quarrel, each claiming – how hopelessly – the primacy in love, because Arcite argues that Palamon is disqualified by not knowing whether Emily was woman or goddess. Arcite says that anyway lovers always break the law for love. He is much the tougher and more ruthless of the two young men, as well as the second to see Emily. A friend procures his release, with ironical consequences, for it places both young men at the extremes of grief; Palamon because still in prison, Arcite because free, but banished from Athens. However, Arcite returns secretly and works his way up the ladder of advancement at court, though still no nearer Emily. Then Palamon escapes, and Arcite, out Maying and sorrowing, accidentally meets him in the grove where he is hiding. They all but fight. Palamon has however no armour, so Arcite in his chivalry brings him next day all the armour and weapons he needs. They meet and arm each other in stony silence.

> Ther nas no 'good day', ne no saluyng   [*was not*; *greeting*
> But streight withouten word or rehersyng   [*repeating*
> Everich of hem heelp for to armen oother   [*each*
> As freendly as he were his owene brother.
>
> *CT* I, 1649–52

They fight madly. Theseus, out hunting in the company of Hippolyta and Emily, finds them. He is at first in a noble rage with them, and condemns them to death. The Queen and Emily go down on their bare knees to beg for pity for them, in a scene which recalls Froissart's famous story of how Queen Philippa successfully begged Edward III for mercy for the burghers of Calais. (The fiery, amorous but magnanimous Theseus might be a portrait of Edward III.) He forgives the two young men, who agree to meet in a year's time each with a troop of supporters to fight for Emily. Theseus has some fun at their expense. How great a lord is love, he says. Here are Arcite and Palamon, who might be living royally in Thebes, and who know that I am their mortal enemy, and here they are, in my presence, fighting each other to the death:

> Who may been a fool, but if he love?
>
> *CT* I, 1799

> But this is yet the beste game of alle,
> That she for whom they han his jolitee
> Kan hem therfore as muche thank as me.   [*owes*
> She woot namoore of al this hoote fare   [*knows*; *hot business*
> By God, than woot a cokkow or an hare.
>
> *CT* I, 1806–10

In a year's time the lists are set up, like a great theatre, precisely measured, and temples of Mars, Venus and Diana are set up. These are magnificently described, though mainly emphasising pain and sorrow – a reminder of the hardness of life underlying all the splendour. The poet participates so keenly, though not ironically, that he continually says in his description, 'I saw' this and that. He makes it all vivid and present to the mind. Arcite prays to Mars for victory; Palamon, who cares nothing for victory, only for Emily, prays to Venus; Emily, who would prefer the life of virginity, and loves hunting,

> And for to walken in the wodes wilde
> And noght to ben a wyf and be with childe
>
> *CT* I, 2309–10

prays to Diana that Palamon and Arcite may be reconciled and neither want her; but if it must be so, let him have her who most desires her. There is real sympathy for the pathos of woman's lot here. Since the poem is a fiction about pagan times these prayers come to the respective god and goddesses to whom they are addressed, in particular Mars and Venus, each of whom by a sign in the temple grants what is asked. The requests of Palamon and Arcite are incompatible, so Mars and Venus are referred by Jupiter to the gloomy Saturn, who promises that each will get what he asks for.

SOME INNER STRUCTURES OF THE STORY

The pagan surface of the story is supported here by the inner structure of scientific truth (as it then appeared) according to which the gods are really the planets, who really do influence people's lives. There is also an ironic pattern within the story: you get what you ask for, but it may not turn out to be precisely what you want. Arcite wants Emily but he asks for the means, victory, not the end. These inner structures of the story do not mean that the story is allegorical: they are not *more* real than the literal meaning, but are the depths below the shining surface, and are part of the whole meaning.

THE STORY RESUMED

The preparations for the tournament are told with unparalleled realism and conviction, and the fighting vigorously described in a pastiche of the rough alliterative style (ll. 2600–13). And Arcite wins. What of Venus's promise then? Saturn sends an infernal fury from the gound which startles Arcite's horse as he rides in triumph, and he receives his death-injury. The description of his sufferings is as detailed and realistic as the description of earlier splendour. The women shriek as he marries Emily on his death-bed, and he generously reconciles himself to Palamon, in a moving speech.

The extravagant sorrow shown by all is corrected by Theseus's aged father Egeus

That knew this worldes transmutacioun   [*changes*
As he hadde seyn it chaunge both up and doun,
Joye after wo, and wo after gladnesse,
And shewed hem ensaumples and liknesse.   [*illustrations*

CT I, 2839–42

The ups and downs of earthly fortune are a favourite reflection with Chaucer.

This world nys but a thurghfare ful of wo
And we been pilgrymes, passynge to and fro.
Deeth is an ende of every worldly soore.

CT I, 2847–9

This Boethian and medieval Christian commonplace is repeated at the end of *Troilus*, and is echoed in the Boethian lyrics 'Fortune' and 'Truth'. One should not expect life to be all roses. One should not mourn too much. Chaucer keeps the speech of Egeus short, but there is no reason to believe that its tone is ironic and self-mocking because it is a commonplace. It is the basic stoic acceptance of life-with-death that underlines both pathos and comedy, and is paradoxically comforting.

Arcite's pagan funeral pyre is described in great detail in an extraordinarily strange device of refusing at great length to describe, which seems to be an example of Chaucer's virtuoso rhetoric, very effective for those with an interest in pure artistic skill. Eventually, after years of mourning, Theseus summons Emily and Palamon to marry. Palamon deserves to succeed. He saw Emily first. He was less ruthless. He prayed for the end, the love of Emily, not the means, the victory in the tournament. Chaucer changes Boccaccio's characters around to bring this about. But the point is that the two young men are nevertheless closely similar. The deeper pattern of the story embodies the unspoken proposition that one stands a fifty-fifty chance of success and happiness in life.

The conclusion is brought about by a noble Boethian speech by Theseus, encouraging Palamon and Emily to make the best of 'this wrecched world', 'this foule prisoun of this lyf', which is however bound by 'the faire cheyne of love'. Death is inevitable, but Arcite made a good death. Why begrudge him his welfare? So let us make a virtue of necessity,

And after wo I rede us to be merye   [*advise*
And thanken Juppiter of al his grace.

CT I, 3068–9

Chaucer's resolute realism will no more deny joy than sorrow.

FLIPPANCY AND VARIABILITY OF TONE

In a very characteristic way he also indulges his flippancy at various stages of the poem. A traditionally sarcastic remark is made about women, when Emily favours Arcite as he becomes successful (ll. 2681–2). A flippant remark about what happens to the soul after death when Arcite dies (ll. 2809–15), is not unlike the flippancy of soliders in battle when their comrades are killed. There are other lightenings of tone, such as the comment on the cost of the paint used for the images in the temple of Diana, which is the earliest comment on such matters in Europe, much earlier even than made in Italy.

WHO TELLS THE STORY?

Who is the 'I' who seems to be telling the poem? There is no doubt it is Geoffrey Chaucer. But when a man writes he inevitably to some extent dramatises himself, especially when writing a poem, and the poet in his writing may in some ways differ from the ordinary mortal whose body he inhabits. This is accepted when we speak of 'the poet', even if we call him Chaucer. We accept the self-dramatisation, just as we accept the poem as a fiction, and not a statement to be tested in a police-court. Chaucer had long ago taken narrative self-dramatisation a stage further by introducing himself as a character within his own poem. As has already been noted, the character *within* the poem is a *persona* who is inevitably only a part of the total poet, who himself is represented by the total poem. In such poems *persona* and poet merge into one by the end. Is there a *persona* of Chaucer in *The Knight's Tale*? Obviously not.

IS THERE A NARRATOR?

How then shall we understand the 'I' who sometimes tells the story? The crucial question is, does he represent a Narrator who is different from the poet? If he is different, then we must be meant to take the literal meaning of the poem, spoken by the Narrator, as different from the real meaning intended by the real poet. Are we thus to take the poem as being meant ironically? Some modern critics who assume that Chaucer was a good man, and that all good men must be liberal humanist pacifists, have assumed that since the poem literally praises bravery in fighting it must be meant ironically; that it must really mean the opposite of what it seems to say and really be condemning war. Other critics have similarly assumed that Chaucer, with his modern sensibility, could not possibly mean seriously the common-places of traditional wisdom about making the best of things, etc., and they have referred to the obvious instances of his flippancy. They have thus supposed that the whole poem is spoken dramatically by a stupid Narrator, who is meant to be laughed at by us, as he is being laughed at by the real poet (for in the end one cannot get away from the real poet). The poem has thus been taken as an ironical liberal pacifist joke. But this is all very anachronistic. For all his modernity of spirit, Chaucer lived in the fourteenth century, when it was normal to think of war as honourable, even if (and because) it was also distressing; and it was normal to reflect sombrely on the vicissitudes of Fortune. Moreover, the flippancies can hardly be attributed to a *stupid* Narrator, because their very quality as obvious jokes denies the character of stupidity we endow him with.

If we were to accept a Narrator who is dramatically different from the poet, we would have to accept that he does not speak, for example, flippantly. We would therefore have to assume that the Narrator is used only intermittently. Sometimes the *real* poet *must* be speaking, and we would understand the poem literally; sometimes the Narrator, and we would have to understand that part of the poem ironically. The Narrator, if he were to exist, could only be understood ironically, as speaking falsely, otherwise he would be identical with the poet, and there would be no need to think of a Narrator at all. But there are no signals to tell us when the Narrator comes on, and the poem is certainly not continuously ironic. It is self-evidently wrong to think of the poem being continuously ironic for the very same reason that prompts some critics to invent the stupid Narrator – the narrative tone is highly varied. The idea of a Narrator is very popular because it does point to the frequency with which Chaucer varies his tone, and to the elusiveness of his implications. (An example of his baffling elusiveness is the description of Arcite's funeral pyre. *How* serious is Chaucer here?) Chaucer is often ambivalent, ironical, flippant. He likes subtle jokes. One is often not quite sure how to take him. But the idea of a Narrator, though attractive, over-simplifies Chaucer's subtlety. We do better to think of an intensely complex poet, who takes up many different points of view within the same poem, and who adopts many different tones. Often he cannot resist a joke, or an ambivalent meaning. We do better to think of the *narration*, the act of story-telling which is variable, as the centre of interest, rather than of a non-existent Narrator. But it should be added that many good critics, especially American, speak of a Narrator.

At this stage one thing is certain: the teller of the poem is *not* the

Knight of *The Canterbury Tales*, who had not yet been invented. The 'I' of *The Knight's Tale* therefore *cannot* be dramatically autobiographical of the Knight. The poet's remark

> But of that storie list me nat to write   [*it pleases me not*
>
> l. 1201

not only shows the real poet himself as storyteller, writing in his study, but shows that *Palamon and Arcite* is unlikely to have been revised for *The Canterbury Tales*. It is highly suitable in subject matter, splendour and dignity to the knight, but it is not a dramatic expression of his particular character; it is not like a speech in a novel, or even a soliloquy in one of Shakespeare's plays.

Chapter 10

A PHILOSOPHICAL ROMANCE: *TROILUS AND CRISEYDE*

Troilus and Criseyde was written about the same time as *The Knight's Tale* and like it is also translated from a poem by Boccaccio, *Il Filostrato*. The translation is much closer than that from *Teseida* but the poem is even more varied and splendid than *The Knight's Tale*. For example, the poet presents himself, and his story, in an even more interestingly complex way, though complexity does not mean confusion. A straightforward reading finds no difficulties. Only analysis shows how rich is the charmingly but in one sense deceptively clear surface of the poem.

At the very beginning the poet presents himself dramatically as a story-teller in our very presence, telling us about his interest in the story, his sad appearance in accordance with his sad story, his devotion to lovers, his own lack of success. This self-characterisation is in line with that of all the earlier poems, yet he is not a named *persona* within the poem as he is in earlier poems. The poet varies his point of view; sometimes he knows much about the characters, sometimes little, and he varies his tone from serious to flippant to an amazing extent. The impression of personal narration, in which the poet acts out his own story-telling, though on the written (or now printed) page, is in the text so striking that it may well itself have inspired the frontispiece of the manuscripts already referred to (p. 54) at Corpus Christi College, Cambridge. Whether or not the picture reflects on actual practice it beautifully evokes the courtly audience and the dominating poet, and allows us in imagination to join the group which is so personally addressed.

THE POET AS EXPOSITOR

Chaucer presents the substance of his story, and himself, both together in the first stanza.

115

> The double sorwe of Troilus to tellen ...
> My purpos is, er that I part fro ye.
>
> I, 1 and 5

Yet he concludes the stanza with an invocation to Thesiphone (four syllables), one of the classical Furies

> Thesiphone, thou help me for t'endite
> Thise woful vers, that wepen as I write.
>
> I, 6–7

The strange conceit of verses that weep as the poet writes them derives ultimately from Boethius. It is inconsistent with the purely oral presentation which line 5 has suggested, but well suggests the Gothic mixture of points of view, of spoken and written, which the poem incorporates. The inconsistency should no more worry the reader than it worries those who look at medieval manuscript pictures, or at Renaissance pictures which show several successive episodes of a story all apparently taking place simultaneously; or even at modern Cubist paintings, where too incompatible perspectives are deliberately juxtaposed. Such pictures do not aim at a plausible naturalistic imitation of the appearances of ordinary life. They use such appearances to create their own pattern, which itself comments on life; which, in literary terms, *tells* as well as *shows*. Chaucer as a story-teller is adept at both telling and showing.

The first fifty-six lines of the poem tell us of the poet's feelings about love, and he dramatises himself for us; hence the understandable enthusiasm for calling the poet the Narrator. But he is rather the traditional story-teller, receiving a known story, as an objective fact, participating imaginatively in it, suffering and enjoying with the characters (else why tell it?), yet also manipulating the story as an artist, altering and creating, in order to have the maximum effect on the audience or reader. Sometimes the poet identifies himself very closely with the characters, and knows their inmost thoughts and feelings; at others, just like one who has only heard a story, he professes ignorance of some aspect of the events or of a character, because he has not been told it; at other times he stands back and comments on the people or the action in a general way, as one might on something that one knew or heard of in ordinary life. The telling varies from the very dramatic, where we are conscious of no one and nothing between us and the character, to a tone which is very detached, philosophical, flippant, or ironical, and we are extremely conscious of the poet telling us the story and reflecting upon it, seriously or satirically.

The best way to think of Chaucer the poet in this poem is as the *Expositor*, the presenter of a play, who also comments on the action and is, though not an actor, present on the stage and deeply engaged sympathetically with the action. Such an Expositor, called *Contemplatio*, appears in the Hegge (or Coventry) Cycle of plays. *Expositor* introduces the Chester Cycle. In the Digby *Conversion of St Paul* the introductory character is even called *Poeta*. In other plays there is a similar character, *Prologue*. The essentially dramatic nature of Chaucer's genius, combined with his compulsive desire to comment, are exactly summed up by this neglected but crucial aspect of medieval drama.

METRE AND FORM

The metre of *Troilus* is the flexible rhyme royal stanza, which occasionally needs padding, but carries the story forward firmly and steadily while making it easy to rise to higher levels of lyric intensity, or of poetic apostrophe. It needs to be strong and varied for the whole poem is over 8,000 words long.

THE SOURCES

Chaucer must have had *Il Filostrato* on the desk before him, translating it stanza by stanza, and adding, leaving out, adapting it in the light of his own interpretation of character and event. The *Consolation* of Boethius gave him material for and depth to his comments. *Il Filostrato* is in eight books, but Chaucer adopted the Boethian five-part structure, and divided his poem into five books.

The poet refers, when it suits him for various purposes, to his sources and authorities, especially to 'Lollius' (I, 394 and elsewhere). There is no such author, but the name probably arises from a mistaken assumption, based on a misreading of a poem by the classical author Horace, that there was an ancient writer of that name who wrote on the Trojan war. 'Lollius' for Chaucer gathers up the tradition of writers on that subject, but Chaucer must also have derived a touch of amusement from referring to him, and apparently did not know Boccaccio's name as author of *Il Filostrato*.

It has also been claimed that Chaucer used a French translation *Il Filostrato* by Beauvau, Seneschal of Anjou. But this is hard to date and was probably written in the mid-fifteenth century. In any case none of the similarities that have been argued for as existing between Beauvau's version and Chaucer's has the least significance, Chaucer demonstrably owes nothing to Beauvau, while there are clear influences from the details of Boccaccio's Italian, most obviously the use of occasional Italianate words or phrases, such as *ambages* (V. 897).

Chaucer used other sources to enrich the story, borrowing most notably from *Teseida* at the end, and in the middle perhaps from another work of Boccaccio's, *Il Filocolo*. He blended in details from other works, as the commentators have made clear. But above all he used his own incomparable experience and observation of life, and deployed his own extraordinarily varied attitudes and responses to the narrative events he read about or invented.

BOOK I: THE STORY

Troilus is one of the sons of Priam, King of Troy, which is closely besieged by the Greeks, and as we know, doomed to be destroyed. Troilus is, after the great Hector, the best soldier in Troy, though very young. We should think of him as about sixteen or seventeen. Fighter pilots and army officers in the Battle of Britain were little older. In earlier centuries soldiers were even younger. The Black Prince was sixteen when he commanded one of the front wings at Crècy. Troilus still practises an adolescent mockery of those who are in love, until one day at church during the festival of spring, he sees the beautiful Criseyde and is at once smitten with desperate love.

Criseyde is a young widow, whose age we are never told, but which is surely near to that of Troilus, or a little older. She stands modestly yet assuredly by the church door, with black dress and glorious golden hair.

> Hire goodly lokyng gladed al the prees.   [*crowd*
> Nas nevere yet seyn thyng to ben preysed derre   [*praised more highly*
> Nor under cloude blak so bright a sterre

I, 173–5

She is rich and independent but isolated, for her father Calkas is a great lord and priest of Apollo who by calculation, presumably in astrology, foreknows that Troy will be destroyed and has deserted to the Greeks. It is as if, at the most desperate stage in England of World War II, when all seemed lost, the Archbishop of Canterbury had proclaimed the certainty of defeat and gone over to the enemy. The mob has threatened Criseyde, but the noble and chivalrous Hector, full of pity, has assured her of his protection.

Troilus sickens with love for the all but unknown lady and eventually lies in his misery on his bed – a bedroom being the only place of any privacy in Chaucer's world. A song of lament is attributed to him; one of the many lyrical moments in· this poem which in some ways, with its wonderful combination of freshness, artificiality and expressiveness, reminds one of opera. Troilus agonises on his situation in long soliloquies which may give the modern reader a misleading impression of softness, but which are best thought of as expressive arias in an opera. The poet imputes to Troilus all a young man's sensibility in heightened terms. What a fool he is, he tells himself, and what a fool others will think him, and so he goes on, repeating the name Criseyde, as the poet says in a neat combination of hyperbole, amused deflation, and sympathy that recalls the attitude of Theseus in *The Knight's Tale,*

> Til neigh that he in salte teres dreynte.   [*drowned*
> Al was for nought: she herde nat his pleynte.
> And whan that he bythought on that folie
> A thousand fold his wo gan multiplie.
>
> I, 543–6

A friend called Pandarus comes into his room unexpectedly and hears him groan. Alas, says Pandarus, have the Greeks frightened you, or have you become devout and suffer from remorse for sin? He asks this as a wild improbability to make Troilus angry and throw off his sorrow, for he knows there is no braver man. So Pandarus makes his first appearance in English fiction, as a vivid dynamic speaker, undescribed, very much what he says, purely dramatic. He is an emotional, shrewd, friendly, energetic man. He well nigh melts for sorrow and pity for Troilus, who replies with an almost comic languidness to his briskness. Pandarus wheedles out of the touchingly and comically shy Troilus the cause of his sorrow. It takes a long time, since traditional wisdom advises against telling anyone private matters and especially all

> That toucheth love, that oughte ben secree.
>
> I, 744

Troilus is silent. Pandarus fears he has had a fit and bellows 'Awake!' Troilus sighs

> And seyde, 'Frend, though that I stylle lye   [*quiet*
> I am nat deef.
>
> I, 752–3

It turns out that Pandarus is the uncle of Criseyde. He praises her beauty and goodness and says he will do his best to obtain her grace for Troilus. Troilus warns him that he would not for anything have harm come to Criseyde; Pandarus laughs, and wishes she could hear Troilus, who kneels and embraces Pandarus in gratitude. While Pandarus ponders how to tell his niece the news, Troilus springs up and does doughty work upon the Greeks. The hope of successful love beautifies and improves his character.

BOOK I: COMMENTARY

Though the modern reader may well be as interested in love as the fourteenth-century reader, our responses will be very different, especially after the sexual revolution. Yet it is still common enough for the sensitive to suffer agonies from shyness, and common enough for overtures of love to be repulsed, for whatever reason. An ideal of chastity for knights, originating with the Church, developed in the fourteenth century and Troilus is chaste before falling in love, as he is faithful afterwards, though in this he was surely an exceptionally refined spirit. Chastity was even more important for a woman. Sexual love may have meant warmth and security but it also meant all the pains, discomforts and downright dangers of childbirth, as Emily says. Virginity apart from its spiritual integrity was desirable for good practical reasons. More profoundly, sex was felt to be more a part of a woman's integrity than a man's, no doubt by the nature of the physical act, and also because of childbearing. Children were felt to be deeply a part of parents, and no man wished to foster other men's children and know that they would inherit his possessions. Jealousy of sexual possession of women was very strong. For many centuries in almost all traditional cultures honour has been felt for a woman to be based on her chastity, or if married on her faithfulness to her husband, while for a man honour resides first of all in his courage. Men have traditionally been permitted, very unequally, greater sexual freedom than women, and women who have been seduced, rather than men who seduce them, have been blamed. For associated reasons, it is always the cuckold who is derided, not the masculine adulterer who is blamed, in traditional literature. (Nor need we assume that such primitive attitudes, though unfashionable and obviously inconsistent now, have entirely disappeared.)

There was, therefore, a tremendous charge of feeling built up about sexual love which followed a different social pattern and met different barriers from those that are assumed by many today, especially among young people. It is no good simply to judge what Chaucer describes by modern standards, and to believe, for example, that Chaucer must be mocking a certain delicacy of feeling because we ourselves mock it.

Chaucer himself recognised this at the beginning of Book II, and comments in a remarkably modern way about the fact of historical change. Language changes over a thousand years, and words then

That hadden pris, now wonder nyce and straunge   [*value*; *foolish*
Us thinketh hem; and yet thei spake hem so   [*they seem to us*
And spedde as wel in love as men now do;   [*succeeded*
Ek for to wynnen love in sondry ages   [*also*; *various*
In sondry londes, sondry ben usages.   [*customs*

II, 24–8

This suggests that Chaucer himself recognised some degree of extremism in his portrayal of Troilus, and wished also to protect his story from being judged on too simply contemporary grounds even then. Chaucer's art is always heightened, and he makes as it were an experiment in *Troilus*, testing an extreme hypothesis of love.

At the same time Chaucer's own warning about difference works the other way too, reminding us that the basis of feeling remains similar throughout many ages, although active in different social forms. Moreover, we must not exaggerate the differences between Chaucer's day and our own. Sexual promiscuity that is now said to be commonplace was always the practice of most of the aristocracy. Edward III and his sons had their bastards before and after their marriages. Their love affairs were separate from their marriages and legitimate families, which were stable for reasons of property and the difficulties of divorce, though death broke them up fairly frequently because women died young, as did Blanche. Chaucer, himself a courtier, though married by 1366, continued to write poems with references to his being in love with some lady who, since she is said to have refused him, cannot have been his wife. No doubt there was much that was empty form, or no more than mild flirting, in such writing. But Chaucer was also accused of rape.

The Church had early set its face against sex save for the purposes of procreation. There was much to be said in favour of that, considering the times. But it cut off from religious support, except through sublimation, some of mankind's most passionate and imaginative experience in personal relations. It is true that mystics used the imagery of marital sexual love to describe the highest form of spiritual union with God, but they did so only by paradoxically relegating actual sexual love to a low level of esteem. Again, the great theologian, St Thomas Aquinas, praised sexual love: but the normal run of moralising and devotional writing, more in touch with what people are actually like, normally condemned it. Sexual love, therefore, became a purely secular sentiment, only tangentially related to religious love, and treated with hostility by religion. Since religion set most of the dominant 'official' values of the culture, love became 'unofficial', though as it was practised by the highest in the land it achieved in purely secular terms the dominance which literature reflects, especially in Chaucer. Official secular culture in this respect could rival and oppose official ecclesiastical culture for a time.

Sex in itself was felt to be 'dirty', being so closely related to the organs of excrement, and perhaps for other deeper reasons too. This feeling is so deep-set in Judaic and Christian European culture that we must believe that it has some justification. We can easily see that distrust of sex had great survival value, and that it protected women and children, or would have done, if more men had taken the concept seriously. But it also hindered natural relations between men and women and gave rise to many uncomfortable inhibitions.

No writer of the fourteenth century was more interested in sex and love than Chaucer. He obviously had a powerful sexual drive, however inhibited it was. He considered sex dirty, as we can see from various remarks and stories in *The Canterbury Tales*. 'Dirtiness' is itself an ambivalent and powerful concept, which encourages interest as well as repulsion. As the anthropologist Mary Douglas has shown, pollution is related to power. The consequence in Chaucer was that though sexual desire is taken for granted as the basis of sexual love, love itself, physically and socially inhibited and controlled, became a highly complex and refined set of attitudes and modes of behaviour based on, but normally superior to mere sexuality.

Much of the pattern of 'refined love', *fine amour*, was established for secular readers in the thirteenth and fourteen centuries in *Le Roman de la Rose*, though as already noted that had also its controversial aspects. Because of Jean de Meun's advocacy of promiscuous sexuality to produce a large population the poem was regarded by many as 'a heresy against love's law', as the God of Love calls it in *The Prologue* to *The Legend of Good Women*. This is because faithfulness to one beloved had long been regarded as one of the absolute necessities of love.

The pattern of behaviour expected in love according to Chaucer is expounded in some detail in his earlier poems where there is no reason to believe it to be ironical. The story of the man in black in *The Book of the Duchess* describes his devoted passion, shyness, continuing loyalty. Love is described very much from the young man's point of view. It is his desire which provides the dynamic. The lady is an ideal figure, superior in moral worth, chaste and passive. She grants the knight her 'mercy' or her 'pity'. To be in love improves the knight in every way. He is a better fighter, but also more gentle – more of a lion in the field, more of a lamb in the hall. He vows eternal faithfulness, which, as in *The Parliament of Fowls*, may produce problems for unsuccessful lovers. In all of Chaucer's work except *Troilus* marriage is the accepted aim of lovers, but marriage is not the point. The personal relationship, intensely individualistic and private, a world on its own, independent of society, is what is sought. It relates however to the cosmos. It has philosophical and even in a sense religious implications, for it is a kind of parallel to deeply personal religious experience.

Like religion, love inevitably involves suffering. This is partly because any ambitious enterprise involves self-discipline, forgoing short-term pleasures in favour of long-term advantages, persistence, and consequently some incidental pain. More deeply, passionate desire itself, when unsatisfied, is deeply painful as well as deeply attractive. Hence the ancient but true cliché of the bitter-sweet nature of love. Suffering is intrinsic to it.

The greater the suffering, the greater the joy of accepted love. It becomes the acme of human happiness, the goal to which all turn.

All this is most characteristic of human experience in youth, when society is less interesting, administration a bore, and social bonds are felt to be restrictive rather than supportive. Yet still for most people the heart of their satisfaction in life is to find satisfying personal relationships in the secular world. The ways of achieving and preserving them which seem natural at any one period will seem artificial and conventional to another. Our descendants will think that our 'natural' behaviour, which we take so much for granted as hardly to think about it at all, is not only strange, but has obviously been 'learnt': for almost all behaviour is indeed the product of the conditioning from the many forces in society that we are subject to, whether we like it or not. And we all try to behave so as to be successful in any enterprise, including how to win a lover.

So it is that in Chaucer's poetry the concept of the 'craft of fine loving', as he calls it in *The Legend of Good Women* (l. 544), or 'Love's craft' (*Troilus* I, 379), combines the desire to please, the desire to win a lover, and a highly moral set of feelings. In *The Legend* it is Alcestis who teaches the craft of fine loving and specially of 'wifehood the living'. She is a faithful wife, and the poem, being about faithful women, is unusual in giving the initiative to women. In the case of Troilus himself, the instructor of faithfulness will be his own heart, and the instructor of ways and means of wooing Criseyde will be Pandarus. Marriage is irrelevant, and it is taken for granted that love is so private as to be secret. No one likes his innermost feelings to be the subject of gossip and jest.

THE CONDUCT OF THE STORY

The conduct of the story in Book I is leisurely. The poet as Expositor works his way slowly into the story, first presenting himself, then allowing the characters to take over as dramatic figures. He is much more interested in the significance of small but crucial events than in a series of stirring events. The poem is concerned with feeling, not action. Thus, the first glimpse of Criseyde by Troilus (l. 273) is explored in a passage extending from l. 204 to l. 308. Chaucer is the Samuel Richardson, the Henry James, of the fourteenth century. And, as Dr Johnson said of Richardson's work, if a man were to read *Troilus* for the story alone he would hang himself. The immediate moment is to be savoured. It is no use being in a hurry. The tiny event of Troilus's first sight of Criseyde is preceded by a mythological reference to the God of Love, an adornment, with a touch of comedy, suitable for the local colour of a pagan past, but part of fourteenth-century contemporary fancy, too. Then the poet reflects on the nature of life:

> O blynde world, O blynde entencioun,
> How often falleth al the effect contraire
> Of surquidrie and foul presumpcioun.   [*pride*
>
> I, 211–13

This dignified language is followed in the next stanza by a reference to horses:

> As proude Bayard gynneth for to skippe
> Out of the weye, so pryketh him his corn,
> Til he a lasshe have of the longe whippe
> Than thynketh he, 'Though I praunce al byforn
> First in the trays, ful fat and newe shorn   [*harness*
> Yet am I but an hors and horses lawe
> I moot endure, and with my feres drawe',   [*must; companions*
> So ferde it by this fierse and proude knight . . .
>
> I, 218–25

The comment is in one sense serious enough, yet it has a flicker of amused sympathy, not derogatory of Troilus, but a little detached. Further reflections follow; a general description of Criseyde, and of Troilus's feelings. Then Troilus leaves the temple and goes back to his palace, where he soliloquises on love. There is a psychological comment on how he makes 'a mirror of his mind' in which Criseyde appears and he thinks of her; then follows the *Canticus Troili* (song of Troilus), the translation of the only one of Petrarch's famous sonnets to Laura which Chaucer seems to have come across, which lyrically expresses the self-contradictory nature of love.

The style of all this varies from the elaborate, the exaggerated, to the plain. It is never dull. The plain, which comes near to ordinariness but it always slightly different, carries the sense on without difficulty, though the needs of the metre often require alteration of the natural word-order. The elaborate is found in the use of less usual words, often recorded in this poem for the first time, or very early, in English, like *entencioun*, first found here, and *presumpcioun*. The passage containing these words is a good example of Chaucer's *sententious* style, uttering traditional wisdom, usually seriously, of which the proverbs that Pandarus uses so much are another example.

Those parts of the style that are exaggerated, or hyperbolical, are often so in traditional ways, expressing exaggerated ideas, as that Pandarus nearly 'melts' for pity and woe, or Troilus is nearly 'drowned' in tears. Ordinary excited colloquial speech often expresses such exaggeration, which no one in their senses takes literalistically. Chaucer occasionally also expresses himself more extravagantly in complex imagery, or even in strained metaphor. An outstanding example is the line

> N'yn him desir noon other fownes bredde.
>
> I, 465

(Desire bred no other fawns in him); i.e. sexual desire aroused no other wishes in him. The idea of subsidiary wishes as fawns, the young of deer, is attractive but strange. Not surprisingly it gave the scribes a lot of trouble and they produced many variations.

BOOK II: THE STORY

We begin with another invocation, this time not to a Fury but to Clio, muse of history, and the promise that we will sail out of these black waves. The poet disclaims responsibility for his story – it is a received story, a piece of history, autonomous, though there is also irony in this assertion, for though a man may not have responsibility for inventing a story, he certainly has for passing it on. Chaucer dramatises his narrative by presenting so many different attitudes of his own towards it. He proclaims his own ignorance anew, and here at the beginning (ll. 22–8) occurs as part of his apology the stanza already noted discussing historical change in language and manners.

We are then told that the date is May 3rd, traditionally unlucky, but a date Chaucer uses several times. Pandarus himself is suffering as much for love as Troilus, tossing and turning in bed all night for sorrow. But he gets up early, finds out by astrology that the time is propitious and visits Criseyde. She is in her paved parlour with two other ladies, hearing her niece read to them about the siege of Thebes. Their meeting is joyous, but she will not dance because she is a widow. They draw aside for private conversation and there follows a marvellous scene of several hundred lines (up to line 595) in which Pandarus slowly breaks to her, at first to her genuine dismay, the news that Troilus loves her. They fence in conversation with wit and slyness; the poet sees into their minds, they each try to gauge what the other is up to.

Equally fascinating, though more beholden to Boccaccio's original, are the succeeding passages in which Criseyde first sits in her own room on her own to think about it all, then sees by chance Troilus returning from battle, richly armed,

> So lik a man of armes and a knyght
>
> II, 631

acclaimed by the people, modest in his battered armour,

> That to hireself she seyde, 'Who yaf me drynke?'
> For of hire owen thought she wex al reed.
>
> II, 651–2

The poet says this was no sudden love, but the beginning of a steady process, brought about by Troilus's good service. Criseyde is shown arguing with herself in an entirely convincing way. Why should she get involved, she asks herself. She is perfectly happy, free and independent, and love is 'the most stormy life'. But she is fatally divided between hope and fear. She walks out into her beautiful formal garden with her three nieces, walking along the sanded alleys between the blossoming green boughs, and one of her nieces, the bright Antigone, sings a song of love, that makes Criseyde feel what bliss there is between lovers, while when she goes to bed

> A nyghtyngale, upon a cedir grene
> Under the chambre wal ther as she ley,
> Ful loude song ayein the moone shene   [*against*; *bright*
> Peraunter, in his briddes wise, a lay   [*perhaps*; *bird's way*
> Of love, that made hire herte fressh and gay.
>
> II, 918–22

She dreams a dream in which an eagle tears out her heart and leaves his own in hers – traditional but almost Freudian symbolism.

The remainder of the book continues with Pandarus rushing between Criseyde and Troilus with extraordinary joy. On one occasion to Criseyde

> He seide, 'O verray God, so have I ronne!   [*run*
> Lo nece myn, se ye nought how I swete?   [*sweat*
>
> II, 1464–5

He gets them to write letters to each other (in Criseyde's case the first that ever she wrote) and advises Troilus on his epistolary style, including how to blot the letter with a few tears (l.1027). Pandarus asks the honourable and generous Deiphebus, an elder brother of Troilus, to give a large dinner party, (ostensibly to arrange help for Criseyde, for a problem purely invented by Pandarus), to which, besides others like Paris and Helen, Troilus will be asked. Pandarus will arrange a private interview between Criseyde and Troilus at which, he exhorts the shy Troilus, he must

> Now spek, now prey, now pitously compleyne ...
> Somtyme a man mot telle his owen peyne.   [*must*

II, 1499...1501

Pandarus then arranges for Troilus to feign sickness, so that Criseyde may see him alone in a bedroom in Deiphebus's house. All this is arranged with zestful bustle by Pandarus and ingenious detail. The domestic intrigue of this second book is really very like a novel in its realism, its chain of cause and effect, and vivid dialogue. The book finishes delightfully with Troilus about to be visited alone by Criseyde, longing to declare his love, and asking himself,

> O myghty God, what shal he seye?

II, 1757

BOOK II: COMMENTARY

Our sense of individual characters and relationships is built up in this book on the basis of realistic domestic and personal detail, much of it, like Pandarus's visit to Criseyde, invented by Chaucer and inserted into the story. The poem approaches the nature of a novel because the characters seem to create the events, and it is no accident that most of the actions of Pandarus, from his first talk with Criseyde to the organisation of the meeting at the dinner party, is Chaucer's invention. None of this invention is of a traditional literary kind. Pandarus manipulates both Troilus and Criseyde, though he is continuously respectful to both. He refers to Troilus as 'my lord', and usually begins a conversation with him, however flippant, using the respectful second person plural 'ye' (e.g. 1.943), though he soon switches to the familiar second singular. He and Criseyde always speak to each other using the respectful plural form. Troilus always uses the singular, as to an inferior, to Pandarus, while throughout the poem Troilus and Criseyde use the plural form to each other. These subtle usages illustrate something of the subtlety of relationship. The action in this book, apart from Pandarus's bustle, is mostly in Criseyde's mind.

CHARACTERISATION

The characters take on clearer Chaucerian shape, except that it is of the essence of Criseyde's character that it is malleable, responding to

127

the pressures on it, ambivalent, therefore charming and interesting. Troilus remains more typical, if extreme; he is the doughty warrior, the devout and devoted lover, whose modesty wins our sympathy. Both these characters, but especially Troilus, are traditional types (none the less true or interesting for that) whom Chaucer has realised with sharp realism. He has changed them from *Il Filostrato*, making Troilus both more warrior-like and more shy than his Italian counterpart, who unlike Troilus is sexually bold and experienced. From this change arises much of the greatness of the poem, for it enhances Troilus's goodness as a young man, allows Criseyde to dally longer in sweet reluctant amorous delay, introduces more philosophical reflection, and causes the need for Pandarus's activity. The story requires that Troilus should seduce Criseyde. This is taken for granted in Boccaccio, and willingly assented to by his heroine. But Chaucer's Troilus is too good and too shy, his Criseyde too cautious, for such promptness, and Pandarus has to do Troilus's dirty work for him, as they both acknowledge a little later (III, 239ff., especially 253–5). Pandarus says that if what he has done were known, everybody would say he had committed the worst treachery possible (III, 278). Thus in a deeper sense, Criseyde and Troilus are independent characters with an archetypal relationship, while Pandarus is, in the end, created by the need for action between Troilus and Criseyde, so that he *is* what he *does* and *says*, no more and no less. Since we know most people only in such a way, by what we hear them say and see them do, this makes him very immediate to our imaginations, and very 'solid'. If ever there were a character like one in a novel, we are tempted to think, Pandarus is he. Yet it is not so, because what we know of him is only his functions, not his essential being. Thus we know he is Criseyde's uncle. This is Chaucer's invention; in Boccaccio's poem he is her cousin. He needs to be Criseyde's uncle, not cousin, because Chaucer conceives of Criseyde so much more subtly than Boccaccio does his heroine. She is not the type of amorous widow, as eager for an affair as her Italian boyfriend. Therefore, Criseyde has to be persuaded, and therefore Pandarus has to be cunning, socially adept, and with some authority over her. He is her financial adviser, and, as she says, her best friend, whose duty it is to *prevent* her having a lover (ll. 411–2). He is *in loco parentis*, as no cousin of equal age could be. He is only her uncle because Chaucer needs him to be so in order to persuade her to love Troilus. We see this more clearly when we recall how Criseyde's isolation, consequent on her father's desertion, is emphasised at the beginning of the poem. On that occasion Pandarus is not mentioned, because his function as go-between, literally as pander, has not yet arisen. (It is not accident that the function of bawd has taken his name in England.) He must presumably be her mother's brother, rather than the brother of her father Calkas, whom he never mentions, and whose defection is not said to bring shame to him. Genuine family relationships are not important in the action and Chaucer leaves them out, for his poem is not after all, a novel, and its realistic surface covers an inner structure of romance, of relationships between two people only. Criseyde in Book II appears to be far from isolated, with, apart from Pandarus, her three nieces who live with her, and her friendly relationships with Deiphebus, Paris, and Helen, apart from Hector.

The impressionistic nature of the poem thus causes some paradoxes of character. Not least important for the vividness of Pandarus as a character is that there is so much we do *not* know about him, as is the case with so many of our acquaintances in real life. The action of the story between Troilus and Criseyde does not require him to appear as a soldier, so in this society of soldiers, though he is the closest friend of one of the greatest soldiers, we know nothing about his fighting ability or lack of it. We hear that he is in love, but the lady is not needed for the relationship between Troilus and Criseyde, so she does not appear.

Although Pandarus shares many of Troilus's activities, and thus would seem to be of about the same age, as he is in *Il Filostrato*, he is *in loco parentis* to Criseyde, and is very much more knowledgeable in all sorts of ways than Troilus, so he also seems older than either. We have ambiguous clues to his age. He seems both middle-aged and young. The ambiguity does not worry us because it arises out of the action itself, and is not irreconcilable to natural possibilities, but to recognise it is to be reminded again that the story is about the relationship between two archetypal characters, and that the character of Pandarus is not in itself of any intrinsic significance.

REALISM AND SOCIETY

The same paradox of practical social surface realism without naturalistic depth (not as a fault in the poem, but as part of its quality) is to be seen in the social circumstances sketched in Book II. We are given a delightfully vivid glimpse of social life in Chaucer's Troy, and as it must surely have been among courtiers in their grand houses along the Strand in Chaucer's London. Enough detail is given for us to begin to describe this society, with its visits, and acceptance of ladies on equal footing in an easy and gracious politeness. It is sociable, rather emotional. People touch each other often in friendly manner, like modern Italians. Helen, for example, in charmingly womanly fashion, puts her arm round the apparently ailing Troilus (1.1671), not amorously, but as a friend, in a society where people feel strong personal warmth. The paradox is that this society, though so vividly presented, only appears when it impinges upon the relationship between Troilus and Criseyde, either as help or hindrance, and the essence of their affair is its evasion of all social structures. It is a relationship of love alone, a bond purely of personal feeling. That is what the poem is about.

WORDS AND THE POET'S ATTITUDES

Feeling in the poem is conveyed by words, in expression *by* the characters; in letters and speech *between* them; and in narrative and comment *about* them, by the poet to us. Pandarus is most eloquent, a well-trained rhetorician, as Troilus and Criseyde are not. He gives Troilus excellent advice on how to write a letter, keeping to the point, but still arousing feeling. Pandarus's rhetorical art to some extent associates him with the poet himself, of whom, it might be said with only a little extravagance, that he himself has to act as a bawd between Troilus and Criseyde, since he has to bring his freshly conceived characters together, and he has had to invent, in the new character given to Pandarus, the means by which they are brought together. A number of critics have seen some similarity between Pandarus and the poet. Each acquires a character by his relationship to the action. The poet's character, like Pandarus's, varies in relation to different aspects of the story; it is ambiguous, and contains inherent inconsistencies. He expresses approval, at one stage, as we shall see, of what he seems to disapprove of at another. Yet since these differences arise from the facets of the action, like flashes from the many different facets of a well-cut diamond, they are all part of the same brilliance. The poet, like Pandarus, is a literary intellectual, a dramatic presenter, an Expositor, drawing speech from the other characters, urging on the action and commenting on it. Both poet and Pandarus love the sententious style, larded with proverbs. Both have zest and fun and a wicked sense of humour. (The poet mocks his own love of rhetoric with a rhetorical joke, ll. 904–5.) Yet Pandarus is a character *within* the action, whom the other characters recognise, and the poet is not. Pandarus is less than, and in the end, different from the poet. When the relationship between Troilus and Criseyde finally breaks down he will have nothing to express but angry frustration. His *raison d'être* as a character will disappear, while the poet will go far beyond, conducting Troilus up to the heavenly harmony of the spheres, then able to turn away even from him to address his learned friends and pray to God. As Pandarus rightly says, echoing the rhetoricians, 'th'ende is every tales strengthe' (l. 260).

BOOK III: THE STORY

We end Book II with Troilus palpitating with nervousness about what he shall say to Criseyde. Was he not, says the poet amusedly, in a 'kankedort' – a strange word, still not properly understood, though its general meaning of being in a 'fix' is clear; those scholars who discuss it are still themselves in a kankedort.

Book III begins on a new note, a triumphant hymn to Venus, based on a later passage from *Il Filostrato*. Then we resume with Troilus in bed, going over in his mind what he wants to say, Pandarus pulling Criseyde in by a fold in her dress, peeping in between the curtains that enclose Troilus's bed, and seeming almost to weep. Troilus tries to spring up, while Criseyde gently lays hands on him to press him back. All that he wants to say flies out of his head. Criseyde perceives and understands his tongue-tied embarrassment very well, and loves him never the less for it. He manages eventually to express what the poet calls his manly sorrow, and Pandarus weeps as if he would turn to water. The talk between the three is serious yet with a touch of pure social comedy, quite without satire or irony. In a moment's sober comment when Criseyde has gone Pandarus remarks to his 'alderlevest lord' (best loved lord) and 'brother dear' that he has done for him what he will never do again for anyone, be he a thousand times his brother.

> That is to seye, for the am I bicomen [*thee*
> Bitwixen game and ernest, swich a meene [*go-between*
> As maken wommen unto men to comen

> III, 253–5

that is, a bawd, what is henceforth called a pandar. Troilus reassures him, and says he would do the same for him, even if it were to concern his own sister. The whole conversation is of the greatest interest for the way in which the whole affair may be thought of. Troilus asserts his total devotion, and they settle down to sleep, for Pandarus has had a pallet made up for him in Troilus's room (ll. 299–31).

A plan is then devised for Pandarus to hide Troilus in his house and invite Criseyde to supper. He does so on a night when a most unusual conjunction of stars (which occurs once only in 600 years and occurred in May 1385) promised exceptionally heavy rain. So Criseyde, half against her will, certainly without her foreknowledge, is persuaded to stay. Troilus is introduced into her bedroom, in one of the richest, most interesting scenes in all English literature. He is fearful, solemn, devout, she surprised, Pandarus comically urgent. Troilus pleads his love, and faints. Pandarus throws him into bed with

Criseyde, says 'Do not faint now, whatever you do', and retires to read 'an old romance' by the firelight. Troilus has been told by Pandarus to tell some lies about his jealousy of one Horaste, which Criseyde repudiates, and Troilus in lyric speech – again, one is reminded of the long expressiveness of operatic arias at the point of action – praises Citherea (Venus) and celebrates 'Benigne Love, thow holy bond of thynges' (l. 1261). Now at last he seizes Criseyde as a hawk seizes a dove. She is fully won, and though their subsequent meetings are few and secret, each is full of joy. Troilus improves still more in manly conduct, in honour, generosity, kindness, even in being well-dressed, achieving fully all the beauty and joy of the ideal courtly life (ll. 1716–36). The book concludes with Troilus's great song in praise of cosmic love (ll. 1744–71) based on Boethius. Troilus expresses the wish that his love may be part of the great bond that unifies and harmonises the universe – that Love, as Dante says in the last line of *The Divine Comedy*, which moves the sun and other stars. It is an aspiration, not an assertion, on the part of Troilus – the operative word in the song, *Bynd*, is in the subjective mood, expressing a hope, not in the indicative, expressing a *fact*.

BOOK III: COMMENTARY

There is far more in the book than can be summed up in brief commentary. It moves from the lyrical intensity of sincere passion, to sensual appreciation, gently comic comment, and slightly bawdy innuendo. There is evidence here for almost any attitude towards love one likes to mention, from moral condemnation to reverence to secular and cynical revelling in sensuality.

The vehicle of most of these attitudes is the self-dramatising poet's narrative, which includes comment of all kinds. Though the sustained realism is unrivalled in English literature until we come to Defoe, the poet remarks that there simply is not space and time enough to record everything fully, and anyway it would be boring (ll. 491–504). And though the poet knows at times the inmost thoughts of his characters, he deliberately distances himself, with a touch of humour, at the very climax of sensual joy. He claims only to be translating from his author, whom he has earlier called 'Lollius' (I, 394), not altogether seriously, but he effectively throws all responsibility on to the reader:

> For myne wordes, heere and every part,
> I speke hem alle under correccioun
> Of yow that felyng han in loves art,
> And putte it al in youre discrecioun

> To encresse or maken dymynucioun
> Of my langage, and that I yow biseche.

III, 1331–6

He gives licence to the critical fashion of the 1980s for 'deconstruction', for reformulating the work of art in the reader's own image. He disclaims, or pretends to disclaim, responsibility, especially moral responsibility, for the story at least at this point. The reader is called on fully to participate, to imagine and create for himself or herself, and is flattered by the imputation of greater knowledge and experience. The requirement is genuine in that all poetry, all art, can only live if the reader, or viewer or hearer, brings personal knowledge, experience and sympathy to come part of the way to meet the artist. It is also more specific to Chaucer, in that he is generally not didactic, but rather questioning, exploratory, ambivalent. Nevertheless, if he *really* rejected responsibility he would not write at all: if the reader were *totally* independent he would not read at all.

Both poet and reader necessarily practise an ironic complicity. Chaucer's awareness of playing with this complicity is part of his many-layered poetic meaning, and of his humour.

HONOUR

The domestic and social realism of the poem continues strikingly and delightfully in Book III. One aspect of it which develops more strongly, and relates to character, is Criseyde's insistence on the maintenance of her honour. Almost the first thing she says to Troilus, in reply to his long first speech is

> Myn honour sauf, I wol wel trewely,   [*provided my honour be preserved*
> And in swich forme as he gan now devyse,
> Receyven hymn fully to my servyse,
> Besechyng hym, for Goddes love, that he
> Wolde, in honour of trouthe and gentilesse,
> As I wel mene, eke menen wel to me,
> And myn honour with wit and bisynesse   [*common sense and energy*
> Ay kepe.

III, 159–66

Honour is mentioned three times in eight lines. The concept of honour in traditional societies is complex and almost totally lost in modern society. It is an aspect both of primitive individual integrity and of primitive collective social cohesion. Honour so to speak looks both inwards into the personality and outwards towards society. Honour is what the individual needs to exist as an effective person, and is simultaneously the recognition by the social group that that quality is actually present. The qualities in question are the primitive masculine and feminine qualities: for men bravery, for women virginity, and these qualities have already been noted in Chaucer's heroes and heroines. They are vital to life at a high level in traditional society, though some sections of society have no honour to gain or lose, for example, priests and peasants. Criseyde, like all of Chaucer's heroines, is much concerned with her honour. She talks about it more than any of them, and the pathos of her story is that she, who is concerned above all with her honour, will lose it. The problem of this essentially two-sided honour is that if only one side is felt to exist the whole is called in question. If a man is brave or a woman chaste but their social groups cannot, or refuse to, believe that they are, how far does *honour* exist? *Goodness* may and does exist without social recognition, we may perhaps says, because it is seen by God; but honour is purely worldly, which is why the Church, especially in England, always regarded it with suspicion and some hostility. On the other hand, if society believes you to be brave or chaste, that is as good as truly being so, as far as honour is concerned, until you are found out. If you are found out you are treated with derision, and cast out from your group.

Criseyde ultimately gets herself into something like this last situation, partly because she cares so much about the external social aspect that she neglects the internal quality. She is very vulnerable. As a widow she is honourable in solitude. By sleeping with Troilus she loses the internal quality of honour, since she is not married to him. That is why the affair must be kept secret, *because if nobody knows* (and nobody except Pandarus and the reader does) *she may be said to retain her honour* from the social point of view. Honour is partly what people think about you and the respect they accordingly grant you.

There is another aspect of honour not so far mentioned. That is, keeping your word. It might be argued that this is not really honour but loyalty or truth or faithfulness; it is at least so closely associated with the integrity that is part of honour that it must be considered with it. The significance of loyalty can be seen most clearly in the case of a married woman's honour. Her honour obviously does not reside in her virginity; her honour resides in her faithfulness to her husband. This is part of the social nature of honour, for her husband's honour also depends on her faithfulness to him. If she is unfaithful to him, she loses honour, and so does he. A cuckold is universally an object of derision. Since sexuality is not itself part of a man's honour, the seducer is not dishonoured. This example again shows that honour is by no means always the same thing as goodness or justice. Nor is it dishonourable to deprive another man of honour, either by defeating him in battle or by dishonouring his wife, though either act is risky since it may well provoke battle and death.

The complexity of Criseyde's position consists in this: she has given her honour as it were into Troilus's keeping. If the affair is known, she is dishonoured but he is not.

Troilus however, is nothing if not loyal. The poem is as much about his loyalty, called *trouthe*, as about Criseyde's ultimate disloyalty. For Criseyde will eventually lose honour by abandoning Troilus for another man. That will be her dishonour, not primarily her loss of chastity in sleeping with Troilus when not married to him. But there will be more paradoxes before the story is finished.

LOVE AS A PURELY PERSONAL RELATIONSHIP

Why does Troilus not marry Criseyde? The simplest, true, answer is that the story does not say that he did, and the story has a traditional 'given', historical character, which does not allow events to be changed. If the events were changed it would be a different story, not this one. The question does not arise in Boccaccio's story about a lusty and lustful young pair. Chaucer creates the problem because he makes both Troilus and Criseyde more thoughtful, more complex and more moral. He seems conscious of the problem when he emphasises at the beginning of Book II how different were manners and morals in time past. In his own day, in literature at least, marriage would be the normal object of such a wooing as that of Troilus. But Chaucer never mentions marriage in the poem, and in life in his own day, as opposed to literature, liaisons of the kind which Troilus, who is a prince, is seeking, were, as has been said, usual for princes. The goodness, not the amorousness, of Troilus is the stumbling-block. Chaucer's presentation has nevertheless the advantage already remarked, that the interest is concentrated on the personal relationship independent of any social support or compulsion. Chaucer presents the romantic ideal of a purely personal relationship, independent of social obligation or constraint, and as such it is highly relevant in the late twentieth century. Social bonds differ from personal; when divorce was difficult they maintained marriage and the marital relationship independent of the respective parties' personal wishes. A purely personal relationship depends on both partners maintaining a continuous wish, or abiding by a personal, not a legal promise. If personal volition is all, and it fades for one of the partners, as it is likely to, then the promise, and the other partner's personal wish, may be treated as of no account, as Troilus found. The rational answer then is for the deserted person to change his or her wish, as now often happens; but we are not all rational, nor can we all control our wishes. So it seemed to Boethius, and to Chaucer, and to Troilus, that the flesh, or the stars, and not the rational mind, controlled desire; and sexual love is seen as the greatest of all desires.

LOVE AND DESTINY

Book III is a curious mixture. It begins and ends with noble hymns to love which are not ironic, while Troilus's sincere love is brought about by a deceitful intrigue. We cannot doubt the nobility of love. The hymn to Venus at the beginning is a wonderful combination of mythology, astrology, historical local colour, and an almost religious warmth of feeling. Of Venus, goddess, and planet, the poet says

> In hevene and helle, in erthe and salte see
> Is felt thi myght,

III, 8–9

as if she were the Virgin Mary, Empress of Heaven, Earth and Hell. Troilus, a pagan, solemnly invokes all the gods, including Hymen, god of marriage, and shows a serious piety which deserves respect, and from which he never swerves. It is an intrinsic irony that the love stories of the gods he invokes are all of rape, atrocity and disaster, with nothing of the faithful tenderness that Troilus himself never fails in. He regards himself as totally committed to Criseyde though they are not married. When they are together she fully avows her love with complete sincerity, but never with such fervour of religious conviction.

Is their love a product of fate or manipulation or chance or their own choice? The poet deliberately creates an ambivalent sense that it is both inevitable and yet chosen. At the crucial moment when Criseyde proposes to leave Pandarus's house after supper in the downpour of rain the poet apostrophises Fortune, another mythological figure:

> But O Fortune, executrice of wyrdes   [*agent of destiny*
> O influences of thise hevenes hye,
> Soth is that under God ye ben oure hierdes   [*shepherds*
> Though to us bestes ben the causes wrie.   [*beasts; hidden*
> This mene I now, for she gan homward hye   [*hurry*
> But execut was al bisyde hire leve   [*carried out without her consent*
> The goddes wil; for which she most bleve.   [*remain*

III, 617–23

In other words, Destiny controlled her through the stars. But Pandarus had calculated that effect from the stars, in the form of the rain, when he invited her. *Wyrdes* is not a pagan concept but an aspect of Destiny, which is controlled ultimately by God, as Boethius argues. So here is a strong sense that Criseyde is helpless. But when

Troilus later that night amorously in bed seizes her and says there is no escape for her, she prettily answers

> Ne hadde I er now, my swete herte deere
> Ben yold, ywis, I were now nought heere. [*been yielded*
>
> III, 1210–11

Here, at least, she willingly co-operates with the universe. Destiny as always remains a mystery.

BOOK IV: THE STORY

> But al to litel, weylaway the whyle, [*too little, alas that it should be*
> Lasteth swich joie, ythonked be Fortune. [*thanks to Fortune*
>
> IV, 1–2

So begins Book IV, in sharp contrast to the calm joy in which Book III ended. Criseyde, we have always known, will desert Troilus, and this sad foreknowledge has always been a dark background to the brightness of the moment. Now the sun goes out and clouds come up. The poet prays to the Furies to help him finish this fourth book in which he will show Troilus's loss of both life and love. He was obviously translating and remoulding with a copy of *Il Filostrato* open on the desk before him, knowing the general outline of what he was planning but changing the details of the plan as he went along, guided by his response to the story at the moment. At this stage he is still with the fourth of *Il Filostrato*'s eight books. He presumably intended to cut *Il Filostrato* as radically as he had cut *Teseida* for *The Knight's Tale*, and tie it all up in one last book. As it proved, the subject matter of loss and betrayal made too deep an appeal. It invited long expressions of sorrow on the part of the characters, and much philosophical questioning of choice and destiny. The long irony of Troilus's self-deception, the precise calculation of time, the chance of a really striking ending, all appealed very strongly to Chaucer both as man and as artist. The fourth book became immensely long (as had happened proportionately with the last book of *The House of Fame*), so he cut it at l. 1700 and made the rest of it a fifth book, without noticing, or without bothering to change, the promise to finish made at the beginning of the fourth.

Criseyde's father Calkas asks the Greeks if they will arrange to have his daughter sent to him. They grant him the Trojan prisoner Antenor to use for exchange, and the proposition for this unfair deal is put to the Trojan Parliament. Troilus is present and in agony. He feels he cannot say anything because Criseyde would not wish him to betray any special interest. The noble Hector resists: she is not a prisoner, he says; tell the Greeks we do not sell women here. But the crowd wants Antenor. Little do people know what is best for them, says the poet, for it was Antenor who later betrayed Troy (l. 204). But Hector is outvoted, and Criseyde must go. Troilus goes home distraught. Pandarus too is distressed, but after all, he says to Troilus, why are you so mad? You have had what you wanted. There are plenty of other ladies in the town.

> If she be lost, we shal recovere an other.

IV. 406

The poet remarks that Pandarus merely uttered such sentiments in order to prevent Troilus dying from sorrow (a good example, acknowledged by the poet, of how what Pandarus says arises directly from the needs of the action between Troilus and Criseyde. He himself has no stable views, no 'stable ego of character' as they have, which is another reason why he seems so modern a character.)

This went in at one ear and out at the other, says the poet, as far as Troilus was concerned. He is wholly Criseyde's whom he will continue to serve till he dies.

Criseyde hears the rumour that she must go with dread, since she cares nothing for her father and everything for Troilus, but she dare ask no one for confirmation. A crowd of silly women come to congratulate her, but she weeps distractedly, and they think it is because she will miss them. When they go she curses her fate and the prospect of separation from Troilus, in a complaint, reproaching the 'cursed constellation' of her stars. How shall she live without him? Pandarus visits her, and she tells him of her sorrow. Pandarus once thought to himself how dim she was (II, 271–2). Now he tells her that since women are 'wise in short avysement' (IV, 936, i.e. 'good at quick consideration' and the earliest recorded use of *avysement*) she should be able by her wits to find a way out of the difficulty.

Then he looks for Troilus and finds him in a temple, in despair, arguing with himself whether there is such a thing as free will and coming to the conclusion that there is not:

> For al that comth, comth by necessitee
> Thus to ben lorn, it is my destinee.   [*lost*

IV, 958–9

This is expanded by a long argument with himself which is a versified translation from Boethius, *Consolation*, V, prose 3. The passage was probably an expansion inserted by Chaucer at a slightly later stage of composition, between what are now lines 960 to 1086, but were once

960 and 961. The passage is an extreme example of the variability of form of the *Troilus*, which can range from detailed realism to this philosophical-argument which makes only the slightest concession to dramatic propriety, and sometimes even violates it. The passage represents by logical argument the actual turmoil in Troilus's mind, and is part of the Boethian deepening of the poem.

Pandarus is genuinely impatient with such depair. Has Nature made you only to please Criseyde, he asks in exasperation (l. 1096). And it is true that such devotion as that of Troilus has something of super nature in it, as well as something supine. Pandarus wants to see some action. So Troilus visits Criseyde. They are speechless for woe; she faints and after lamenting he draws his sword to kill himself. Though this may all seem very extravagant it is translated from *Il Filostrato*. The fourteenth century was a period almost as sentimental as the Romantic late-eighteenth century, when Goethe's *Werther* was all the rage. In the fourteenth century young men did not, as in the Romantic period, actually commit suicide for love. Troilus is saved by Criseyde recovering and calling to him. They go to bed to talk things over like an old married pair. This is in Boccaccio, but the very long speech by Criseyde (ll. 1215–414) is much expanded from Boccaccio's quite brief report of her speech. The style, which combines the colloquial, the sententious and the learned, like a gloriously varied aria, is entirely Chaucer's: the subject matter of lines 1317 to 1414, plus the next stanza, is Chaucer's own without any corresponding lines in *Il Filostrato*. Criseyde says, echoing Pandarus in both word and idea (from IV, 935–6), that being a woman she is 'avysed sodeynly', and that they ought not to make half this woe, for she has a plan. She will return of her own accord from the Greeks. She reveals a foolish over-confidence which complements her usual and more sensible nervousness. Chaucer, having taken the framework of event from Boccaccio, fills it in with his own substance of Criseyde's motive and attitude, his own further colouring of style. Criseyde is shown to be touchingly inventive and enthusiastic about how she shall manage and what she shall say. Chaucer adds the comment, as Expositor, ll. 1415–21, that she really meant what she said, and that she intended to be true. Is this remark ironical? I do not think so, though others do. The later event, which we already know, turns sincerity into an ultimate irony, but need not impugn her present actual intention.

Troilus is dubious, and in language more humble, expressive and religious than that of Boccaccio's hero Troilo, prays her to elope with him, since, as Boccaccio's hero does not mention, Troilus has, 'vulgarly to speken of substaunce' (l. 1513), enough money. So the discussion goes to and fro, enriched with much comment. Criseyde rightly says her life would be impossible if she lived with Troilus openly: her reputation for chastity would be besmirched for ever. She emphasises that she will return on the tenth day of her exile. She also warns Troilus against making love to any other woman in her absence, because she would be so distressed if he were untrue – an extra emphasis by Chaucer which is part of the irony of the total narrative, since we know that it is Criseyde who will prove unfaithful. She also emphasises that she has loved Troilus not for his position or power, but for his 'moral vertu, grounded upon trouthe', his 'gentil' (i.e. noble) heart, and his manhood (ll. 1672–4). The sentiment does credit to both lovers, and has the effect of emphasising the centrality to the story of Troilus's own natural goodness and 'trouthe'. Then Chaucer inserts an extra stanza, not suggested by Boccaccio (ll. 1660–6) in which Criseyde says that she will always behave, since he has been so true, 'That ay honour to me-ward shal rebounde'. Chaucer's Criseyde is always concerned for her own status and there is more narrative irony here. They lament and make love. Dawn comes; Troilus must dress and go, in deepest sorrow.

BOOK IV: COMMENTARY

The characters are enriched still further and more facets of Criseyde's character are shown dramatically. As with people in real life there is no single key to her personality. She is loving, gentle, nervous, spirited, rash, well-intentioned; but her governing concern, as Chaucer envisages her, is with her honour, which ought to be, but is not, associated with her 'truth', i.e. faithfulness. Her concern determines her actions, and it is a general irony that she who is more obviously concerned than any heroine in Chaucer with her honour is the one who notoriously loses it because she is untrue. Troilus rages against Fortune and is unshakably true, but honour does not come into the question for him.

THE EXPLORATION OF A DILEMMA

Although the characterisation is rich, the essence of Book IV is a realistic version of a *demande d'amour*, a question of love; in other words the main point of the book is to express dramatically a frantic exploration of possible ways out of a distressing dilemma. The three characters discuss many possible courses of action, even marriage, or the violent abduction of Criseyde; too many to summarise here. Character or circumstance foils each possible solution, and we attend with sympathy to the expression of passionate frustrated feeling, while contemplating the apparently ineluctable course of events.

VARIATION OF STYLE

In this exploration of possible solutions the style is wonderfully varied. There are realistic touches of description, as in the mention of the knight who guards the door of Troilus's darkened room (ll. 351–4); there are vivid colloquial touches, as Troilus calling himself a 'combre-world' (l. 279) (an expression invented here by Chaucer and only used again by Hoccleve), and Troilus referring to 'nettle in, dock out' and 'playing rackets' (ll. 460–1) with love; or Troilus described as paying deep attention with 'heart and ears spread out' (l. 1422). But in general the style in Book IV is less naturalistic, less dramatic, and more abstract or general, more intellectual. The extreme example is Troilus's soliloquy in the temple, where for a while all naturalistic imitation is abandoned (ll. 960–1078), but Criseyde's long speech, and the poet's comment, ll. 1254–421, express high sentiment in a high style, which makes no attempt at novelistic imitation, though mingled with more homely notes. The learned words *conclusioun* (l. 1284) and *redresse* (l. 1266) (each of which Chaucer used several times later but are first recorded in English here); *mocioun* (l. 1291); and the strange *amphibologies* (l. 1406), (meaning 'ambiguities'), are examples of an intellectual vocabulary which could be much extended.

This fourth book contains much less comment by the poet. Nor does there seem any need to attribute irony or mockery to such comments as there are. On the other hand, the promises of faithfulness by Criseyde are examples of what may be called dramatic or narrative irony, because we know, though she does not, that the future will show them to have a different, opposite meaning to what she at present intends.

BOOK V: THE STORY

Book V begins without an invocation but with two stanzas of solemn comment in high style added by Chaucer and not in *Il Filostrato*, which also begins here at Book V:

Aprochen gan the fatal destyne	[*fated*
That Joves hath in disposicioun,	[*at his disposal*
And to you, angry Parcas, sustren thre ...	[*three sisters*
The gold-ytressed Phebus heigh on-lofte	[*golden-haired; aloft*
Thries hadde alle with his bemes clene	[*bright*
The snowes molte, and Zepherus as ofte ...	[*melted*

V, 1...10

There is no question here of a stupid, pretentious, ironical or cynical Narrator. The poet speaks grandly, a dignified *Expositor*, *Contemplatio*, or *Poeta*, independent of the action but sympathetically engaged with it. We know the story: these premonitory introductory chords lead into the last act.

Fatal destiny does not mean '*deadly* destiny'. There is no notion here of a Hardyesque malicious Fate, or of a modernistic fatalism. Destiny is the expression of Providential order, which by a poetic fiction we think of as the action of Fortune (*Boece* IV, pr. 6; *LGW*, 2580; *Troilus* III, 617). It may be painful because to us beasts here below the causes are hidden. The world is both tragic and good. The poetry here expresses a natural human mood, for which the underlying logic, such as it is, must be sought at much greater length in the *Consolation*, or in theology.

The Greek Diomede is ready to fetch Criseyde, who feels her heart bleeding, in this extravagantly if traditional expressive image which Chaucer adds to his source. Troilus accompanies her to the gate, hiding his sorrow, and his anger when he sees Diomede, in a manly way. Chaucer both adds to and cuts from his source as usual, tending to add a Gothic extravagance to the expression of feeling, and adding equally Gothic concrete detail, as when Troilus takes Criseyde's hand 'full soberly' 'And Lord!' so she gan wepen tendrely' (ll. 81–2), details which are not in Boccaccio.

Diomede, as he takes the bridle of her horse, thinks to himself – for the poet here knows his inmost thought – that he may as well have a try at seducing her, if only to make the way seem shorter. So he courts her immediately in an odious unconscious parody of the high love-language of Troilus, swearing to her, 'as a knight', that he will be 'her own man', never having loved a lady before, but now unable to strive against the God of Love – though he only asks to be her friend and brother. The speech is not exactly a joke, either by Diomede or the poet, yet there is an almost painfully comic wit in the dramatic aptness of expression of this cynical, treacherous womaniser. Criseyde is so distracted that she pays little attention, but all the same, with her usual fatal readiness to collaborate with whoever is urging her, she thanks him, accepts his friendship, and says she would gladly please him, and will trust him. We see that she is effectively already lost. All this passage, which is both social comedy, and personal tragedy (ll. 92–189), almost a hundred lines long, is inserted between stanzas 13 and 14 of the fifth book of *Il Filostrato*. And then she is warmly welcomed by her father.

Troilus returns to Troy and rages, soliloquising in torment, in a long speech plus poetic comment added by Chaucer between two lines of *Il Filostrato*'s Book V, stanza 21.

The poet continues,

Who koude telle aright or ful discryve   [*describe*
His wo, his pleynt, his langour, and his pyne?   [*torment*
Naught alle the men that han or ben on lyve.
Thow redere maist thiself ful wel devyne   [*guess*
That swich a wo my wit kan nat diffyne.   [*intelligence; express*
On ydel for to write it sholde I swynke   [*labour*
Whan that my wit is wery it to thynke.

V, 267–73

The refusal to describe is a rhetorical device, which characteristically of Chaucer calls on the reader to participate. There seems no reason to doubt that the poet does genuinely sorrow for Troilus. If we, as readers, not only of this poem but of other stories, feel sorrow, as we surely do, for characters in distress, then equally surely the writer too must feel genuine pain, or else why should he write? Art objectifies and distances our feelings, but also extends and enhances them precisely in this way, by imaginative participation in fictional sorrows and joys, which yet may be more 'real' to us than real life.

Yet we also notice here that the poet, by his very comment, withdraws himself, and us, a little, from full participation, even as he invites it. The address to 'thou reader', a habit perhaps caught from Dante, is also interesting as inconsistent with other addresses apparently to an attentive *audience*. This is another example of Gothic multiplicity of perspective.

A very beautiful stanza of a quite different kind immediately follows with sharp Gothic contrast:

On hevene yet the sterres weren seene
Although ful pale ywoxen was the moone . . .   [*become*

V, 274–5

It is translated from Boccaccio's *Teseida*, with suggestions from the *Consolation*. In this fifth book are a number of such beautiful evocations of the starry heavens.

Pandarus comes to assuage Troilus's sorrows and speaks with his customary colloquial and sententious vehemence, fullness of information, and worldly *savoir-faire*. Ten miserable days must pass before Criseyde will return. Pandarus makes Troilus spend a sociable week at the house of Sarpedoun, 'to lead a lusty life in Troy'. Social life is torment to Troilus and Chaucer makes us intensely aware how slowly the time passes for Troilus. He visits Criseyde's house, that desolate palace (Chaucer constantly heightens the social level and physical circumstance, as well as the feelings expressed: in Boccaccio the 'palace' is only a 'house').

Pandarus, like Boccaccio's Pandaro, is completely sceptical about Criseyde's return, but unlike Boccaccio's young man does attempt to console Troilus, in a mixture of kindness and hypocrisy that is humanly entirely convincing.

Troilus sickens, soliloquises, makes another song, and walks on the walls to look at the Greek army (a concrete detail not in *Il Filostrato*). And

> Upon that other syde ek was Criseyde,
> With wommen fewe, among the Grekis stronge;

V, 687–8

moving lines, translated straight from Boccaccio except that 'strong' is substituted for Boccaccio's colourless 'armed'. But for the next hundred lines Chaucer considerably expands the direct speech given to Criseyde, making her more sympathetic, and pathetic, in her distress. She weeps and sickens, and reflects in Boethian style on the nature of happiness. Meanwhile Diomede gets to work on her. Chaucer makes his cynicism and progressive success quite clear. At this stage Chaucer, following a hint from *Il Filostrato* which actually occurs some thirty stanzas later in the Italian, slots into the narrative formal descriptions, physical and mental, of Diomede, Criseyde and Troilus (ll. 799–840), with an effect of summing-up. Then on the very tenth day, as Chaucer, not Boccaccio, tells us, Diomede makes another attempt on Criseyde, with a subtle mixture of bullying, threatening, flattery and cajolery, reminding her of the fate that her father himself foresees for Troy. He even reminds her of his own high lineage (l. 931). What a contrast to Troilus. Criseyde cannot but be polite. She temporises, but Chaucer shows her saying she will speak with Diomede 'tomorrow', which was when she had promised to be back in Troy. The hundred lines from l. 995 correspond to only three stanzas, that is, twenty-four lines, of Boccaccio, and are a masterly expression of the complex development of Criseyde's thoughts and feelings, when she goes to bed beneath the beautiful starry skies and turns over in her mind what this 'sudden Diomede' has said. Her soliloquy is a wonderful passage of psychological drama, and finishes most remarkably

> But al shal passe; and thus take I my leve.

V, 1085

Such speeches are a familiar rhetorical device, but it is hard to avoid the impression that Chaucer has been thinking of her as a character on a stage, giving a soliloquy. She is vividly before us on the stage of our minds, all ordinary realism left far behind. But truly, says the poet, in what is almost a farewell comment, no authority tells us how long it was before she actually forsook Troilus for Diomede. The comment is neutral, as it were historical, distancing her. The poet continues in his rôle as sympathetic Expositor,

Ne me ne list this sely womman chyde   [*simple*
Forther then the storye wol devyse.   [*tell*
Her name, allas, is punysshed to wide,
That for hire gilt it oughte ynough suffise.
And if I myghte excuse hire any wise,
For she so sory was for hire untrouthe,
Iwis, I wolde excuse hire yet for routhe.

V, 1093–9

The tone seems genuinely sympathetic. Her fault is plain. 'Trouthe' is the highest value. Yet of course only the reader and author *outside* the frame of the work, beside Troilus inside it, know that she is untrue, for her affair with Troilus is quite unknown to every other character *within* the fiction.

Chaucer has taken us far beyond the tenth day, and the narrative returns to Troilus on that very day. We now see him against the background of the desertion which is yet to come, to sympathise with the sickness of hope deferred. Criseyde has in every sense left the scene, and the story continues centred only on Troilus, on a foreboding dream he has, and an exchange of letters with an increasingly deceitful Criseyde. Chaucer draws swiftly to the end, making no use of long passages by Boccaccio in *Il Filostrato* describing Troilo's misery and a visit from Trojan ladies to Troilo. Chaucer adds Cassandra's foreboding interpretation of Troilus's dream, more historical and mythological allusions, and more addresses to Fortune. In particular the poet comes forward more and more as Expositor, referring to his sources, summarising events, steadily withdrawing us from close participation in the action. Criseyde is given one last indirect appearance by means of her most deceitful letter (ll. 1590–632). This is entirely Chaucer's invention, though he draws on earlier material from *Il Filostrato*, and illustrates her degeneration. A brooch that Troilus had given Criseyde is captured from Diomede. Troilus is at last convinced of her unfaithfulness and yet, he says, with profound human truth, he cannot find it in his heart

To unloven yow a quarter of a day.
In corsed tyme I born was, weilaway.

V, 1698–9

This is not in *Il Filostrato*. Troilus must suffer.

Swich is this world, whoso it kan byholde:
In ech estat is litel hertes reste.
God leve us for to take it for the beste.

V, 1748–50

The poet speaks movingly. Such true and appropriate comments can surely not be attributed to a stupid Narrator. They arise naturally from the story. That they are not original, but are part of traditional wisdom, part of common human experience, seems their strength, though some critics consider them to be commonplaces intended to arouse our derision.

As the poet moves increasingly into the foreground, the persons of the narrative become more distant. The long slow withdrawal is amazingly rich. The story is finished, but not the poem. There is a lightening of tone, with an injunction to the poem itself, first as 'a little book', then implicitly as a person itself (as stories seemed 'persons' to Chaucer), to kiss the footprints of the great poets of the past, Virgil, Ovid, Homer, Lucan and Statius.

There is an astonishing last flourish. Troilus is killed by Achilles, reported in one line (l. 1806), and his soul is taken up into the heavenly spheres, to laugh at those who mourn his death, and to go 'wherever Mercury shall place him. And then again a surprise, as the poet says emphatically, in a moving stanza with repetitions like a tolling bell, yet ambiguously, so that we are uncertain if it is praise or blame, such was the end of Troilus. What was his suffering worth, what relevance had it? The poet counsels young fresh folk to love the true God. The heathen gods are mere 'rascaille'. The poet then dedicates this courtly poem to his middle-aged learned friends, the poet 'moral Gower' and the 'philosophical Strode', and concludes with a noble prayer to the Trinity, translated from Dante.

BOOK V: COMMENTARY

Book V is an artistic *tour-de-force* and a most moving account not only of the sadness of betrayal, the sickness of hope deferred and extinguished, but also of a robust modification of tragedy. The *story* is a tragedy, but the *poem* is something larger, longer, more varied.

THE ENDING

The ending has attracted a great variety of response. It is not, as it is sometimes described, an epilogue, a mere tailpiece, nor a palinode, a rejection of what has gone before. It is the expression of yet another point of view, another response; and though it may be the last, it does not deny the truth, within their own terms, of the joys and sorrows and interim values expressed before. The long-drawn-out ending is a deliberate disengagement from the story, held together by the poet as Expositor, who continues to comment on the action. The flight to heaven, adapted from *Teseida* and not in *Il Filostrato*, is an immense strengthening of the poet's exposition, rather than a part of Troilus's story. Its placing is very deliberate. It both condemns and validates Troilus's love, which is inseparable from his 'trouthe'. The ancient motif of the flight to heaven suggests both questions and answers, which are obliquely followed by the injunction to love Christ. None of this should be taken as ironical. It would be too silly, as well as historically impossible. But it does leave a fascinating set of underlying ambiguities, opening out multiple perspectives within this extraordinary poem. As in so many of the greatest stories we are left with the sense of a profound enigma at the heart of it, which prompts a series of different yet related answers, none final.

THE USE OF THE *CONSOLATION* IN *TROILUS*

The essence of the *Consolation* is that mind is superior to matter. Its two main topics are, first, 'what is true happiness', which Chaucer calls 'felicity'; and, second, how to obtain it in the light of our material conditioning, both inner and outer, which amounts to what Boethius calls Fortune, Destiny. In *Troilus and Criseyde*, Criseyde is more interested in 'felicity', Troilus in fate and free will. Troilus is in the position of the 'lesser' Boethius, inside the *Consolation*, though Troilus, unlike Boethius, never becomes reconciled to his destiny.

Criseyde is clearly aware that worldly happiness is only false felicity (e.g. III, 813–17). According to Boethius true felicity consists in *gentilesse* and *trouthe*, which is exactly what Criseyde says she loves Troilus for (IV, 16, 72–4). *Trouthe* is for Chaucer the highest, most complex quality, which can refer to God himself, as in Chaucer's short poem with that title. But Criseyde, though she can recognise *trouthe* does not possess it. She is always worrying about what other people think, but you can only find *trouthe* inside your own mind (though it is not subjective, or limited to yourself alone); and you must have peace with yourself, as Boethius says (II, p. 4, as also does Pandarus, I, 893). *Trouthe* is that inner integrity which assures loyalty to what is outside ourselves.

We can only love *trouthe* 'outside' us if we have it 'inside' us. Now it is clear that Troilus has *trouthe*, yet comes to disaster in his life, as did Boethius himself. It must be because of Troilus's *trouthe* that after death he goes, if not to heaven, which the poet is not explicit about, yet presumably to bliss, although the poem ends in condemnation of pagan life and of 'feyned loves'.

Boethius has as it were a circular model of the spiritual universe, the opposite of the Ptolemaic model of the physical universe (above, p. 95). In the Ptolemaic model earth is the almost dead lump at the centre, with Hell inside it at the very mid-point. Above the moon all is stable and beautiful in the successive starry spheres which mediate God's plans for earth. In the spiritual globe by contrast, God, not the earth, is the centre; next comes the sphere of Providence, which is God's planning, and outside that, Destiny and Fortune which are the physical universe of appearances, the ups and downs, the chains of cause and effect, of ordinary life. In practice for Chaucer Destiny and Fortune are the same. Fortune is the poetic personification of that level of reality represented more philosophically by Destiny.

Boethius claims that man can either stay at the level of superficial ordinary experience, the level of Fortune, or he can move 'inwards' towards God's providence. Fortune is chaotic yet unfree, bound by chains of material and astrological causation. Moving towards God is towards love and freedom (they must go together for as *The Franklin's Tale* will tell us 'Love wol nat been constreyned by maistrie', 'Love is a thyng as any spirit free'.)

There are plenty of paradoxes and problems here, but one of them is particularly significant. Beothius represents himself inside the *Consolation* as at first arguing in Book V, prose 3, that men cannot have free will to choose the good if God foreknows all, since if he can know it now, it must be bound to happen. Therefore there is no real choice for men. This is the longest speech by Boethius within the whole *Consolation* and is clearly of great intellectual and emotional significance to Boethius; so it is to Chaucer, for Troilus's repetition of part of Boethius's argument here is the largest single section that Chaucer directly borrowed from the *Consolation*. Boethius's argument contains a logical fallacy which his mentor, the Lady Philosophy, analyses in order to break out of the circle of necessity. She thus convinces Boethius of his mistake. But Chaucer does not employ the refutation, since he is concerned with the dramatic relevance to Troilus, who uses and believes the demonstrably false argument of Boethius without correction. Troilus, though good, is not represented as learned, and this long philosophical excursus as already noted is not part of a naturalistic characterisation. His speech represents the nature of his feelings as the good rationalist pagan 'who found no end, in wandering mazes lost'.

This raises important points for understanding the intellectual nature of the poem. We, the audience, are clearly meant to dissociate ourselves from Troilus's point of view, while sympathising with his sorrowful dilemma. He accepts a total determinism which we know to be mistaken. Yet the course of the poem, of which we know the outcome from the very first line, if not before, may seem to exemplify Troilus's deterministic view. We are therefore, *vis-à-vis* the poem, in a position like that of God *vis-à-vis* the world, while in a sense the poet, in the poem, is like the philosopher who has to reconcile God's (the audience's) foreknowledge of the outcome with local immediate participation in the hopes, fears, lives and potential freedom, of the characters. Both choice and necessity must be seen to coexist. This involves the shifting of perspectives upon the narrative events, which has already been remarked. To put it another way, to do justice to the complexity of the action different attitudes are required to different parts of the poem. For example, the attitude to love expressed or implied in the whole of Book III, is different from that at the end of the whole poem. This is the nature of a 'Gothic' poem which, unlike a novel, straddles fiction and reality. The unity of the poem lies in the continuity of the story as presented by the Expositor; different persons may validly judge the events differently, and so may the poet himself at different stages of the story, in various contexts. The events are presented with, and for, sympathetic rationalistic participation, though the degree of participation, or distance, between us and the events, varies. The realistic non-mythic, or non-folkloric story, told mainly in terms of naturalistic cause and effect, here serves Chaucer much better than a mythic story would have done. The chain of cause and effect so efficiently linked in *Troilus and Criseyde* provides a connected, coherent, continuous and almost self-enclosed simple structure, round which the poet as Expositor can wind a much less continuous or consistent commentary, which is certainly not self-enclosed since it can address itself to actual living people (Gower, Strode) and evoke real, non-fictional standards. The commentary at any point tends to take its tone from the nature of the specific action being described, but then relates that action to the audience or reader.

The chain of cause and effect is an effective Boethian image of worldly events. The various attitudes taken towards them by the poet contribute to our sense of wonder, our speculations, and our own sense of the possible alternatives and choices. The poem is always presented for our godlike contemplation; we always know more than the characters, and the poem cannot fully exist unless sustained by our godlike loving participation, just as the world itself, in Boethius's and Chaucer's thought, could not exist without God's sustaining participating love.

THE QUESTION OF LOVE

In the question of love Chaucer goes further than Boethius. Although Boethius does indeed write nobly of the bond of love throughout the world, the general effect of his work is to recommend an ascetic denial of the world for the sake of loving God. Troilus loves Criseyde who represents worldly joy, the gifts of Fortune, and is badly let down as we expect. The paradox is that because of his virtue, his *trouthe*, he cannot cease loving Criseyde. Stable people cannot just switch love off – not even Pandarus can. Stability is the crucial value for Boethius, as it was for Chaucer. It is an aspect of *trouthe* (cf. *Consolation* III, m. 11.), an aspect of God, dwelling within oneself. What makes worldly felicity false is precisely its own transience, its instability. Troilus's stability involves him totally with an unstable person; a painful and hopeless paradox. The simple answer to the paradox at the end of the poem is that it is less painful and more satisfying for stable true love to direct itself to the only really stable true person, to wit, God. But the totality of the poem's commentaries, in whatever way we resolve or fail to resolve their logical inconsistencies, adds up to a more complex assertion of the reality of the joy of human love, even if it is transient. This thought is at best only implicit in Boethius. Chaucer brings it out much more fully.

The usefulness of the *Consolation* to Chaucer lay in its rational appeal within the general Christian tradition. Of course, scholasticism was rational, and no doubt Aquinas was a greater thinker than Boethius. But for Chaucer Boethius with his literary flavour was a better teacher than Aquinas, and was secular; he was neither ecclesiastical nor technically philosophical, nor theological. Had he been so Chaucer would have lacked training and perhaps sympathy to understand his work. Being secular the *Consolation* was historically apt for a poem set in pre-Christian times; even more, it could bypass what by Chaucer's time was the rather sour asceticism of the ecclesiastical tradition.

This great long poem was Chaucer's supreme artistic achievement in which tradition is handled with startling originality. Having achieved it Chaucer went on to different kinds of work, of even greater originality, but first he followed the vein which he had in fact almost exhausted.

Chapter 11

THE LEGEND OF GOOD WOMEN

The years following 1386 were as usual troubled, and Chaucer's political friends were in eclipse until 1389. The thin stream of references to him in the official documents continues. Their interpretation is often doubtful, and from none of them would it be gathered that he was a well-known court poet. Thomas Usk's reference to him in about 1387 in his Boethian prose work *The Testament of Love* as the 'noble philosophical poete' is worth the whole of them. It establishes a contemporary's estimate of his work, and the typical line of appreciation of the next two and a half centuries.

There are two main bodies of poetry filling Chaucer's later years, each composed of a Prologue introducing a collection of stories. The first of these is *The Legend of Good Women*, and the second, *The Canterbury Tales*. *The Legend* is a pendant to *Troilus*, yet in its form it provides a half-way house to the *Tales*. Its plan is simple. *The Prologue* recounts a dream of the poet's, in which the god of love accuses Chaucer of holding it folly to serve love because he has published the untruth of Criseyde, thereby casting a general aspersion on woman's constancy. He also accuses Chaucer of translating the 'heretical' *Roman de la Rose*. The god's consort, Queen Alceste, with womanly kindliness, endeavours to soften the charge, by recounting Chaucer's other works in praise of love. She also mentions such 'other holyness' as his translation of Boethius, and his life of Saint Cecilia. To include such 'holiness', as he also calls these works in the final *Retraccioun* to *The Canterbury Tales* which condemns his secular works, is a queer inconsistency, but perhaps Chaucer was taking a useful opportunity to list, and, so to speak, to 'sign' some of his major works, as he does in the Prologue to *The Man of Law's Tale* and even in his *Retraccioun*. At all events, Chaucer denies the god's accusation, and Chaucer is right; he is no heretic to love, no defamer of women. But nevertheless he has to pay the penalty, which is to write a glorious 'legend' (i.e. a Saint's Life) of women true in love. This is a half-humorous secular parody of the true saint's life, in

151

which love was normally repudiated. The poet agrees, although the god of love says there are so many of them that he will only be able to make a short tale of each.

THE PROLOGUE ITS VERSIONS AND DATE

The Prologue is one of Chaucer's most delightful poems, and a quite extraordinary mixture of old and new. In substance it is something of a throwback to the old-fashioned French love-vision, and several French poems about the marguerite are followed at times quite closely. But the metre is the new five-stress rhyming couplet and the manner is that of Chaucer's maturity, often apparently only half-serious. The jests go along with a real tenderness and beauty of description. The preciosity of daisy-worship is indulged without becoming mawkish, or being sneered at.

The poem was sufficiently interesting to Chaucer for him to have two goes at it, and *The Prologue* exists in two versions.

The first appears in eleven manuscripts or parts of manuscripts. The best of these manuscripts is Bodley Fairfax 16, a notable anthology of Chaucer's minor poems. This version of *The Prologue* has therefore been labelled F. The second version appears in only one manuscript, University Library Cambridge Gg. 4.27, the biggest manuscript collection of Chaucer's poems in existence. Its spelling is odd but its texts are usually very good, and close to the originals. Hence this version has been labelled G. Each manuscript is of the early fifteenth century (and like many others, is now available in facsimile). The first version, F, must have been written, because of the content, sometime after *Troilus*, say after 1385. There is a kind of dedication to Queen Anne, for Queen Alcestis says,

> And whan this book ys maad, yive it the quene
> On my byhalf, at Eltham or at Sheene
>
> *Pro LGW* F. 496–7

(Eltham and Sheene were favourite royal palaces not too far from Westminster.) Since Anne died in 1394 *The Prologue* must have been written before then, and it seems reasonable to date it soon after the completion of *Troilus* around 1385, and before the beginning of *The Canterbury Tales*, which has been plausibly suggested as around 1387. The later version of *The Prologue* omits the reference to the Queen and was probably produced some time after 1394.

A GLIMPSE OF SOCIAL CIRCUMSTANCES

The Prologue gives us a rare glimpse at something like the social circumstances of Chaucer's poetry. He addresses an 'audience', or readers, especially in *Troilus*, of lovers, ladies, middle-aged friends and scholars, that 'sire' (*Troilus* III, 83) who may be the king, and even 'Thou reader' (V, 270), but powerful as the imaginative grouping is, there remains in *Troilus* a certain freedom from social context. In *The Prologue to the Legend of Good Women* the poet tells us very clearly about his own personal tastes and habits. He makes explicit his love of books, in a reversion to his earlier manner in *The Book of the Duchess, House of Fame* and *Parliament.*

> On bokes for to rede I me delyte

F. 30

Only in May, when the birds sing and flowers bloom, farewell his book and his devotion, and he walks the meadows at dawn to observe the daisy, the flower of all flowers. Granted that this derives from French poems devoted to the cult of the marguerite, it seems fairly specific to Chaucer's own situation. There is a reference to Saint Valentine (F. l. 145) which may associate *The Prologue* with St Valentine's Day celebrations. A reference is made to the divisions of the Flower and the Leaf (F. l. 72), which were court parties or associations, probably with some political overtones. In F, Chaucer seems to declare for the flower (F. 1.82), but in the revision he adds a passage which denies adherence to either side (G. ll. 71–80). Whatever its significance, the brief reference gives a further social depth to the setting, hard as it is to understand.

The poet tells us how he retreats to his house at dusk and sleeps in a little arbour he has had made in his garden. One is bound to feel that all this refers to his new house at Greenwich, then so near the meadows. He has a couch made up for him by his servants on a bench of turves. As so often, one does not quite know how seriously to take this. He fell asleep, he says, 'within an hour to two' (F. l. 209) – surely a wry joke about an uncomfortable bed, a touch of irresistible comic realism? Then he dreams of the god of love coming to him over daylit meadows, hand in hand with a queen, clad in green, with a golden fret upon her hair, and a crown with white 'fleurons' – the small protrusions of medieval royal crowns – which were made of pearl, and resembled the petals of a daisy. The queen is the human transformation of a daisy, and a most entrancing, poetical creation she is. Chaucer does not usually create such almost mythical characters. However, both the god of love and his queen speak very humanly and at times tartly to the poet, reproaching him, as already noted, and eventually commissioning from him the stories of ladies loyal in love.

The commissioning is unique in Chaucer and sounds like an actual command or request from a patron and patroness of a kind completely lacking elsewhere in his poetry. One aspect of Chaucer's modernity is his normal freedom from patronage. Perhaps he was not free here.

WHO DOES ALCESTIS REPRESENT?

But who was the queen? We later learn she is Queen Alcestis, most famous in Greek Antiquity for her loyalty to her husband, whose death she took on herself. Who does she represent? A natural guess is that the god of love is King Richard II and Alcestis Queen Anne. It may be so, but it seems odd that she should suggest that the poems be presented to the Queen, that is Anne, at Eltham or Sheen. The god of love was not married, and Alcestis had a husband, and conceivably Chaucer intends a compliment to the Queen Mother, Joan, once the Fair Maid of Kent, now the widow of the Black Prince, with whom it is possible that Chaucer served in Aquitaine. Whether or not this very pretty scene represents an actual reproach and commissioning of compensatory stories by some great lady, no reward is mentioned. The scene is allusion rather than allegory, and teases us with its possible meanings. Whoever the god and the queen are, the poet permits himself a fairly light-hearted dramatic portrayal of them, not disrespectful, but far from obsequious.

LITERARY POINTS

The Prologue has many interesting literary points. Chaucer's listing of his writing has already been noted. The G version has the additional item of *The Wretched Engendring of Mankynde*, witness to Chaucer's continuing pursuit of serious, not to say gloomy, devotional subjects, in his maturity, which accompanied his equally vigorous development of the far from moralistic bawdy comic stories in *The Canterbury Tales* at the same time.

Another interesting point is his insistence on his interest in old stories, and his desire to revere and believe in them. But in the revised version, G, he is more clearly ironical about this – 'leveth hem if you leste' (believe them if it pleases you) G. l. 88. It is here that he declares his intention for the narratives that will follow: to declare them in 'the naked text'. He aims at a sort of narrative literalism, without allegory. The plain or naked text, without the 'glose', without, that is, the interpretation that came to signify falsification or flattery or deceit, appealed to Chaucer, and he always uses the word 'glosing' unfavourably.

THE REVISION OF THE PROLOGUE

The revision itself gives us a unique opportunity to see Chaucer at work on the craftsmanship of writing, and at the same time gives us some insight into his changing attitudes.

The structure of F is somewhat rambling, and there is an awkward confusion between Alceste and 'my lady' (cf. lines 249 ff., 432, and 540). G does a certain amount of tidying up and the confusion about Alceste is removed. In F the subject of the fashionable controversy between the Flower and the Leaf is approached in l. 72, but is not actually developed until ll. 188–96. In G these two references are consolidated in ll. 65–78. Again, in G the dream starts earlier. The effect of this alteration is to put the famous description of the beautiful morning and the charmingly anthropomorphic behaviour of the birds *inside* the dream. This is an improvement. The morning, for all its freshness, is nothing like the chilly hours just following dawn of an ordinary English May morning. It has the warmth and sweetness of a kindlier clime, as in the French literary tradition, and is much easier to accept as part of the Dream. The general effect of this and other structural changes is to consolidate, to make the development less wandering and casual.

G also develops certain matters more lightly touched on in F. In the earlier version Chaucer says that a king's subjects 'are his treasure and his gold in coffer' – a very appropriate sentiment for a customs officer. In the later version he substitutes six lines about the duty of a king to hear his subjects' complaints and petitions. This is an echo of increasing anxiety about Richard's irresponsible and autocratic behaviour. Nevertheless, in G the central occasion of *The Prologue* seems to be taken less seriously. As he grew older Chaucer was even less able to refrain from a little mocking with a solemn face. In the long and important insertion, G. ll. 258–312, he gives the god of love a much livelier and fuller speech. The god accuses Chaucer of heresy against him, although he remarks that Chaucer owns a lot of books telling the lives of women, 'and ever a hundred good against one bad':

> What seith Valerye, Titus, or Claudyan?
> What seith Jerome agayns Jovynyan?
>
> G. 280–1

But this is a joke at the expense of the God of Love. What Jerome said against Jovinian is touched on in the *Wife of Bath's Prologue*. He and 'Valerian' (i.e. Walter Map), far from praising women, were perhaps the most satirical and effective of all the many slanderers of women in the anti-feminist Middle Ages. Chaucer loved them as much as he loved the tales of noble women. Here he is deliberately making a fool of the god of love. He makes other ironical additions. The queen defends him by suggesting that he translated poems, and 'knew not what he was saying'. On the other hand he cut out F. 1. 152, which is rather a feeble joke about sex.

Most of the alterations are obviously aimed to improve the sense and the poetry. Thus he cut out the last twenty-five lines of F. They are somewhat verbose, and are little loss. At the beginning he much modified the expression of his love for the daisy. It is difficult not to sense some personal feeling in the early, F, version of this – perhaps it was a courtier's address to the Queen. Chaucer may have modified it later because the Queen's death made it inappropriate, or even simply because the daisy cult was no longer a fashion in sentiment which was current or still appealed to him. Some of the alterations at the beginning forced him to abandon the charming four-line song which in F introduces Alceste's attendants. Chaucer's willingness to abandon these excellent few lines in the interests of the whole is a mark of his maturity and self-confidence as craftsman and artist. Other changes are often minute, but hardly less interesting. Thus he tones down the rather mechanical emphasis on the brightness of the god of love. For 'holiness' (F. 1. 424) he substitutes 'busy-ness' (G. 1. 412). Where F. ll. 348–9 describes Love as a God who knows all, G. ll. 323–7 substitutes the remark that all is not true which the god of love hears. Occasionally the alteration merely cuts out the clumsy repetition of the same word, e.g. the repetition of 'serve' in F. ll. 326–7. The later version also writes at somewhat greater length of Geoffrey Chaucer himself, in the familiar image of an amiable simpleton.

In general, the revision gives a stronger sense of the poet's personality, a better construction, and a strengthened style. The G version is livelier in humour, and also warmer in its praises of noble women. It varies much more in tone; some parts of G are more serious, other parts more flippant, than in the earlier version. Chaucer intensifies his original, even when it is his own earlier composition as he intensified the style of *Il Filostrato*. Nevertheless, for all the tinkering, it is still the same poem. The wonderfully fresh sense of spring remains, with the poet's heart-warming confession of inability to read in that stirring time of the year. There is still the delight in books, together with a little more information on the books Chaucer has read or written.

Perhaps between the two versions of *The Prologue* Chaucer's interests turned away from the courtly subject of love and of the fundamental problems raised by love. He may have felt he had worked that vein. It is also a matter of common experience that as a man grows older he becomes less interested in fundamental questions, for willy-nilly he has made up his mind about them. Interest tends to turn from philosophy to ethics; from theories to facts. We may perceive this happening even in the difference between *The Parliament* and *Troilus*. *The Canterbury Tales* are evidence of the continuation of the process.

THE LEGENDS THEMSELVES

When we come to the stories themselves we find that there are only nine of these love's saints and martyrs, beginning, somewhat surprisingly, with Cleopatra, and continuing with Thisbe, Dido, Hypsipyle and Medea in one, Lucrece, Ariadne, Philomela, Phyllis, Hypermnestra. They derive from Ovid's *Heroides*, and two works of Boccaccio on the falls of famous men and women. In the *Introduction to the Man of Law's Tale* in *The Canterbury Tales*, undoubtedly written later, Chaucer gives another list of his works, along with a jest against himself, and lists fifteen of these 'saints of Cupid', while in yet another list, his *Retracciouns*, written in a quite different spirit, he refers to his Book of the Twenty-five Ladies. He clearly wrote many if not all of the stories we now have after writing *The Prologue*, and he intended to continue, but got diverted to *The Canterbury Tales*. It is unlikely that any are lost.

Each of the tales has, in effect, the same theme as *Troilus* (for *Troilus* is a story of true love), though reversed in sex, and is essentially a counterpart to *Troilus*. The tales certainly are not a repudiation of the so-called repudiation of love at the end of *Troilus*. They are written to assert the trueness of women against what is said to be Chaucer's imputation of their falseness. *The Legends* are thin when compared with Chaucer's other treatments of closely similar themes. There seems little doubt that in writing *Troilus* Chaucer had exercised that sense of loss and betrayal which had haunted his early work from *The Book of the Duchess* onwards. But he did not at first realise that. Another reason may have been that there seemed so many stories to be told that each was rather cramped. Like the later project of one hundred and twenty *Canterbury Tales*, it was too ambitious a scheme. Moreover, all Chaucer's work shows how ready he was to change subject matter and treatment. *The Legend* has for him and us the major disadvantage of a single theme and type of subject matter. Chaucer seems to have liked variety above all.

LOVE AND MARRIAGE

The recurrent theme makes clear the centrality of marriage to Chaucer's general conception of love. Everyone of the betrayed heroines has been married or been promised marriage. Love is genuine, thought to be mutual, and free from concepts of service and humility. The plight of those who are betrayed is rendered with genuine pathos. Chaucer does his best to stick to the bare essentials of plot and character, and on the personal relationships which as always are at the centre of his interest. Nor are these as monotonous as sometimes claimed; if the theme is the same the circumstances are all different.

Gower told several of the same stories in his *Confessio Amantis* and Chaucer's principal aim seems to have been to achieve a rapid, plain, brief narration of the kind in which Gower excelled. Perhaps Chaucer set out to imitate Gower. Like him he always maintains the interest in the succession of events. Chaucer's difficulty was in restraining himself from adorning and enriching the narratives, and in preserving the benevolent even tone in which Gower is so tireless.

DESCRIPTIONS

Yet Chaucer cannot resist some vivid descriptions, for which the reader must be grateful. In the story of Cleopatra there is a sea-fight in which, as in a similar passage in *The Knight's Tale*, Chaucer evokes hints of alliterative poetry, which he seems particularly to have associated with this sort of subject matter;

> Up goth the trompe, and for to shoute and shete   [*shoot*
> And peynen hem to sette on with the sunne.   [*strive*
> With grysely soun out goth the grete gonne   [*horrible sound*
> And heterly they hurtelen al atones   [*violently*
> And from the top doun come the grete stones.
>
> *LGW* 635–9

Heterly is a word particularly characteristic of the alliterative school of the North-west Midlands poetry. The description in full is so remarkably vivid an account of a contemporary sea-battle that one wonders if Chaucer had been in one himself.

The account of Thisbe is longer than most and genuinely affecting. Like others it has some touches of striking if slightly grotesque realism, as when Thisbe finds her beloved in the throes of death

> Betynge with his heles on the grounde,
> Al blody, and therwithal a-bak she stert   [*started*
> And lik the wawes quappe gan hire herte   [*waves heave*
>
> *LGW* 863–5

The story of Dido is also told with some fullness, and worth comparing with the account from the *Aeneid* in *The House of Fame*.

As in all these poems there is a refreshing response to goodness. Thus Dido is attracted by the noble Aeneas:

> And saw the man, that he was lyk a knyght,
> And suffisaunt of persone and of myght,
> And lyk to been a verray gentil man;   [*truly noble*
> And wel his wordes he besette can,   [*apply*
> And had a noble visage for the nones
> And formed wel of braunes and of bones.

LGW 1066–74

This is an admirable summary of the good qualities of a knight. The cumulative descriptive style with frequent use of *and* is one of the characteristics of Chaucer's later manner. The apparently simple style may have more subtlety than at first appears. The conjunction of qualities given here expresses Chaucer's genuine ideal of the knight and gentleman, sympathetic to Dido. Yet the empty and possibly mocking phrase 'for the nones', and Aeneas's handsome appearance, such as Chaucer does not make for his real heroes, like Troilus, signals a satirical or sarcastic implication about Aeneas, as do other stylistic touches. He promises, or seems, better than he really is, as the story shows. This little passage is a masterpiece of veiled criticism of Aeneas.

VARIETY OF NARRATIVE STYLE

In these stories Chaucer cannot altogether refrain from his usual habit of taking the story so seriously as to address the characters, or make exclamations about them. Critics rarely if ever speak of the Narrator in these poems, and quite rightly, because the concept gives us no new insight, but the narrating poet or Expositor is evident enough. An example, together with Chaucer's irrepressible tendency to hyperbole, is found at the beginning of the Legend of Hypsipyle and Medea where the poet addresses Jason:

> Thow rote of false lovers, Duc Jasoun   [*root*
> Thow sly devourere and confusioun
> Of gentil wemen, tendre creatures ..
> O, often swore thow that thow woldest dye
> For love, whan thow ne feltest maladye
> Save foul delyt, which that thow callest love.
> Yif that I live, thy name shal be shove
> In English that thy sekte shal be knowe,   [*kind*
> Have at thee Jason! Now thyn horn is blowe.   [*Now the game is up*
>   *for you*

LGW 1368...83

None of this is in Chaucer's sources. The concepts are serious and familiar enough, but the style, especially in the last three lines is irrepressibly lively. The horn that is blown is presumably that which signifies the finding and expected death of the quarry in the hunt.

ATTITUDE TO PAGAN HEROES

The attitude expressed towards Jason appears elsewhere and may remind us of the 'rascaille' of heathen gods referred to at the end of *Troilus*. Although the stories are fascinating, Chaucer has a genuine medieval contempt for the vices of pagan heroes and disgust at the horrors which are the frequent subject matter of classical mythology. He expresses this most forcibly in the *Introduction to the Man of Law's Tale* when, after listing the stories in the *Legend* that he has written, or is going to write, he draws attention to his refusal to write about the incest of Canace and Antiochus. Although here again he diverges into humorous asides, there seems no reason to doubt, in a poet who so often expresses tenderness and pity, a real squeamishness on certain topics, a real moral conviction that some things are beyond the pale, even though he has a robust enjoyment of the misadventures of the popular traditional comic tale. Chaucer's idealism is as certain as his realism, his satire and comedy; and the Gothic mixture of them all is part of his attraction.

The stories in the *Legend* are very much a mixture of this kind, but there is a certain lack of control. The relative frequency with which the poet encourages himself to get on with the story and not to take too long, betrays a sense of strain. The ninth and last story breaks off unfinished, though obviously near the end. Other projects must have seemed more attractive. The plan of the *Legend* was too constricting. Their own attractions, and the insight they give into Chaucer's literary methods, development and interests, are nevertheless considerable. The *Legend* is a sustained evocation of genuine pathos, drawing extensively on a great range of classical and other narrative, with some corresponding variety, yet also with a new concision and drive. It is energetic, forward-looking, not tired. The style is often subtle. Were it not for Chaucer's other works we should admit without question that the *Legend* is a remarkably good, complex poem. If suffers by comparison with them because it is different, a paradoxical example of Chaucer's constant search for new material and forms of expression.

Chapter 12

PROLOGUE TO *THE CANTERBURY TALES*

THE PLAN

The Canterbury Tales have always been by far the most popular of Chaucer's works. There are some eighty-four full manuscripts or fragments and six early printed editions, compared with twenty manuscripts and three early printed editions of *Troilus and Criseyde*. The reason is not far to seek: *Troilus* is long, subtle, learned and magnificent; *The Tales* are short, varied, and often humorous. *Troilus* is more often mentioned in early records because it is more obviously splendid. The ordinary reader has always been more easily captivated by *The Tales*. Their demands are less uncompromising, they contain some of Chaucer's best work, and they offer more opportunities for skipping. There is something for everyone in them, and their richness is inexhaustible.

The plan is very ambitious. Originally two stories each way for each of about thirty pilgrims were planned. This was drastically curtailed, and all the signs are that Chaucer cut the plan to one story each, and finally decided to conclude with the arrival at Canterbury. He even began to envisage Canterbury as a sort of secular New Jerusalem, if we so interpret a remark by the Parson in his *Prologue* to the last tale, which the Parson tells, and which is not a fiction but a concluding religious meditation on Penance. Chaucer did indeed finish *The Canterbury Tales*, but at the cost of leaving much of it unrevised and incomplete. He had changed his mind continuously as the scheme developed. The whole work is a fascinating mixture of complete and incomplete, of 'being' (and thus stable, conclusive) and 'becoming' (and therefore fluid, uncertain, with inconsistencies). It is a very Gothic mixture, but one to which all centuries, and especially the twentieth, find it easy to respond.

THE MANUSCRIPTS

Chaucer must have left a box full of written papers, with stories partly in groups, partly on their own. We have none of his preliminary notes, which may have been made on lightly waxed tablets, but his working copies of poems would have been loose sheets or pamphlets of paper or parchment which he bound up in booklets of at most a few stories at a time. When satisfied with what he wrote, he sent a section off to a professional scrivener to have one or more copies written out fair. Scribes were liable to make many mistakes, so Chaucer corrected the copy when it came back (scratching mistakes out with stone or a knife), cursing the scribe meanwhile. Much of this we know from the short poem which is the uneviable monument of his usual scribe.

> Adam Scriveyn, if ever it thee bifalle   [*scrivener*
> Boece or Troylus for to wryten newe,
> Under thy long lokkes thou most have the scalle,   [*may you have*
>   *the scab*
> But after my makyng thou wryte more trewe   [*unless according to*
> So ofte a-daye I mot thy werk renewe,   [*must*
> It to correcte and eek to rubbe and scrape;
> And al is thorugh thy negligence and rape.   [*haste*

Chaucer published a poem in two ways; either by reading it aloud or by allowing copies to circulate. The famous *Troilus* 'frontispiece' depicts Chaucer himself reading to the Court. However, as already noted, the 'frontispiece' is by no means realistic and was painted after Chaucer's death; and it is curious that there seems to be no other reference to the reading of longish poems in a court except Froissart's account of reading his own *Meliador* at the court of Gaston de Foix in the south of what is now France. Perhaps the more usual situation was similar to Criseyde's 'reading-party', where a book is read to a small group of friends. The court at large seems to have been fonder of music and songs. Many people heard literature; some, like Chaucer himself, read it. Even when manuscripts were lent out and copied, there might be many who heard for one who read. A manuscript was read until it fell to pieces. It was also copied, by amateurs and professionals. A bad copy might be made of a manuscript which had already lost several pages and was itself a bad copy of another. Copyists made every conceivable error – missing out letters, words, lines, pages; misunderstanding, miswriting; often they wrote in different dialects; sometimes they altered passages which for some reason seemed wrong to them, or of which they disapproved. Chaucer himself complicated the situation when, as happened with

The Tales, he continued the work piecemeal, and never issued it whole in his lifetime. There are many inconsistencies which we may guess Chaucer would not have noticed, or bothered about, but others which he would have removed on full revision.

None of Chaucer's original manuscripts survives, unless the manuscript of the astronomical work *The Equatorie of the Planetis* is his, and that does not help us much, since it is non-fictional. Our manuscripts are the descendants of his through the hands of an unknown number of copyists, a few of whom made their own attempts to sort out the sequence of Canterbury tale, occasionally even by adding their own verses. It is not necessarily the best manuscripts which have survived the accidents of flood, fire, children, vandals, and other enemies of books, including those who love them so much that they read them to pieces. A good deal of uncertainty exists as to the date of writing the various stories of *The Canterbury Tales*. But by this time, variety not development is the mark of Chaucer's genius. The internal chronology of the later *Tales* is not important for understanding them.

THE SEQUENCE OF TALES

Chaucer did not group the *Tales* according to any intellectual system, but rather for the sake of variety. The whole work is like a Gothic manuscript miscellany, such as Thornton's book, or the Auchinleck manuscript, but is, almost incredibly, the product of one extraordinarily diverse creative mind.

The intended sequence of tales can be made out to some extent by internal references to stages of the journey between Southwark and Canterbury along the Pilgrim's Way. This was worked out by Professor Skeat in his now outdated edition, and since this was the order which Chaucer was clearly aiming at it is followed here. However, the earliest editor of Chaucer was the scribe of the famous Ellesmere manuscript, now at the Huntington Library in California, and the order he follows is slightly different. The Ellesmere order has been followed by Professor Robinson in his edition and by most later editors. Robinson's text, though not perfect, is the one followed here, and his numbering alone is used, giving ten 'blocks' or groups of tales, a group sometimes being one tale alone, though with preceding and/or following material. Such material between tales, which is brilliant realistic comedy, is referred to in general as the *Links*.

THE RAW MATERIAL OF STORIES

Chaucer probably began to work seriously on the idea of *The Canterbury Tales* around 1386–7, when he went to live down in Kent. The idea of gathering stories into groups was fairly common. From Classical Antiquity comes the great example of Ovid's *Metamorphoses*. More collections of stories held together by some single idea, or placed in a single framework came to be written in the fourteenth century. Gower was in process of writing such a collection, and Chaucer's own *Legend of Good Women* is another example. A collection of short stories was perhaps the most characteristic form of fourteenth-century literature. It conveyed all kinds of literary effects. An audience, as opposed to a reader, can better understand and remember a story than any other form of literary expression. For the more sophisticated, a story could be analysed, and there might be as many as three or four different levels on which a story might be understood. There were many folktales current of all kinds, pious, amusing, improper. A number of these, as habits of reading and writing spread, were caught up by literary men. Apart from what he might hear Chaucer also read many stories and we may well understand the attraction they had for him, both as a typical man of his times, and as a literary artist seeking satisfactory forms. A collection of stories of different kinds obviously created an attractive variety.

Many stories were heard as oral narratives, or were developed orally from being read in some manuscript. Many other stories had been written down and recopied for centuries. In general it was the more serious stories which had been written down, the lighter ones told. Often a story was believed to be historical and therefore true simply because it was written down. The *Clerk's Tale* of patient Griselda is the subject of two illuminating comments in this respect, quoted by Professor Manly in his edition. One of Petrarch's friends doubted whether the story could be true. Petrarch replied that such stories as those of Alcestis (who went to the Underworld in place of her husband, and was rescued by Hercules) *seem* to be fables (*fabulas*) – 'Atque historiae verae sunt', 'but they are true histories'. The sensible fifteenth-century citizen who wrote the *Ménagier de Paris* also tells the story of Griselda, and says, 'I do not believe it ever happened, but the story is such that I dare not correct or change it, for one wiser than I compiled it, and gave it its name'. There was therefore a clear difference between a 'fabula' and a 'historia'. Yet whereas the plot itself could not be altered, a great part of the aim of such rhetoricians as Geoffrey of Vinsauf, whose work Chaucer knew, was to teach how to dress up an old story in a new signification. It was also taught that style should suit subject matter – high subject, high style. 'Low' subjects, therefore, which dealt with humble people and trivial or amusing events, were not to be dressed in the panoply of high style, unless the poet's aim was burlesque.

STORY AND CHARACTER

The quality of Chaucer's genius and originality is especially clear in the use he made of the raw material and the ideas which he shared with Gower and Boccaccio. It was natural to the Gothic spirit to attempt to gather in every kind of story, to put the serious subject by the amusing, the parody of the high style not far from the high style itself, the 'pious fable' by the 'dirty story' – in a word, to sum up as much of human experience as possible, to let 'contraries meet in one'. Even in Boccaccio's *Decameron* there are a number of serious and pious tales. Chaucer goes further than his contemporaries, however, in his variety; and especially in accounting for it by the characters of those who tell the tales. We may guess that his characters were first the product, so to speak, of the tales they were to tell. It is certain that Chaucer had some stories by him which were already written before the *Tales* as a whole were conceived. He may have wished to use these, and to provide characters as a series of pegs on which to hang the many more stories he wished to write. Perhaps he wrote *The General Prologue* to *The Canterbury Tales* at this stage of his idea. However that may be, stories for him, as we have seen, had as it were a personality of their own. Then furthermore the human characters once conceived took on almost a life of their own, and the whole scheme continued to develop under his careful fostering and pruning. We can see a good idea succeeded by a better, for example, when he substituted the present *Wife of Bath's Tale* for the tale originally given to her which is now called *The Shipman's Tale*. The change is apparent because the present *Shipman's Tale*, although unquestionably attributed to him according to the manuscripts, is written for a woman to tell. It belongs to the period of the *Tales*, and could only fit the Wife of Bath. Here is a case where the speed of his own development as it were outpaced Chaucer; he had no time to complete the other half of his plan, and change the wording of *The Shipman's Tale* to make it accord with the new speaker. From similar inconsistencies in the text it is usually assumed that the prose *Tale of Melibeus* was first assigned to the Man of Law, and then later switched to its position as Chaucer's own second tale, perhaps to add its weight of contrast to the brilliant sequence of Fragment VII. When this was done, the Man of Law was given his present tale of *Constance*.

The developments of the plan involving a change of attribution of the stories went hand in hand with Chaucer's writing of the links between the tales. These are no mere connections. They have been called the finest tale of all, for the characters who in the general *Prologue* are somewhat static for all their brilliance, talk among themselves on the road between stories – and when people begin to *talk* in Chaucer we hear the very tones of living voices. The coarser characters quarrel, Miller against Reeve, Friar against Summoner. One tells a story against the other, churls tell churls' tales. Who shall say here which came first – such stories as make a pair and give rise to characters, or characters who quarrel, giving rise to stories in which they attack each other? We may as well ask which came first, the chicken or the egg. Nevertheless, in at least one case, the character came first; this is the Wife of Bath, for since she was presumably first meant to tell *The Shipman's Tale*, her present tale may be thought of as particularly hers, arising out of her character. Even so, it is not nearly so much the product of her character as, say, one of Hamlet's soliloquies is a product of his. Her tale of Gawayn is a fairy-tale, a wonder, told in a mood of delicate fantasy (though the plot was not invented by Chaucer). Delicacy is not one of the Wife of Bath's characteristics. To understand and enjoy the story and its placing to the full, the tale's reflections on sovereignty in marriage should be compared with the similar reflections – how differently expressed – in the Wife's own lengthy *Prologue* to her tale, which is very much more a product of her character. There is a most delightful contrast between her own comic and lusty coarseness (itself a satire upon her whole argument) and the charm of her *Tale*. In the succession of *Tales* which follow hers (Fragments III, IV, V) the theme of marriage relationships is raised fairly frequently, though the sequence is hardly to be regarded as a debate on marriage, as some critics imply, though it may be convenient to retain the name of the Marriage Group, and we shall miss some of the significance of *The Wife of Bath's Tale* if we do not recognise its contribution to the theme of marriage. Thus only a small part of its significance lies in its expression of character.

From this brief survey, it is clear that the essential quality of *The Canterbury Tales* as a whole lies in the interplay of stories, rather than in the interaction of the characters who tell the stories. The method may be compared with that of a painter who plans the area of colour on his picture, some passages to support each other, some to contrast. Just as Chaucer seems to have planned *The Parliament*, balancing and contrasting Nature with the lascivious Venus, and the *Somnium Scipionis* with both, so he seems to have planned his *Tales*, though he got no further than Fragments. Or in other words, the sequence of stories is similar to the events of a plot, and the characters are motivated so as to make their actions (i.e. their stories) seem suitable. By so regarding the *Tales* we may appreciate their total design. On occasion the demands of the pattern of stories cause minor inconsistencies of character, as when that fashionable and self-confident huntsman, the Monk of the *Prologue*, tells his string of bookish and sententious Tragedies. Chaucer needed someone to relate them, and the Monk, though not a perfect candidate, was because of his profession the most suitable of the pilgrims. In many cases the story told is neither particularly suited nor unsuited to the teller. We also find that within a given tale the conception of the character who is supposed to be telling it is now strong, now weak. Chaucer often seems to speak in a tale of his own poetic person.

Such variation in the narrative point of view is a Gothic character-istic. It also reminds us that the realism of the *Tales* is superficial and not to be taken too seriously. We cannot know whether Chaucer was recording in any way an actual pilgrimage, nor need we expect him to display characters in action like a modern novelist. It is also doubtful whether we can draw any valid conclusions about the chronological developments of his scheme from variations in the presentation of a character at different parts of the work.

We do not only hear the pilgrims speak, we see them before us in their very habits as they lived, for Chaucer with the apparent simplicity of truly original genius paints their portraits in the general *Prologue* before he sets them on their way to Canterbury. For all its simplicity there seems to be nothing in European literature like it, before or since.

THE PROLOGUE

The Prologue opens with a passage about Spring of a superficially familiar medieval kind. Boccaccio has one in his Latin handbook of mythology, Creton in his French chronicle of Richard's deposition, and there are many others. So familiar a subject could surprise no audience. Nor was it always a prelude to a love-poem. The joy of spring was justification enough after a medieval winter. The triumph of the opening as literary art lies in its purposive structure and its style. This elaborate introduction takes less than twenty lines, and in it we have smelt the spring air, and have swooped in imagination down from the Zodiac to the Tabard. The focus has carried us from a general view of the season to fix sharply on the nine-and-twenty pilgrims gathered in a well-known inn near London. The vision is both spacious and precise. The passage is written in a modified 'high style' which is not personalised or dramatised at all. It would be quite pointless here to think of a 'Narrator' who is saying something different from 'the poet'. There is no irony, folly, dullness or anything but splendidly vigorous poetry which is active through description. The first two lines are simple and direct, so that no listener or reader can miss the point. The next three lines, with their almost scientifically elaborate mention of the nourishing of plants, are written in that poetic diction for which Chaucer was so venerated in the following two centuries; he calls water, *licour*, the west wind *Zephirus*. The third line combines the decorative mythological touch of the image of Zephirus in the first half, with the realistic 'sweet breath' in the second. The fanciful personification of the west wind provides a colourful and musical word and presses home the sensuous realism of 'sweet breath'. There is the same mixture of splendour and directness in the next two lines, and by this time the poet can well afford one of his favourite astronomical references to the date – it heightens the style, and cannot be misunderstood. He continues with a line of striking simplicity and musical beauty:

> And smalé fowelés maken melodyé.

The commonplace reference to the song of birds in spring becomes beautiful and arresting partly from the music of the line, and partly from its position in the poetic unit, which is the paragraph. In this rhetorical and superbly poetic beginning to his poem, Chaucer gives us the delights of both narrative and lyric.

THE PORTRAITS

The portraits of the *Prologue* have the same concentrated brilliance. Chaucer describes a man as if his eye were wandering over him, noticing a bright detail here and there, which he haphazardly records. There seems nothing more natural in the world, but this very impression of casualness, this economy, significance and variety of detail clearly tell of that supreme art which conceals art. There is no pattern of description. Sometimes the visible details of dress come first, and through them we see the character. The Knight's gipoun is still marked by the rust and oil from his armour, and his horses are good. Mere factual information, it seems; yet from these we learn that he has wasted no time after his safe return home to go on his pilgrimage. He is not concerned with a smart outward appearance, but he is not poor, nor neglectful of his essential equipment as can be seen from his horses. Sometimes Chaucer describes a person's character, and adds almost as an afterthought those details of dress which set him vividly before our eyes and reinforce what is already known of him. There is a different order of description for almost every pilgrim. The sketches are very brief, yet by including snatches of conversation, and by describing in many cases the past history, present opinions, usual activities, or dwelling place of a person,

Chaucer conveys a strong sense of individuality, and depth of portraiture. The necessary shortness of the description leads Chaucer to lay detail close by detail, often in a non-logical order. The impression of naivety which this compression sometimes gives may be compared with Chaucer's fondness for portraying himself in his own poetry as a simple man. The sugar-coating of naivety contrasts pleasantly with the sharpness of wit it pretends to conceal. Thus of the Cook Chaucer says:

> But greet harm was it, as it thoughte me   [*seemed to*
> That on his shyne a mormal hadde he.   [*shin*; *ulcer*
> For blankmanger, that made he with the beste.   [*chicken blanquette*

CT I, 385–7

Poetry, comedy, satire, characterisation are all created by this apparently innocent juxtaposition.

THE BREAKING DOWN OF FORMAL PATTERNS

The absence of a formal or regular pattern of description of the persons is the more effective because medieval literature in Latin and in the vernaculars has many verbal portraits which do follow a regular pattern. The formal portrait in words goes back to Classical Antiquity and was reinforced by the teaching of such medieval rhetoricians as Matthew of Vendome and Geoffrey of Vinsauf who wrote treatises on rhetoric in the early thirteenth century. They gave several patterns. The most famous is the one of the Lady. All medieval heroines, including Criseyde, conform to her type. The appearance and the sequence of description is always the same; golden hair, dark eyebrows, teeth like pearls, slender shoulders, small breasts, broad hips, etc. – the detail sometimes leaves nothing to the imagination. Chaucer knew and at first followed and benefited from the work of the rhetoricians, who were, after all, teaching the tricks of the trade of creative writing. The portrait of the Duchess Blanche in *The Book of the Duchess* follows the rhetorical scheme very closely. So does the briefer portrait of Criseyde, with one or two significant exceptions, such as her joined eyebrows, which were thought to be a sign of unreliability. Chaucer could have found a series of such portraits of the characters in a story at the beginning of the Anglo-French poem *Le Roman de Troie*, which he must have known, and which may have contributed to the idea of *The General Prologue*. When Chaucer actually came to compose his own portraits he deliberately avoided systematic rhetorical portraiture, and part of the pleasure of the vivid arbitrariness of the sequence of details derives from our underlying sense of the scheme which is broken. It is refreshing to see inconsequential 'reality', the apparently accidental event, break down preformulated rigid patterns, codes, ideals. There is at times something deeply iconoclastic in Chaucer, as in the Lollards. Break the images, the forms! Spontaneous life surges in. We feel the release of vital forces. This breaking of the mould helps to make him seem modern. But the forms must have existed first in order to build up pressure against them, and for the sense of freedom to arise from their destruction. Rhetorical discipline is the necessary prelude to free expression, if freedom is not merely chaos. There must also be purpose in breaking down the pattern, which reveals itself in a new creative building-up.

THE VOICES OF POETRY

It is not surprising that there are some sharp differences between critics about the real meaning of many of the portraits and the point of view from which they are described. For example, it has just been seen that the notion of Narrator is not helpful in our response to the opening lines. But how about our response to the mention of the Cook's ulcer, juxtaposed with his delicious chicken or white-meat stew? There can be no question but that Chaucer meant the juxtaposition of the ulcer and the food to be comically disgusting. The tone of simple-minded pity for the ulcer and simple-minded admiration for the 'blankmanger' is offset by the implications of their placing. There are thus two levels of meaning simultaneously presented, one naive, one jesting. It is possible to divide these 'two voices', which speak the same words with different implications, and attribute the naive voice to a naive Narrator and the jesting voice to the 'real' poet. One can go further. Chaucer tells us early in *The Prologue* that he himself was one of the Pilgrims, and it is he who speaks to each of them and describes them. Later in the work he attributes to himself the absurd *Tale of Sir Thopas*. In other words he reverts to the device of his earlier love-visions and introduces himself into his own poem, presenting himself again as plump, modest, naive, and bullied or patronised by talkative assertive men. There may be some justification for seeing the pilgrim-Chaucer as Narrator, but not for seeing, as some critics seem to, yet another Narrator, also stupid, behind the pilgrim-Chaucer. But however many Narrators we have, one behind the other, we are bound to come to the 'real' poet at last, unless we 'deconstruct' Chaucer completely: but if we do that we come only to our own minds, and lose the poet altogether. There has to be a base-line, so to speak, if there is any meaning at all. If there is no stable meaning; if anyone can impose any meaning he likes upon the words, independent of history and society, then there is no point in discussing the words at all. They have no identity.

To divide the separate 'voices', the 'naive' and 'real' of the poetry, may sometimes be useful for analysis, but reconstruction must follow, because the poetic effect depends on the maintenance of both voices simultaneously, as in musical harmony, or as in metaphor. In a metaphor, when the comparison of two things is expressed simultaneously in the same word, the essential pleasure comes from the maintenance of both aspects of meaning together. If 'the ship flies over the ocean', we need to keep together the notion both of flying and of ordinary sailing. If they are separated, one is ridiculous and the other dull: their relationship gives them life. So in *The Prologue* and much other poetry by Chaucer, the totality of voices, all the layers of meaning together, is what gives the tang. Chaucer's poetry is in some ways like medieval polyphony – music in which a number of different voices are singing the same words to different melodic lines. Except that Chaucer's poetic line, until the mind is alerted, may seem deceptively simple, and the careless reader may notice only one of the voices.

POETRY OF ASSOCIATION: METONYMY

Chaucer's poetry is not especially rich in metaphor, though there is more metaphor present than is often realised. A more characteristic effect is one that has only recently been discovered as important for poetry in general, let alone Chaucer. It has already been mentioned briefly in this book. The effect is that of juxtaposition, or association, known technically as metonymy (from the Latin rhetorical figure of that name). Metonymy, or association, whether of ideas or things, is potent in medieval poetry, but relies heavily on the reader's preceding knowledge for its full effectiveness. Even in *The General Prologue* foreknowledge is more important than might be expected. Chaucer minimises the problem because he concentrates on description, but he necessarily relies on our understanding of the associations of the objects he describes in order to get the tone. Luckily many of these associations are based on common human nature, such as disgust at a running ulcer. But one has to learn what *blankmanger* is. That is not so difficult, however, since appetite for food is common. Less easy to grasp are the associations of such matters as the dirty marks on the Knight's 'gypoun' or tunic, left by the armour he normally wore on top of it. The traditional interpretation, already noted above, is that the Knight, as Chaucer tells us, had come so lately from his travels, was so anxious to go on pilgrimage, that he had not had time to get another cleaner garment. Poverty is always honourable in Chaucer, and though the Knight is not poor, he disdains mere smart appearances. But some critics have argued that his dirty appearance shows that he is a scruffy mercenary thug, though they are certainly mistaken.

This is connected with wider questions of associations. What are the associations of the victory of Alexandria, where the Knight had fought? It was generally at the time regarded as a tremendous success, which had regrettably not been followed up. The proof of this lies in Machaut's poem *La prise d'Alexandrie* which Chaucer probably knew. But it was certainly an unprovoked attack on an unprepared city. Modern attitudes to war rightly condemn such attacks. From a modern point of view the capture of Alexandria can be regarded as an outrageous unprovoked massacre of innocent civilians and disgraceful looting of a rich and peaceful city. If that were the normal view of the fourteenth century the Knight would be a wicked man, and that case has been argued vigorously. But the associations of war, as of love, were very different in the fourteenth century. It is anachronistic to impute our standards to those of earlier periods. We can, if we wish, 'deconstruct' Chaucer's poetry so as to remake it in our own image, but this is a pointless intellectual exercise. Why bother with Chaucer at all? Why not write our own modern liberal humanist pacifist poetry? Chaucer wrote none. He was not a modern liberal humanist pacifist.

THE FRAMEWORK OF THE ESTATES

The true pattern of association for the Knight, as for a number of other characters described in *The General Prologue*, is the long tradition of descriptions in what is called 'Estates literature' as Dr Jill Mann has shown. Some of these 'estates', i.e. social classes, were regularly idealised; for example peasants and certain clergy (not all, for friars were equally regularly satirised). Chaucer creates a social frame of the ideal medieval estates as the three basic orders of society, knighthood, clergy, ploughmen: ploughmen to work with their hands and gain food for all; clergy to foster and protect the souls of all; knighthood to maintain justice and protect the lives and property of all. Chaucer does not satirise those pilgrims who represent this ideal of society. Thus, although details of the Knight's career can be paralleled in the lives of contemporaries, the total impression of his character is somewhat different from our impression of many fourteenth-century representatives of his Order. That does not make him any the less pleasant and inspiring to read about, loving as he does, 'Trouthe and honour, fredom (i.e. generosity of spirit) and curtesie'; he has fought for our faith against the pagan, a lion in the field, a lamb in hall. With him goes the Squire, youthful, romantic, courtly, in whom love upgroweth with his age, but who, when the time of young love is passed, we may suppose will take on the sterner duties of knighthood. Clergy is represented partly by the Clerk, who speaks for the life of learning. These three ideal portraits are also entirely convincing, for Chaucer was writing well within the range of his own experience and personal ideals. The other representative of clergy is the Parson, in whom is seen the humility and holiness, the active well-doing, praying and preaching, enjoined upon priests. The Ploughman, brother to the Parson, represents the third order of the ideal medieval society. The Parson, and especially the Ploughman, are the most idealised of all the pilgrims, and the least individually realised. They are theories rather than persons. But the concrete details of the descriptions, and the moral beauty of the ideals when understood in their proper contexts, are extremely attractive and effectively presented. Once again we note that Chaucer's natural interests and ideals are secular, not cloistered, otherworldly nor mystical.

Judged against the accepted ideals of estates literature most other classes have serious shortcomings. The Lawyer appears to twist the law to allow him to acquire land improperly. The Merchant is usurious (a sin according to the Church) and indulges in shady exchange practices, the Physician will only cure people for money and neglects to read the Bible. The Prioress is gently satirised for her genteel over-refinement of manners and feelings. Chaucer appears to be the first English writer to notice compassion for animals, that notable late-twentieth-century concern which in general begins in the late eighteenth century. The Prioress is tender towards her little dogs. Chaucer mocks her for it.

The portrait of the Monk similarly portrays usual monkish vices. He does not stay in his cloister, but is essentially a rich, fat, sport-loving, travelling businessman. He does not care to labour with his hands, as St Augustine says he should. The poet adds

And I seyde his opinion was good.

CT I, 183

How do we intepret this? Is it a stupid Narrator, or naive pilgrim – Chaucer saying the opposite of what the 'real' poet means? Is it ironical, or to be taken literally?

Before answering we may note that though Chaucer lists traditional vices he is much less condemnatory in tone than is traditional 'estates literature'. Dr Mann shows how far these characters are presented in terms of the work they do, and how far Chaucer advances towards a modern world of individual consciousness of 'relativised values' which are, of course, no values at all. This is another aspect of the freedom inherent in the poem. The tendency towards 'relativised values' is there in the portrait of the Monk, though value, if unorthodox value, is apparently attributed to him. But relativism is not dominant. It is not apparent in other portraits, where the values shown are to be admired, as in the idealised characters, or in those where the tone is a good deal sharper, and hostile value-judgements are implied against such characters as the Friar and Summoner. The Pardoner is treated particularly scornfully, not only because of his deceitfulness but especially for his absence of virility (thereby illustrating another traditional masculine attitude, of contempt for effeminate men). If the portrait of the Knight is ironical we would be equally justified, by modern standards, in taking the portraits of Summoner and Pardoner also as ironical, that is, as really in their praise. If the Knight is really a thug, the Pardoner is really a distributor of alms, which is absurd.

The point is that Chaucer, the 'real' poet, constantly takes up different points of view in *The General Prologue* as in *Troilus*, and not all of them may be consistent with each other, and not all of them may be equally firmly held. Some remarks are indeed ironical, some not. In the case of the Monk there seems no reason to think that the poet's praise is ironical. He is deliberately, provocatively, pushing his secular views forward and approving of a profitable busy active life. There were plenty, including the Lollards to whom Chaucer was sympathetic, who disapproved of traditional monkish virtues, or who simply disliked them. So does Chaucer. He is daring rather than simple-minded. Even so, he leaves a trace of ambiguity in the portrait of the Monk, as of others.

REAL PEOPLE

The portraits are continuously rich and stimulating, with far more implicit in them than at first appears, by way of attitude to work, to money, to social classes, etc. They must be left for the reader's pleasure to follow in detail. One further aspect must be mentioned. Some of the portraits were certainly based on people in real life, thus adding another layer of implication, a further dimension of interest, and at least for the earliest readers, of amusement. One quite well-documented figure is the Host of the Tabard Inn in Southwark (which certainly existed) where the pilgrims foregathered. Harry Bailly must have been known to many in the court, as an innkeeper of a famous inn within a city of only 45,000 inhabitants. He was twice Member of Parliament, and often acted as tax-collector, coroner, etc., as well as being an innkeeper on the much-frequented London-Canterbury-Dover road. Whether he was as Chaucer describes him we shall probably never know. The Merchant may possibly be meant to suggest a well-known merchant and money-lender named Gilbert Maghfeld, from whom Chaucer and several other courtiers are known to have borrowed money, and who went bankrupt. The Man of Law is probably meant to call to mind the distinguished Serjeant-at-law Thomas Pynchbeck, on the opposite side politically to Chaucer. He had offended Chaucer's friend Sir William Beauchamp, and had once signed a writ to arrest Chaucer for a small debt. Other less certain identifications of other persons have been proposed, and even in uncertainty they enliven our sense of the social context and vigour of *The General Prologue*.

VARIETY OF SUBJECT: ABSENCE OF DIDACTICISM

The quality of those real people whom we can fairly certainly identify, and who are all of inferior status, with some reason for Chaucer to tease them, and the idealising framework of the three estates against which all other characters are measured, allow a lightly comic tone to prevail. On the other hand, the presentation of people in terms of their functions, whose excellence is expressed with Chaucer's usual hyperbolic zest – the very perfect knight, the best beggar in his house, never such another pardoner, etc. – gives a warmth of appreciation which makes it difficult to speak of satire, even comic satire. He avoids the social extremes of nobility and of peasant poverty, so that more troubling notes are avoided. We see men and women of the world through Chaucer's eyes and he observes them, as Blake said in 1809 'as a master, as a father, and superior, who looks down on their little follies from the Emperor to the Miller; sometimes with severity, oftener with joke and sport'. Though tragic emotions are not evoked, and there is no Romantic expressiveness, no twentieth-century anxiety, any more than there is facile optimism of sentimental indulgence, this is great poetry of rich human interest, deeply humane, amazingly subtle, extraordinarily varied, perhaps a Divine Comedy, certainly a human one.

Chapter 13

THE CANTERBURY TALES

The Host's good wine and cheerful enthusiasm easily persuade the pilgrims, some thirty in number, to give their oath to tell two stories each on the way to Canterbury, and two on the way back. The tales that shall 'shorten their way' must be either instructive or amusing; either of 'sentence' or 'solas'. Stories of downright moral instruction in particular seem to have been relished by Chaucer and his audience as much as amusing anecdotes. What is missing is the idea of later Neoclassical literature, which continues through Romanticism even to the present day, that literature instructs *through* delight. Chaucer does not confuse comedy or art with moral uplift. 'Sentence' differs from 'solas', though 'sentence' is appreciated. His dramatic audience is the group of pilgrims; his real audience was composed of the members of the court, of important city merchants, of such clerics as the 'courtier bishops', and of such fellow writers as Hoccleve, a clerk in the Chancery offices, the poet and lawyer Ralph Strode, the poet and small landowner Gower.

To begin *The Tales* Chaucer fires off his heaviest broadside, *The Knight's Tale*. Written some years before, it was now used with probably no change to begin the series. It has already been discussed (Chapter 9) and no more need be done here than to agree with young and old among the pilgrims, and especially with the 'gentils', that it is a noble story. It seems likely, however, that the Miller has been occupying his time otherwise than by listening, for he is by now very, very drunk. Not even the Host, by command or entreaty, can control him, and he insists on telling his 'churl's tale'. Chaucer apologises, but pleads the duty of *exact* reporting; he has not invented the tale. If you do not wish to hear it, you may turn the page; there are plenty of 'storial' things, concerning nobility, morality, and also holiness. So Chaucer neatly puts the onus for any shock to the feelings upon reader rather than writer. He obviously had readers more than hearers in mind in this last great work.

THE MILLER'S TALE

The contrast between *The Miller's Tale* and *The Knight's Tale* is very refreshing, and very typical of Chaucer. Though not a parody of *The Knight's Tale*, it also tells of two young men in love with the same girl. Since this is undoubtedly the greatest comic poem in English it will be worth discussing it in detail.

The plot of *The Miller's Tale* is as fantastic as that of any romance. It is based on a common folktale: variants of the story are found in several languages. A young Oxford student lodging with an old man tricks his simple-minded landlord, who has a young and beautiful wife, into believing that Noah's flood is coming again. So all three must spend the night in wooden tubs slung in the roof, in order safely to float out on the waters when need arises. The elderly husband falls asleep and the two young persons skip downstairs and into bed together. But along comes another lover of the wife, a fastidious, squeamish, village dandy. He serenades the wife and asks her for a kiss. The bedroom is on the groundfloor, and she puts out her bottom which the unfortunate man kisses. It is a moment of awful comedy. He goes away in fury and returns with a red-hot piece of iron, a ploughshare. Again he serenades the wife. Her student-lover proposes to repeat the same exquisite joke, and puts out *his* bottom, and receives a jab from the burning-hot ploughshare; he withdraws with a scream of agony. To cool himself he shrieks for 'water!' The cry awakes the husband, who thinks the Flood has come and cuts the rope that holds his tub, and crashes to the floor, where he knocks himself out and breaks his arm. The wife and lover by their cries rouse their neighbours, and since many of these are students all take sides with the lover and tell the husband that he is mad, and laugh at him. Thus he suffers, and the poem wastes no sympathy on him, concluding 'and thus his wife was seduced (though a blunter word is used), her lover scalded in the rear, and the dandy has kissed the lady's lower eye'.

I have told the story without names to emphasise how much the persons are rôles or types: jealous old husband, lecherous student, lecherous village dandy, lecherous young wife. The wife is the centre of their attention, but the story is not about her: it is not even primarily about the men who circle round her as a sexual object: the story is, at its deepest, or, as we may well say, at its lowest level, the articulation of a deliberately fantastic insult, common to all the languages of Europe, I should guess, in the Middle Ages; common even today, perhaps; the insult is the regrettable expression, 'Kiss my arse'. The insult is only funny in so far as coarse invective is funny, but there seems no doubt, to judge from the received history of comedy (as in the *Oxford Classical Dictionary*), that coarse invective

177

is indeed the oldest form of humour. In the case of *The Miller's Tale*, however, the articulation of the insult into a fantastic story turns it into a classically comic structure; there is a reversal from top to bottom, if one may put it that way, yet in a context which prevents any tragic implications: the face-to-face human personal relationship of the kiss is grotesquely transformed, parodied, and insulted; the spiritual or at any rate the emotional, imaginative, delicate, higher, relationship of love is conquered by the grossly and disgustingly lower physical connection. Furthermore, the repetition of the first kiss by the burning second one produces further parody – we have all heard of burning kisses. And, of course, the further connection of the cry of 'water' brings down, lowers, the husband, in every sense. The very structure of the narrative is poetic. The story is a general lowering of the pretensions of the men; the wife never had any. In a way, it is a comic assertion of natural physical reality, though not of justice – an assertion of the reality of a young wife's natural lustfulness which is juxtaposed against the jealousy of a silly old man who would unrealistically restrain his wife, and against two deceitful and conceited young men, who want to exploit the wife's nature. We may well remember Aristotle's remark that comedy portrays people as worse than they usually are. Let us hope it is true. In origin the story is anti-feminist. All the men suffer: the woman unjustly escapes scot-free. The implication is that women trick men and make them suffer. But comedy is always ambivalent. And it always takes two to play the wife's game. So the story is not without sympathy for the wife. Chaucer is very sympathetic to women, and he makes the wife very charming and attractive, though he mocks her too.

Chaucer's narrative is more complex than that of any other version. It is filled in, as ordinary popular literature is not, with descriptive detail of the highest artistry, so that we see the very dimensions of the physical setting. The characters are brought to life to enable us to enjoy the richness of the joke without going so far as to feel sorry for any of them. None of the analogues of this common folktale in any way rivals Chaucer's telling of the tale. There is, for example, a kind of poetry of absurdity in the way the carpenter is taken in by the tale of the tub. Some of the analogues miss this out completely; others attempt the impossible task of making the trick itself seem reasonable; Chaucer creates his carpenter as the very kind of man to believe such nonsense. The physical realism, the 'visibility' of characters and setting was never more brilliantly conveyed.

Comic poets particularly need to ground their fictions on territory familiar to the audience. This is an elementary principle, and thus the Flemish analogue of *The Miller's Tale* is set in Antwerp, the Italian in Naples, the *The Miller's Tale* itself in Osney near Oxford, a place well known to many of Chaucer's audience. The very house can almost be measured – the height of the window from the ground (an important point), the hole in the door of the student Nicholas's room big enough for a cat to pass though. We are conscious of the whole life of the village, as when we see the dandy-ish Absolon, who is also village barber and parish clerk, about his business and pleasure, or as when the old carpenter mentions with just the right touch of consternation that a man has just been carried dead to church whom 'last Monday' he saw at his work.

The characters are not pale shades, or types, as they are in the analogues. They are named. Alison is not simply the type of lustful and unfaithful young wife. Chaucer avoids the mistakes of the analogues. One analogue makes her a prostitute. This loses all the comic capital of the deceived husband and the need for secrecy. In another, the wife intends to receive three lovers in succession, which degrades the story. Chaucer's Alison has some individuality.

She is described with the same care as that with which he described the Duchess Blanche, though with greater art, and to vastly different effect. Thus she has the conventional and fashionable beauty of a white forehead, but this is how Chaucer praises it:

> His forheed shoon as bright as any day,
> So was it wasshen whan she leet hir werk.   [*finished*

CT I, 3310–11

She wears an apron white as morning milk, plucks her eyebrows, and has a lecherous eye; she sings like a swallow.

> She was a prymerole, a piggesnye,   [*primrose*; *a sweet little thing*
> For any lord to leggen in his bedde,   [*lay*
> Or yet for any good yeman to wedde.

CT I, 3268–70

This must qualify as one of the most snobbish remarks in English poetry. There never was 'so gay a popelote or swich a wenche' (both of these nouns are 'low' words). She has a well-washed, luscious, vulgar (and genuine) allure. Chaucer does full justice to the allure as he does to the vulgarity. She is a comic figure to the courtly audience, and to us because our eyes by Chaucer's art are adjusted to his vision of her. The formal description of Alison is a kind of parody of the rhetorical portrait of the beautiful courtly heroine (above, p. 31) but here not the courtly element but the vulgar element is chiefly mocked, even if the very use of the courtly ideal for mockery shows some ambiguity of feeling about the ideal itself. Alison is amusing in action by descriptions such as that of her hoity-toity air (no more) when Nicholas begins his rough and direct wooing and by her speedy capitulation; by the way she gently struggles when firmly in his grasp, and promises only to cry out in the future.

The portrait of Absolon is painted with similar amused care and light satire. The village clerk and barber, he is a dandy, according to his lights, with a high-pitched voice and affected accent, and is, 'somewhat squeamish'. He is an amateur actor, and fancies himself with the women. His hair is long and curly. He wears the current fancy gear; in the fourteenth century it was the pattern of St Paul's windows cut on his shoes.

The character of the old husband is as remarkable for what is left out as for what is put in. Great care is taken to make him a clear, but decidedly background character. We are briefly told of his age and jealousy. We see his blend of respect and contempt for Nicholas's learning, his simple conceit of the practical man. We are made aware of his unthinking piety and clumsy good intentions. This is sufficient to make him real enough for the stratagem to have point, but not enough to make us think in terms of real life about the actual pathos, injustice and bitterness of his situation. All art depends on limitation of view and in this case the limitation is that of ordinary derisive popular humour without too much sympathy, reinforced by courtly snobbery about the antics of the provincial lower classes.

There is even more to *The Miller's Tale*. In it Chaucer makes fun of the miracle-plays, not only through Absolon, who used to play Herod 'upon a scaffold high', but also by larger allusions, for it was the Carpenters' Guild which usually put on, for obvious reasons, the play of the Flood. The language of the poem mocks the old-fashioned provincial English love-lyrics, with their use of what had become low-class hackneyed words like *gent* and *hende*. Polished rhetoric, neatly inverted, is used, as already noted, to mock a vulgar village-wench. It is altogether a most courtly poem, and Chaucer has the nerve to call it 'a churl's tale'! It does indeed share general popular feelings, but these are common to high and low. In the fourteenth century 'courtiers' were just as much part of 'the folk' as were peasants.

THE REEVE'S TALE

The tale takes its place in the larger comedy of the pilgrimage in that it grieves the Reeve who, being a carpenter himself, takes to heart the misfortune of the carpenter of Osney. He falls into a self-pitying monologue about old age, spoken in a Northern accent fitting his Norfolk background (the Reeve being also probably an identifiable and unpopular character among Chaucer's friends). This poem and *The Miller's Tale* form as it were a diptych and *The Reeve's Tale* also deserves a somewhat full account to reveal the new reaches of Chaucer's art, and its extreme enjoyability.

This time the setting is the University of Cambridge, also well-known to Chaucer and his friends, though intellectually less influential than Oxford. And again the core of the narrative is a folktale, enriched by high art. The tale is set in the mill of the village of Trumpington. The village remains; the probable site of the mill is known; the fen is drained now but the mists still rise at evening from the damp meadows by the slowly flowing river.

The poem begins by describing Simkin the Miller in a realistic vivid portrait. He is proud, peacock-like, extraordinarily skilful, a bully and totally bald. The baldness is important. He is also a thief, as all millers were traditionally thought to be.

After this comes a portrait of his handsome wife, described as come 'of noble kin' because her father was the local parson. This is itself a joke, because the parson, being a cleric, ought to be celibate and therefore his daughter was illegitimate. She, like Simkin, is a snob in her degree and as proud and pert as a magpie. It is a fine sight to see them walking about on a holiday, brightly dressed. Simkin, the miller, is such a bully that nobody dares call his wife anything but 'dame' lest Simkin should beat him up. Forty-odd lines of description give us a wonderful character study of this well-to-do, efficient, proud pair whose pride is not entirely well-founded. The courtly audience might well laugh at the social pretensions of village worthies. They have a daughter twenty years old, of a lusty attractiveness, and perhaps somewhat improbably they also have a baby six months old. The miller reckons to marry his daughter well, since he is prosperous and she is of such distinguished lineage.

One of the miller's best customers is a Cambridge college, two miles away, the King's Hall. The King's Hall is referred to with remarkably convincing detail. (It happens no longer to exist because it was merged with a couple of other halls into Trinity College in the sixteenth century.) As the story tells us, the chief officer of King's Hall responsible for looking after the grinding of the College's wheat is ill, so two of the members of the College, both young men, called Alan and John, decide to take the grain to the miller and to make sure that the thefts which he has been committing shall not continue. They ride to Trumpington on a single horse with their grain and meet the miller and express the intention of supervising the grinding so as not to be cheated. The conversation between the two clerks and the miller is entertaining in itself. They have been there before, and know the miller slightly, though (a fine touch) they get his name slightly wrong. The students are characterised not only by the cheerful bumptiousness of young men, but also by the fact that they speak in a northern dialect, which always seems comic in the south. The miller puts up with their supervision and their condescension but he slips away and lets their horse loose, so out the two young men have to go to chase it, and only return in the evening, weary and wet. They know very well that their corn has been stolen. Moreover, it is so late that they are caught by the curfew and cannot return to

College because they are locked out. They have to ask the miller to put them up and he, not without some jeering, agrees to do so when they pay for the food and drink, although he has only one room. His daughter is sent into the village for ale and bread, a goose is roasted, they have a splendid supper and the miller drinks so much that, as Chaucer says, he has varnished his bald head. It shines bright with sweat, and he is stupified, while his wife, on the other hand, has so wet her jolly whistle that she is extremely merry. All three of the family, miller, wife and daughter go to their various beds, fall fast asleep and snore resoundingly, having allocated another bed in the same room to the two students.

The cradle of the baby is at the foot of the bed of the miller and his wife. The noise of their snoring keeps Alan and John awake. They talk and Alan (who probably studies law) says that law allows them some compensation for the theft and humiliation which they have endured that day. He creeps in by the daughter and shortly to say it, they were soon at one.

John, as in all the other versions, lies gloomily awake on his own, reflecting on what a fool he will seem when the story is told later. Then he has a marvellous idea. He gets up and moves the cradle to the foot of his own bed. Soon after this the wife arises to answer the call of nature, payment for having drunk so much, and coming in again, misses her cradle at the foot of her bed – 'Alas', says she to herself, 'I'd almost got into terrible difficulty, I nearly went into the clerk's bed and then I'd have had a terrible time'. So she gets into the other bed where she does indeed get an unexpectedly warm welcome.

When Alan returns from the daughter's bed, he goes first to his own bed, sees the cradle, thinks he is mistaken, gets into bed with the miller, wakes him up, thinking he is John, and tells him how he has fared. The miller, with a tremendous roar bellows out, 'Yea you false scoundrel, have you so? Ah you false traitor, you false clerk. You shall be dead by the dignity of God. Who dare be so bold as to disparage my daughter who is come of such lineage?' He catches Alan by the throat and they fight and roll on the floor like two pigs in a bag until they fall on and wake up John and the miller's wife. She cries to her supposed husband for help. John immediately understands what has happened and gropes around the walls to find a staff to help his friend. The wife does the same and knows the interior much better than John. This is the passage which describes the next events.

> This John stirte up as faste as ever he myghte
> And graspeth by the walles to and fro
> To fynde a staf; and she stirte up also,
> And knew the estres bet than dide this John,   [interior
> And by the wal a staf she foond anon,

And saugh a litel shymeryng of a light
For at an hole in shoon the moone bright
And by that light she saugh hem bothe two
But sikerly she nyste who was who   [*did not know*
But as she saugh a whit thyng in hir ye.
And whan she gan this white thyng espye
She wende the clerk hadde wered a volupeer   [*thought; night-cap*
And with the staf she drow ay neer and neer,   [*nearer and nearer*
And wende han hit his Aleyn at the fulle   [*thought to have*
And smoot the millere on the pyled skull   [*bald*
That doun he gooth and cride 'Harrow! I dye.'   [*alas!*

CT I, 4292–307

The rapid pace of the narration here keeps just ahead of our delighted anticipations. The miller has been punished once by Alan sleeping with his daughter, twice by John sleeping with his wife, and now, three times, with gloriously farcical appropriateness, since he is such a bully, by being hit on the head by his own wife. To have been hurt once is a shame, twice could be tragic, but three times is proneness to accident. It is absurd and one might say, poetic. The students beat him up a bit more, then dress and go away. To crown all, the daughter gives them a cake of baked flour which is the proceeds of the theft of wheat which the miller has committed.

The passage quoted is an extraordinarily concrete and syntactically simple piece of story-telling. Of fifteen lines no less than nine begin with *And* and two more with the similar word *But*. Only one and a half lines have grammatically subordinate clauses of purpose and explanation. There is a continuous series of concrete nouns which gives a vivid impression of simple solid appearances – a staff crashing down on a bald white skull. There is a huge predominance of one-syllable words and a very large vocabulary. Of the 75 separate words used 22 are nouns including the names John and Alan, 21 are verbs, and the remainder are other parts of speech, so that there is a high proportion of other words of action to nouns. There are only five adjectives and these are simple and structural. There are, however, 11 or 12 adverbs or adverbial phrases which outline and animate the action. For example, *up, fast, to and fro, near and near*. Although the vocabulary is concrete, full, simple, some key-words are repeated. The vigorous word *stirte* is repeated twice in the first three lines and the word *staff* is also repeated. *Light* is twice mentioned. It is great poetry but not at all our usual idea of poetic language. It is full and sinewy, with many links and associations with the rest of the action. It gives us the poetic culmination of the cross-patterned dualism on which the adventures of the night are based. Great artistry creates powerful effects in this poem, which is an extraordinarily full verbal realisation of a very complex pattern of place, people and events, much more logically connected than in the other versions of this story. The poem creates a much more vivid sense of the world than we can get from the other versions. For example, only Boccaccio in his version of the tale, and Chaucer, provide names for most of their characters; but only Chaucer actually gives us a character sketch of the significant character, the miller. Moreover, he makes him a character who causes us to feel that even if he does not quite deserve all the punishment he gets, at least he is an unsympathetic person, a bully, who only gets what he has meted out to others elsewhere. Measure for measure is suitable for a miller. We also notice that Chaucer establishes a motif of pride coming before a fall, which is absent from the other versions. There is derision for social pretensions. In Chaucer's story the action is not premeditated by the two students and it has a freshness and spontaneity and therefore an innocence, which is lacking in Boccaccio. Chaucer's version alone has the wife stun her husband by hitting him on the bald head with the staff, caused by thinking that his white bald head is the nightcap of one of the students. There is a comic irony of event in Chaucer's version whereby the wife, who is intending to help her husband, in fact strikes the culminating blow. Chaucer has a tremendous sense of the irony of circumstance. What is brought out by Chaucer's treatment of a traditional fantastic plot like this is the way in which he links the events and characters together. He is deeply interested in material cause and effect and in motivation and this gives him a remarkable modernity of outlook. In some ways Chaucer is even in advance of Boccaccio. He is much more realistic, and more interested in character. He is more atmospheric and more poetic in his treatment of a narrative.

THE COOK'S TALE

The pilgrim Miller's reaction to this tale is not told. It is the Cook who chimes in next, almost beside himself with joy at *The Reeve's Tale* and enthusiastically determined to cap it with one of his own. This begins with a description of the wild habits of a London apprentice called Perkyn Revelour which aptly illustrates how the interests of Court and City mingled in Chaucer's audience. We seem to be starting that comedy of City life which Chaucer could have written so well. But alas, he never wrote it, for *The Cook's Tale*, hardly begun, finishes abruptly, though strikingly. Perhaps three such tales in a row would be too much of a good thing. Chaucer never made up his mind as to what should follow *The Reeve's Tale* and the whole Fragment ends here.

THE MAN OF LAW'S TALE

The contents of the next Fragment are in some doubt. It certainly begins with *The Man of Law's Introduction and Tale*. Chaucer seems not to have finally decided which tale should follow, as appears from the variants in the Epilogue to *The Man of Law's Tale*, and the omission of the Epilogue itself from many good manuscripts. The section begins with the curious Introduction to *The Man of Law's Tale*. There are several puzzles here. Why does Chaucer give a list of the contents of *The Legend of Good Women* through the mouth of the Man of Law – especially as it is a list different from the tales he had actually written? Then the Man of Law condemns two stories about incest. Chaucer's dislike of tales about such 'unnatural abominations' was probably genuine, and a similar fastidiousness appears elsewhere in the *Tales*, but is this passage merely a hit against his friend Gower, who had recently written these very stories? The Man of Law promises to speak in prose, though his tale is actually in verse, and *The Tale of Melibeus* was perhaps first assigned to him, but was later transferred to Chaucer. The Invocation which is the Lawyer's Prologue has nothing to do with his story of Constance, to which it makes hardly more than a grammatical bridge. The whole Introduction cries aloud the lack of revision.

Not so *The Tale*. It is written with care and elaboration. The 'matter' is a pious tale of folklore origin. Chaucer translates the story straightforwardly into verse from the Anglo-Norman Chronicle by Trivet, enriching the source here with borrowings from Pope Innocent III's *De Contemptu Mundi*, with touches perhaps from Gower's version of Trivet's work, and above all with his own understanding of how such things could come to be, with vivid evocations of speech and scene, with his own pity for suffering. These rhetorical embellishments arise naturally enough from contemplation of the 'moving accidents' of the story. In this tale, in contrast with *Troilus*, there are only two places where Chaucer is inclined seriously to suspect that his source may be mistaken, both marked by the doubting phrase 'Som men wolde seyn' (II (B), 1009 and 1086), where Trivet is in fact quite unequivocal. Both these examples refer to minor details which seem to Chaucer not to be in accord with what would have been expected from the characters concerned.

This caution is the more striking in that the tale as a whole is of the kind of impossibility that pious legend delighted in. It tells of Constance, daughter of the Christian Emperor of Rome, who is twice married to a pagan king, twice converts her husband, is twice betrayed by an irreconcilably pagan mother-in-law, and twice committed to the sea in a boat without oars or sails. In each case she is afloat for several years. Her first husband is killed by his mother but she is eventually restored to the second. Such a plot does not aim to reproduce a complexity of relationships. Its purpose is quite different. Repetition is a favourite device of traditional literature and is powerful in emphasising with variation the major point. Chaucer handled it with all his mature skill. He accepts the miracles – he is not misled by his capacity for realising detail into giving, as for instance Trivet does, a list of stores for a three-year voyage. He sees it as a Miracle of the Blessed Virgin, who supported Constance in her trials. He comments now and again on the vicious men and women who so afflict the pure and gentle Constance, taking the material for these comments from the *De Contemptu Mundi* which he had recently translated. With his remarkable historical sense he takes the story seriously. He sets the action very vividly in its time and place. The diplomatic overtures for a state marriage (which he must have known so well); the geography of the seas around England; the state of languages in England in about the fourth century; the usage of courts; the felicities of home – all this and much more is suggested or described.

Even more notable, as we would expect, are the very great beauty and sympathy of the accounts of Constance. They have no artificiality and there is perhaps nothing more exquisite in all his work than the passage, entirely his own, where Constance for the second time is to be abandoned to the sea, on this occasion with her baby (ll. 834–40). We see the very movement of her hand as she draws the kerchief off her own head to put it on the child; another phrase tells of the large crowd following her, sympathetic, but silent and helpless. Her prayer is the most moving of all, where she asks pity for her child from that mother who saw her own child torn on the Cross, with whose woe the woe of no man can stand comparison. Yet in the end the world of Constance, for all its miracles, is recognisably part of the same world as that of *Troilus and Criseyde*. The same astronomical and astrological forces govern it under Providence. Constance is steadfast, as her name suggests, in her love of God, and neither pagan intellectual error nor pagan mythology intervenes between her and God; nor are virtuoso embellishments or distractions employed in the narration of what is practically a saint's life, though the poet comments plentifully as Expositor.

The story is exemplary, not allegorical, and the example of constancy is explicit. The repetitiousness of event in the story, though it does not contribute to such matters as characterisation, is necessary for making the point about endurance under repeated sorrows. We may also legitimately draw conclusions from the more general narrative structure which lies beneath, so to speak, the verbal surface or realisation. The propositions inherent in the structure of *The Man of Law's Tale* imply that mothers-in-law are difficult for daughters-in-law; and that strong opinions, especially strong religious beliefs, are divisive in families. The story implies the essential solitariness of religious belief, that ultimate internal value, which must justify itself when deserted by society, by friends, even apparently (as in the Crucifixion), by God himself. Constance is frequently cut off from society because she is a Christian, and we are invited to applaud this painful individualising lonely integrity, as in several other works of Chaucer. Constance is the precise opposite of Criseyde. Criseyde is always thinking of her own honour. She is mainly governed by what other people (not Troilus, particularly) will think about her. In consequence the essence of Criseyde's character is that she cannot say 'no'; she is *slydynge of corage*, 'unstable'. To be able to say 'no' is often the measure of integrity. The irony for Criseyde is that although she always does what society or its present representative wants – Pandarus, Troilus, the Trojan Parliament, Diomede – she is even more completely sacrificed by society than Constance, who never yields. Criseyde wants to be loved by everyone and ends up loved by no one; Constance is difficult, but the best people love her. *The Man of Law's Tale* thus offers yet another variant of the favourite Gothic propositions that love means suffering and paradoxically often causes solitude, as it attracts jealousy. Truly life in the world is hard and full of tensions. Yet the *Tale* also argues that to the constant mind the physical structures of the universe are more sympathetic, more open to God's guidance, than people are. Constance is safer on the sea than often she is among men.

It is fitting that such an austere yet in the end encouraging tale should focus on a single character, and the single perfect flower of her loving fortitude. There are dozens of realistic and historical touches, such as the comment on Constance's Late Latin language ('A maner Latyn corrupt was hir speche', 1, 519) which the Romano-British Celts of what is now Northumbria were able to understand. Another vivid passage is the comparison with the pallor of one who is being led to his death (II, 645–51). So the story is fully 'realised': but it quite properly does not seek to evoke the sense of interplay of character and society of such a work as *Troilus*.

It is written in the rhyme royal stanza of *Troilus*, which so beautifully balances meditative narration with lyric expressiveness. The poet addresses the reader or audience, and apostrophises the characters in the story, in his accustomed way:

> O Sowdanesse, roote of iniquitee!
>
> II, 358
>
> This Sowdanesse, whom I thus blame and warye   [*curse*
>
> II, 373

recalling somewhat the manner of parts of *The Legend of Good Women*. It is part of the Expositor's technique of engagement from a detached position. At times it seem artificial, but there is no reason to think it ironical. The Expositor is not represented as foolish or ignorant. There is a genuinely Chaucerian comment when Constance is married that

> thogh that wyves be ful hooly thynges
> They moste take in pacience at nyght
> Swiche manere necessaries as been plesynges
> To folk that han ywedded hem with rynges
> And leye a lite hir hoolynesse aside ...   [*little*

II, 709–13

The assumption that good wives do not enjoy sex, and that holiness excludes sex, is very deep in Chaucer, though not always exclusive of other assumptions.

There is no reason anywhere in the poem to see it as in any way expressive of the character of the Man of Law. It was a poem Chaucer had by him, which he rightly thought was worth preserving, and he attached it to a sober serious pilgrim on the grounds of general suitability.

Harry Bailly calls it a 'thrifty' (fine) tale and then asks the Parson for a tale. Receiving a rebuke for his swearing, the Host cheerfully calls out he 'smells a Lollard in the wind', and sees a sermon coming, but the Shipman bursts in to prevent so dire an outcome. The Shipman's introductory words have a witty pun on 'cockle in our green corn' based on the Latin *lolium*, 'tare', 'weed', which the orthodox associated with the word Lollard. But the Shipman goes on to deny his knowledge of Latin and proves it by mangling various Latin words. So the earlier wit we must attribute to the poet, not the character. Misuse of Latin words by the uneducated has always been a source of amusement to the English upper-classes. Both errors and amusement derive from the divisive wounds in communal national feeling inflicted by the Norman Conquest and which festered for centuries.

THE SHIPMAN'S TALE

The actual tale told by the Shipman begins with a paragraph about rich merchants which though fairly impersonal in actual style is clearly written from a woman's point of view:

> The sely housbonde, algate he moot paye: [*simple*; *always must*
> He moot us clothe, and he moot us arraye.

VII, 11–12

The story is yet another example of the 'international medieval popular comic tale', and it exists in many variants, both written and found orally in recent times virtually all over the world.

The theme is known to folklorists as 'the lover's gift regained'. In Chaucer's version the wife of a rich merchant of Saint Denis near Paris is kept somewhat short both of money and sexual satisfaction. The merchant is friendly with a smart young monk of thirty, who frequents his house. Like the Monk in *The General Prologue* he is an 'outrider', a kind of steward or estate-manager. (Chaucer shows no knowledge of, or interest in, life *inside* monastic cloisters.) The wife tells the monk that she has incurred a debt of the then large sum of a hundred francs. He promises to help her, and fondles her. The merchant must go to Brugge (or Bruges) but before he goes the monk borrows a hundred francs. In the merchant's absence the monk seduces the wife at the price of the hundred francs, which he gives her. The merchant on his return calls first upon the monk, for he wants the money. The monk remarks that he has paid it back to the wife. The merchant on his return greets his wife fondly and they go to bed and make love vigorously. But then the merchant gently reproaches his wife for not telling him about the returned debt. She dismisses the charge lightly and says she had not realised it was re-payment, but a gift, and she happens to have spent it on clothing, but she will repay him in bed. The merchant has anyway made a great profit, so he has to rest content.

In a sense the tale is anti-feminist, and most versions present the wife unfavourably, but Chaucer gives it a twist that makes it sympathetic to women, good-humoured, and not ungenerous. All these tales bear witness to a layer of common European secular adult culture of relatively middling folk, who relish an improper joke provided it does not go too far; who accept the ordinary morality of society but find it amusing to indulge fantasies of breaking it, provided order is reasserted. Much the same layer exists today, indulgent of dirty jokes, or financial trickery up to a point, but outraged by any real assault on conventional moral standards. On the whole it seems very sensible and tolerant, recognising where fantasy starts and stops. In general the humour is derisive, not satirical in the sense of seeking to correct by ridicule, but not sympathetic either. Such is in general Chaucer's attitude as we have seen with *The Miller's Tale* and *The Reeve's Tale*, and as we shall see again. But he does bring a modifying gentleness and feminist sympathy as well, which we can see well in the strangely-attributed *Shipman's Tale*. He also brings the marvellous realism of description of setting, action, character and psychology which we have come to expect. He paints a genre-picture of the merchant in his counting-house with his wife walking in the garden, like a seventeenth-century Dutch picture, exquisite with the poetry of everyday detail, yet never encumbered by excess. The precision of accounting for money is also a part of Chaucer's arithmetical interest (above, p.15). These anecdotes are the early equivalent of the travelling salesman's repertoire of dirty stories, but raised to a level of unique artistry.

THE PRIORESS'S TALE

The mood changes again through the link which tells of the Host's gentle and respectful words to the Prioress, who freely and court-eously agrees to tell a story. Her Invocation to the Blessed Virgin is fully in character and establishes the mood of pious exaltation in which the tale is told. There can be no doubt that this tale was written with the teller in mind.

The story is just as much an adult folktale as the preceding comic popular tale and really just as secular, but it illustrates secular affective piety and parental love, which are just as much part of secular culture as amusement at sexual impropriety.

The story is set in Asia, in a great city, though it evokes at the end the equivalent story of little Hugh of Lincoln. A seven-year-old child's widowed mother teaches him a special reverence for the Blessed Virgin, and then

> This litel child, his litel book lernynge
> As he sat in his scole at his prymer   [*primer*
> He *Alma redemptoris* herde synge   [*Loving (mother) of the Redeemer*
> As children lerned hire antiphoner   [*anthem-book*
> And as he dorste, he drough hym ner and ner,   [*dared; drew nearer
>   and nearer*
> And herkned ay the wordes and the noote,   [*tune*
> Til he the firste vers koude al by rote.   [*knew off by heart*

VII, 516–22

He asks a slightly older friend what the anthem means, and then determines to learn it before Christmas. He sings it as he goes home daily through the Jews' quarter. This is the point of placing the story in Asia; there were no Jewish communities in England from the thirteenth to the seventeenth centuries, which saves the gentle Prioress from an otherwise ugly anti-Semitism. She is talking about bogeymen. The Jews take the child's song as an insult, and murder him. The whole of the story up to here is told with remarkable realism. The dialogue between the two little boys will convince any parent with its charm. In other versions of the story, which was very popular in the Middle Ages, the boy is ten years old. By making him only seven, Chaucer increases the pathos, but also the realism, and he is extremely accurate about the child's academic schooling. All hangs together; a boy of seven is more innocent than one of ten, more docile and eager to learn. With all this, we still see the child from outside and as it were, from above. We do not, as with nineteenth-century authors, attempt to enter into his view of the world. We do not feel with him; we feel with the mother, her joy in the child implied by her terror when he does not come home from school. After his murder a miracle follows:

> This gemme of chastite, this emeraude,
> And eek of martirdom the ruby bright,
> Ther he with throte ykorven lay upright,   [on his back
> He *Alma redemptoris* gan to synge
> So loude that al the place gan to rynge.

VII, 609–13

His miraculous singing leads to the discovery of his body, and he explains that it is a miracle of the Virgin, who will fetch his soul when he actually dies. He is given a splendid burial. The last description of his mother comes before the explanation of the miracle, though after the discovery of his body, and tells how she lay swooning by his bier. There is no word of consolation for her. The Jews are put to death by torture.

There is naturally no psychological or other probability – it is, after all, a *miracle*. The poem draws its full strength from a pattern and a story which can hardly be called realistic in its *total* effect, though it employs realistic methods and materials in part. The force and beauty of the tale are based on the realistic description of the 'little clergeon'. On this foundation are built the walls and roof which are largely supernatural. In terms of language we move from realistic dialogue and description to the idealising and more metaphorical phrases 'gem of chastity', 'emerald', 'bright ruby of martyrdom'. We move from playground to altar, and each strengthens and sets off the other.

Chaucer's treatment of children falls in with the general pattern of his art; his amazing juxtapositions of the comic and the pathetic, the realistic and the idealistic, the bawdy and the sincerely devout, the natural and the supernatural. The general pattern of development from nature to supernature is also found in *Troilus and Criseyde*.

The Prioress's Tale is an exemplary traditional religious tale which wonderfully appealed to high and low in Chaucer's day, as its reception among the pilgrims shows, but which has aroused varied response in modern times. Some critics, conscious of the appalling crimes of anti-Semitism in the twentieth century, have wished to attribute a similar conscience to Chaucer. They argue that the Prioress must be satirised because after the ecstatic praise of the Blessed Virgin's mercy the story refers to the cruel punishment of the

Jews. But the story, though it suits her, is not a dramatic soliloquy, and such a reading is another example of the rejection of the straightforward, traditional, 'naive' reading in favour of an anachronistic critical literalism. Chaucer shares with his gentle Prioress the normal love of children and hostility to the Jews of the Middle Ages. The story-structure is another demonstration of the closeness of love to suffering, of Gothic pity and tearfulness, of the truth that to love the innocent and defenceless leads to hatred of their oppressors. Nor is such a combination of love and hatred solely Gothic – only his particular version of it; it is very easily translated in the twentieth century into political terms, with no less sentimentality and cant than in medieval Miracles of the Virgin. Chaucer is not guilty here of cant, but we may again notice in his adaptation of a popular tale a sort of artistic extremism, achieved partly by greater realism, as of the child, partly by more exalted religious fervour at the end. He twists our feelings several notches higher up than do other versions of the story. But in recognising the pathos we should not forget that the final point of the story is, after all, triumph and gladness.

SIR THOPAS

Even the Host is sobered by this story of miracle, but begins to jest and, says the poet, for the first time 'looked at me'.

>   'What man artow?' quod he,   [*art thou; said*
> 'Thow lookest as thou woldest fynde an hare
> For evere upon the ground I se thee stare.
>
> Approche neer, and looke up murily.
> Now war yow, sires, and lat this man have place!
> He in the waast is shape as wel as I;
> This were a popet in an arm t'enbrace   [*puppet*
> For any womman, smal and fair of face.   [*slender*
> He semeth elvyssh by his contenaunce,   [*not human*
> For unto no wight dooth he daliaunce.   [*he does not chat with anyone*

VII, 695–704

This is a precious glimpse of Chaucer the man, although a self-mocking one. It recalls and is consistent with the self-description in *The House of Fame* (above, p.74). He is plump, abstracted in manner, keeps himself to himself, and is patronised by more self-assertive men. This is surely one side of the truth, and perhaps to Chaucer's contemporaries the most obvious. There was another side, that of the pilgrim-author who tells us at the beginning of *The General Prologue*, if only for verisimilitude, that he had before

nightfall spoken to every one of twenty-nine pilgrims and had been
accepted into their company (I, 30–2); and the solitary reader
reproached by the Eagle in *The House of Fame* was as desperately
eager to hear stories of real people, as he was to read books late at
night. There is a genuine modesty and introvertedness in Chaucer's
authorial make-up, which is compensated for by an at times incom-
patibly powerful set of feelings, shown by extravagant apostrophe of
characters in a story, a deep sense of pathos, irresistible attraction
towards women. The whole set of contrasts of attitudes in him is
perhaps the basis of his irrepressible sense of absurdity.

The latter now triumphs. The great learned European poet as we
know him to be (though he is not presented as such on the dramatic
level inside the fiction), can only offer a 'rhyme' he learnt long ago.
He goes back to his origins in the English stanzaic tail-rhyme
romances, and begins the tale of the Flemish knight *Sir Thopas*. It is
the funniest parody in English. It is full of clichés, beginning

> Listeth lordes in good entent
> And I wol telle verrayment   [*truly*
> Of myrthe and of solas;
> Al of a knyght was fair and gent   [*nice*
> In bataille and in tourneyment
> His name was sire Thopas.
>
> VII, 712–7

Gent and *verrayment* are typically vapid words of the English
romances. This 'doughty swain', with red and white checks and
saffron yellow beard is a good archer and wrestler – rather old-
fashioned, though not impossible qualities for a knight.

> Ful many a mayde, bright in bour,   [*bower*
> They moorne for hym paramour,   [*in love*
>   Whan hem were bet to slepe: [*it were better for them*
> But he was chaast and no lechour
>   And sweete as is the brembul-flour
> That bereth the rede hepe.   [*bears the red rose hip*
>
> VII, 742–7

The bathetic comment about it being better to sleep, the comparison
with the common bramble flower, i.e. the dog-rose, and its red hips
are all part of the cumulatively ridiculous effect, as, one fears, is the
knight's chastity. (A very different attitude is found in *Sir Gawain
and the Green Knight*.) The jog-trot metre makes the traditional
description of spring, the knight's love-longing without a lady, the
riding out into Fairyland, fighting a giant, ceremonially putting on his
armour, sleeping in it in the open, all delightfully absurd. Chaucer's
lack of sympathy with certain traditional literary topics, and with
mythic romantic narrative, is well illustrated. The elaborate descrip-

tion of arming, for example, is a commonplace of epic and romance from Homer, through Virgil, medieval European romances, down to twentieth-century Yugoslav folk-epic. It is superbly handled in *Sir Gawain and the Green Knight*, which apart from the metre treats seriously all the elements which Chaucer mocks, and is as great a poem, in its different way, as any that Chaucer wrote. Chaucer's 'modernism' is nowhere better seen than in his mockery of traditional romance, and surely his taste was shared by many readers. Yet the list, itself a parody of a rhetorical commonplace, of 'romances of price', which he quotes at the end, and the very act of parody, suggests that for many of his courtly readers these romances had been favourite reading. Several appear in the Auckinleck Manuscript (above, p.40) and as he implies here, Chaucer had read them with great pleasure when he was young. He had grown up on them (above, p.41) and out of them. He also takes the opportunity of some comic satire at the expense of Flemish knights, who were not thought much of generally, and that his father-in-law, the herald Sir Payne Poet, was Flemish, may have added some extra zest.

The poem, being a parody, is a good example of 'two voices' in poetry, or of two levels of understanding. One is within the fiction and certainly to be attributed to the plump, shy ignorant *persona* of the pilgrim-Chaucer, also fully within the fiction. At this literal level the poem is a genuinely feeble attempt. At the other deeper level, in reality outside the fiction, the poem is a most amusing parody of what it pretends to represent. The work of art in its unity straddles both fiction and reality, as the poet does, and for its full effect both levels must be appreciated. Indeed the second level cannot be perceived without seeing first the primary literal level. So with the poet: he is both inside and out. We murder to dissect, to divide too clearly the poet inside from the poet outside the poem.

THE TALE OF MELIBEE

Within the fiction the Host cannot stand this feeble poem and calls on Chaucer to stop rhyming. A little plaintively, but courteously, the pilgrim-Chaucer agrees, and says he will tell a 'little thing in prose', and goes on most interestingly to comment on variable verbal accounts of the same material, as seen in the Gospels, and uses it to excuse any variation he may employ in quoting proverbs. Literal accuracy, a very modern concept, always interested Chaucer, as we have seen in his address to his scribe (above, p.162) although verbal variation of a given story is a characteristic of traditional literature which he himself makes full use of. Proverbs also are a form of the 'sententious style' which characterises popular and traditional literature, and which Chaucer, like Shakespeare, was so fond of that many of his phrases which sound like proverbs were probably actually invented by him. The teachers of rhetoric also recommended the use of proverbs. Proverbs were well thought of by both learned and popular writers, and only fell from esteem in the seventeenth century, when Neoclassical standards created other assumptions about the need for originality and the avoidance of what was 'low'. The *Melibee* is full of proverbs 'to enforce the effect of the matter'. It is written in a fairly elaborate prose style.

Chaucer calls this long prose translation a 'little' thing, more modestly than accurately. It is a serious discussion of various ethical problems. It is sensible, moderate, sober, understanding, and Chaucer had every reason for respecting the original as he must have done to have felt it worth translating. The *Melibee* is out of date now, but full of interest to anyone who will read it with the historical imagination. There is a thread of story, and some obvious allegorical interpretations arising from it. But the main body of the work is debate, the balancing of conflicting authorities often summed up in the 'crystallised thought' of proverbs. The topics discussed are the worth of women, the justice and injustice of war, true friends, flatterers, the fickleness of 'the people', the need to love God, obey the law, etc., etc. *The Tale of Melibee* is a most useful collection of the common opinions of well-educated people, not ironically presented. We should take it 'straight'. We are harassed by the same troubles as were they. We do not see our problems in the same light, but that is due to historical change. Where we tend to see the working of blind mass forces, they saw either astrological influences or, as here, intentional human ill-will, or accidental error.

The Host is too eager to say how different his own wife is from Prudence, the wife of Melibeus, to comment on the tale. And indeed comment would only remind us of the extreme unrealism of the long prose treatise delivered on the way to Canterbury. The joke of the masterful man mastered by his wife is an old and good one, but as we do not know what the real Harry Bailly's wife was really like, we cannot tell if the humour lies in the truth or the falseness of the description of her; it might be either. At all events, the Host's remark provides welcome relief after the ponderings and ponderousness of *The Tale of Melibee*. Chaucer may have introduced this new element in the Link because he was abandoning the well-used device of contrasting tales. The Link itself provides the contrast both to the preceding and to the following tale. The description of the Host's termagant wife also underlines one of the themes of the *Melibee* – the relationship between husband and wife – which becomes more and more prominent as the *Tales* proceed. At the moment, however, it is the Monk whom the Host calls on for a tale. He answers the Host's half-saucy, half-respectful sallies stiffly enough, and embarks upon a series of solemn tragedies in eight-line stanzas with intricate rhyme, telling 'the harm of those who stood in high degree' and fell.

THE MONK'S TALE

Chaucer here adapts the character of the Monk to the nature of the stories he will tell. He is a patient, worthy, learned monk who has a hundred 'tragedies' in his cell, and the poet takes the opportunity, through him, of giving us the definition of tragedy just referred to, which is taken from Boethius. Medieval tragedy does not necessarily include death, but death is traditionally seen as one of the greatest tragedies that can, and must, befall a man. The modern notion of tragedy as an ennobling spectacle is not found here. Rather it is pathetic. At times it may be a salutary warning.

The Monk's Tale is mainly based on a Latin work of Boccaccio's, which itself is very Gothic in its mingling of Biblical, Classical, legendary, historical and modern instances. It is rather archaic, with its disregard for different kinds of story, for different historical periods. All the subjects from evil Satan, through Hercules and Samson, Nero and Julius Caesar, to Chaucer's contemporaries Peter of Cyprus and Bernabò of Lombardy, whom Chaucer considers worthy men foully betrayed (though we regard them as cruel tyrants), are treated much as if they had lived around the same time in the same conditions. What they have in common is the fall from high to low. This work is strikingly unmodern.

The most moving and pathetic of the stories is that of the death of Count Hugelino of Pisa and his three small children, which Chaucer took from Dante. Parenthood and small children always evoke an easy pathos from Chaucer, as this story, *The Prioress's Tale*, and the stories of Constance and Griselda, all illustrate.

How far Chaucer himself began to feel uneasy about the quality of *The Monk's Tale* is impossible to tell. Since the modern instance of Bernabò must be later than December 1385, when he was killed, Chaucer was content to work on the poem in full maturity. He must have worked intermittently on various poems simultaneously. In this one he may have been attracted by the need to exercise his ingenuity over the rhymed stanza, which is more difficult than the rhyme royal. Perhaps he got tired of it all the same, but with ever-flowering ingenuity covered it by having the Knight interrupt:

'Hoo' quod the Knyght 'good sire, namoore of this!'

VII, 2767

The Knight prefers to hear of people going up in the world, not down, and speaks rather roughly to the Monk, recalling the character given to the Monk in *The General Prologue* by asking him to speak of hunting. The Monk abruptly refuses. The Host then cheerfully calls on the up to now characterless priest of the Prioress, riding on a poor horse, to tell a tale, and he immediately agrees.

THE NUN'S PRIEST'S TALE

The poem and the story start immediately and simultaneously with the description of a poor widow, living a simple life in patience with her two daughters, on a bare, if healthy, diet of plenty of milk and brown bread, eggs and fried bacon, and 'hertes suffisaunce'. She has a glorious cock, Chauntecleer, whose brilliance outshines all comparison and who rules his roost with seven wives, of whom his favourite is Pertelote.

Chauntecleer is the hero of this well-known traditional story, which is the conflation of two even older stories. The first is Aesop's Classical fable of the fox and the crow. The crow in the tree has a piece of food in his beak. The fox flatters him into singing, upon which he drops the food. It is a crisp and amusing anecdote illustrating perennial truths about flattery and keeping one's mouth shut, and the non-human actors make the human point all the more memorably. Another similar story first found in the eighth-century work of Alcuin of York tells how a wolf catches a cock and runs off with it until the cock flatters the wolf into opening his mouth to show off his beautiful voice, thus allowing the cock to escape. These two stories were first combined in the eleventh century with characters of wolf and partridge, and become popular. In the twelfth-century Latin poem *Gallus et Vulpes* some unknown genius finally created Cock and Fox as they have became familiar. Thus stories may grow and be improved.

The underlying pattern is one of reversal, which by simple repetition of the same kind of incident gives pleasure, but with the reversal of the incident, so that fox cheats cock, then cock cheats fox, gives extra aesthetic and moral pleasure. The fox's reputation for cunning, based on natural observation, makes him more suitable than the wolf as one character, while the cock, so commonplace a creature, so 'cocky', as we say, by nature, makes him amusing in his temporary discomfiture, and fittingly triumphant in his final escape. The cock is also notoriously sexual, and is symbolically associated with fertility, self-renewal, resurrection. That does not make him or his story allegorical but indicates the resonances which the story-pattern may subconsciously arouse, and makes him suitable for such a fable of variety, quick-wittedness, and survival. In the predominantly rural Middle Ages, cock and fox were extremely familiar, and also natural enemies. *Gallus et Vulpes* also introduced the episode of the chase after the fox who is carrying off the cock in his mouth. It is only briefly mentioned but the seed flowered in the fourteenth and fifteenth centuries in popular art, and especially in Chaucer's poem. There are two essential figures, the woman chasing (usually shown with 'her distaff in her hand') and the fox with his prey; hunter and hunted. This image of the chase set between the two main acts of reversal which make up the plot helps to tie them together as cause and effect, but is also in itself an image of reversal, for the fox who was the hunter becomes hunted, and by a woman, who is not a natural hunter, but is carrying the image of female domesticity, the distaff. When so many others join the chase it becomes a cluster of potent images, a rush together of excitement joining many different individuals in one spontaneous desire. It both witnesses and contributes to the breaking down of boundaries, the rush to freedom, but also the rush to reassert the natural order, to prevent theft and punish the criminal. It has a certain ambiguity. We share both the bloodlust and desire for revenge of those who chase, and the temporary triumph, and final fear, of the offender. The whole episode is transitional, crossing and recrossing boundaries so as both to refresh and reassure us. Yet it is also a comedy, that is, by the medieval definition, a story with a happy ending, and at last we come to laughter.

No poet anywhere so richly fulfils the potentialities of this whole narrative sequence as Chaucer. One thing he does not give us, and that is, an allegory, though many critics wish to extract one. The author of *Gallus et Vulpes* tells the story in 136 lines, but adds a further 152 elaborately allegorising the traditional tale. The cock's dungheap is penitence, the beating of his wings while he crows, says the author in a triumph of bathetic ingenuity, signifies teachers who add gestures to keep their audience awake while being addressed. The fox signifies Satan, etc. All this illustrates a habit of mind common to clerics in the Middle Ages and to some critics today, but it is alien to Chaucer's secular and artistic interests. He does indeed enrich and elaborate the structure, but by adding associative, metonymic details, by hyperbole (the colours of the cock), and by adding illustrative anecdotes, not necessarily comic, like the story of the death of the little Anglo-Saxon royal saint, Kenelm. The fable of Cock and Fox is in origin comical rather than satiric and Chaucer adds marital, sexual, rhetorical, social, linguistic jokes. A neat illustration of several of these elements is Chauntecleer's own joke after praising (in comical poultry terms) the beauty of his beloved Pertelote, quoting

> *Mulier est hominis confusio –*   [*Woman is man's trouble*
> Madame, the sentence of this Latyn is,   [*meaning*
> Womman is mannes joye and al his blis.
>
> VII, 3164–6

This is also a joke between Chaucer and his audience, perhaps at the expense of any ladies present, who were much less likely to know Latin, though this Latin is easy enough to guess.

By naturalistic standards there are inconsistencies of narrative and point of view, but no reader was ever puzzled by them because they are inherent in traditional story-telling.

Although so comical, the main action of the story is postponed to the end because Chaucer embellishes the talk between cock and hen, exemplifying husbandly pomposity and wifely brisk good sense with all the panoply of his usual learning and rhetoric. All the subjects of Chaucer's most serious thought are here. The comedy is in the neatness of the disproportion. Chaucer plays with serious ideas; while pretending to treat his frivolous 'matter' seriously, he treats serious matters frivolously. Thus he ponders yet again the problems of predestination and foreknowledge, but they arise out of the concern of a farmyard fowl who has dreamt about a fox. This does not mean that he is satirising concern with the problem of predestination, but that it was so much a part of his thought that he enjoys it whether serious or light-hearted. This kind of joyful burlesque is the play of the mind, taking the same kind of exercise for pleasure, without concern for ultimate causes, as it normally takes when seriously at work. The attitude to rhetoric is an outstanding example. The poem is in the best sense of the word 'rhetorical', using all the devices of persuasive elaborate language, yet Chaucer also mocks and parodies the chief rhetorical author he knows, Geoffrey of Vinsauf, in an affectionate way.

The poem ends with continuing parody – you that think this is only a story of a cock and a hen – take the morality! Chaucer knows that some people need to take a serious message from the lightest literature. And indeed we may cheerfully accept the profound if commonplace exemplarymoral. But more than that, we may accept, without distorting the entertainment, the genuinely refreshing quality of the poem, its juxtapositions and associations of splendour and simplicity, purpose and accident, learning and commonsense. It celebrates the surprising nature of life. It is not an allegory: as Chaucer says, it is about a fox, a cock, and hen. The poem is about itself, its own morality, its own reversals, its own fun; there is everything in it; it sums up the whole *Canterbury Tales*. It has an underlying, entirely recognisable, unfragmented Chaucerian identity.

The variations and fruitful inconsistencies of narrative points of view forbid us to attribute any specific character, beyond that of the poet, to this poem, and even the poet's direct address is less in evidence than usual. The centre of the piece is the narrative itself which can well stand on its own; the unity based on this is a certain inclusiveness by which each element subtly modifies the other so that all co-operate in a service that is perfect freedom. A brief epilogue in which the Host comments on the Nun's Priest's brawny physique and presumed sexual powers does not appear in all manuscripts, and was probably cancelled either because it repeated, or was used for, the similar remarks made by the Host to the Monk, which Chaucer changed to an earlier stage (see above, p.195).

D. BREWER. 1984

THE PHYSICIAN'S TALE

The long and varied sequence we have been following from *The Man of Law's Tale* ends here. A group of two tales only, *Physician's* and *Pardoner's* may be taken here, though Chaucer had probably not finally decided where to place it.

The Physician's Tale, ultimately from Livy via *Le Roman de la Rose* is another traditional tale, with some similarities to the widespread folktale known most familiarly as that of Jephthah's Daughter, from the Bible (Judges XI), who is mentioned at line 240. It is a story from the cluster of motives and tensions I have called in *Symbolic Stories* (Cambridge, D.S. Brewer, 1981) 'the family drama', telling how a father kills his daughter to preserve her virginity from the demands of an unjust judge. Parental feeling often interested Chaucer: so did problems and dilemmas. This story concerns both. The wide distribution of the tale attests its general appeal to traditional societies who believed that personal honour, virtue and integrity were values that should if necessary be preserved at the cost of life. To have to make the choice between virtue, however conceived, and death for oneself is bad enough, though one that many people have been called on to make even in the twentieth century. To have to make the choice on behalf of one's child is even more dreadful. The actual dilemma presented by Chaucer is perhaps less striking to us now because we have so effectively trivialised sex and we tend to believe that life is sacred above anything else. Few traditional societies have shared our belief. Chaucer, or a part of him, was fully traditional. But a part was modern, and he so consistently jokes about sex that he may well have been unable to deploy his full powers on this particular subject, much as part of him wished to. Furthermore, his realism and flippancy also worked against the type of folkloric or mythic psychological structure represented by this story. The poet who wrote *Sir Gawain and the Green Knight* and

Pearl might have made more of it. But Chaucer could hardly write a bad, or at least, an uninteresting poem, and the death of the heroine Virginia is finely pathetic. There is an earnest address to fathers and mothers, and a curious, not quite fully earnest address to governesses. The tale is, for Chaucer, plainly narrated, and with an unusually moralistic ending quite without flippancy. Why it should be attributed to the Physician is hard to see, but there is no doubt that the attribution was designed as we soon see from the Host's words.

THE PARDONER'S PROLOGUE AND TALE

As if to make up for a certain flatness in *The Physician's Tale*, the Host is represented as so moved by the tale that he swears as if mad. He lets loose a string of commendations of the Physician and his urinals and other useful pots, with various mispronunciations, which immediately lighten the tone. He then calls on the Pardoner. The Pardoner must have a drink of 'moist and corny ale'. The 'gentils', that is, the more refined members of the group, cry out against being told 'ribaldry'. Their wish is an important part of the medieval audience's requirement of literature.

> Telle us som moral thyng, that we may leere   [*learn*
> Som wit, and thanne wol we gladly heere.   [*knowledge*
>
> VI, 325–6

They get what they ask for, in a quite obvious way, as a moral exemplum, traditional, but told with originality and dramatic ambiguity.

'Lordynges', begins the Pardoner, and thus establishes the fictional level at which he speaks his *Prologue*. Chaucer the poet *never* addresses his real, courtly and learned audience in this popular, half-patronising, half-obsequious word, a favourite with the Host and a number of the pilgrims. (Chaucer cannot even bring himself to put it in the mouth of the pilgrim-Chaucer telling *Sir Thopas*, though it would fit metrically, and some manuscripts, judged to be wrong by editors, do use 'lordynges' instead of 'lordes'. It is never used at all in *Troilus* or *The Knight's Tale* or the earlier poems).

The Pardoner explains how he preaches, revealing all the cunning tricks by which he cheats simple folk of their money, preaching against avarice in order to feed his own.

Jean de Meun in his part of *Le Roman de la Rose* had begun the satirical device by which a villain 'confesses', though with glee rather than penitence, the treachery he practises (cf. the English *Romaunt*,

6153 ff.). Such 'confession' possibly stems from the increasing pressure for real confession after the Lateran Council 1215–16, which must have promoted greater self-awareness and more introspection. But Jean de Meun's literary satire gives confession an amusingly secular twist, especially in soliloquy, and proved particularly useful in dramatic contexts, Shakespeare in particular using it for several villains from Richard III onwards. The dramatic element in Chaucer's work continually increased – Criseyde's final 'soliloquy' will be remembered (p.144) – and in the *Pardoner's Prologue* the device becomes almost fully dramatic. Chaucer does not achieve a fully independent dramatic characterisation, for we are shown no motive or reason why the Pardoner should reveal, and revel in the revealing of, his shameful exploitation of the ignorant and pious. To that extent the *Pardoner's Prologue* remains a satire which is the more ingeniously effective for the substitution of the first person 'I do this' for the third person 'He does this'. But a deeper impression of the man is given by making the Pardoner give himself away, and though it is unmotivated it has strangely enough a greater authenticity. It is not even ironical. We cannot speak here of the Narrator, even if we want to: it is the Pardoner who speaks. It is a fascinating, self-absorbed explosion of cunning.

His Prologue merges naturally into his *Tale*, set like others in Flanders, and he describes a company of young rioters and debauchees. The Tale now takes on as well the canting ranting tone of the popular preacher, sanctimoniously and extravagantly condemning carnal men. The Pardoner quotes St Paul weeping, and says he weeps himself to tell it,

> 'That they been enemys of Cristes croys,
> Of which the ende is deeth. Wombe is hir god.'   [*Belly*
> O wombe! O bely! O stynkyng cod,   [*bag*
> Fulfilled of dong and of corrupcioun!
> At either end of thee foul is the soun.   [*sound*
> How greet labour and cost is thee to fynde!   [*provide for*
> Thise cookes, how they stampe, and streyne, and grynde,
> And turnen substaunce into accident,   [*turn essence into attribute*
> To fulfille al thy likerous talent.   [*lecherous desire*

VI, 532–40

There is an element of caricature by the poet here in creating the Pardoner's character. We read this extravagant outburst in the light of the Pardoner's own self-revelation. The reference to the foul sounds that come out of either end of the belly is certainly meant for a laugh, especially as medieval people, including Chaucer, always found mention of the breaking of wind hilariously funny. Similarly extravagant, and delightful, is the great length of register of style from concrete realistic homely bags of dung to the scholastic witticism of cooks changing real essence into subsidiary qualities as they grind meat into sauces and so forth.

The listing of vices goes on with great zest, as the poet fully enters into the Pardoner's spirit and indulges his exaggerated style, so that gradually our sense of poet and Pardoner merges into one.

The actual story is relatively brief, another folktale. Three rioters whose dialogue is vividly reported, look for that thief Death, who has recently caused so much distress in the country. They meet an old man and ask him roughly has he seen Death. The old man longs to die, but must await God's will, and meanwhile walks the earth knocking on it with his staff crying 'Leeve (*dear*) mooder, leet me in!' He directs the three violent men to a place by a tree in a grove. Hastening there, they find a heap of gold and immediately forget their quest. They discuss cagily between themselves how to store and divide it. They decide to guard it till nightfall then steal it away. The youngest is sent into the town to get food and drink. The other two plan to kill him on his return, so as to have more for themselves, and so they do. But he has bought, as well as food and drink, rat poison from an apothecary's shop, so when the murderers settle down to feast after his death they themselves die.

The Pardoner again hits his almost hysterical ranting tone:

> O cursed synne of alle cursednesse!
> O traytours homycide, O wikkednesse!

VI, 895–6

and so he goes on, and turns the same flow towards the audience of pilgrims, producing his usual sales talk which he has so effectively given away at the beginning. It is improbable but gloriously funny, especially as he singles out the Host as the one most enveloped in sin to come forth first and give money and kiss his bogus relics. The Host replies with a robustness and violence of expression which is surprising even in Chaucer – he would like, he says, to cut off the Pardoner's testicles and enshrine them in a hog's turd. The Pardoner is too furious to speak. The others laugh, but the Knight, great and good man that he is, courteously prays them to be reconciled, so that

> Anon they kiste, and ryden forth hir weye.

VI, 968

The section ends in the wonderfully calm fullness of Chaucer's plain style, utterly without extravagance or adornment, which is perhaps the unifying foundation of all the fantastic and colourful structures laid upon it.

The whole episode is astonishing and interesting in every line. The story illustrates yet again how a non-naturalistic folkloric narrative structure, which makes no attempt to 'imitate' life in a plausible

Neoclassical way, may be embellished with satisfyingly realistic detail, and create a penetrating sense of life, its ironies and difficulties and rewards.

The tale itself, apart from the homiletic passages, is told almost entirely through excellent dialogue. Brief as it is, it has a touch of awe, even of horror, found nowhere else in Chaucer, as we watch the three criminals rush on their fate. The most striking figure is that of the mysterious Old Man who walks the earth, poor and longing for death, knocking with his staff upon the ground which is his 'mother's' gate. This strangely haunting character seems to be largely Chaucer's own invention. He is the weariness of old age incarnate. Yet Death takes the young rioters, who have questioned the old man so rudely to discover where they may find death. Is it Death only that cannot die? A sense of the ineluctable mystery of life lies beneath the simple plot.

THE WIFE OF BATH'S PROLOGUE AND TALE

We now come to a new section, a large one, since it may reasonably be held to be composed of Fragments III, IV, V. We plunge straight in.

> Experience, though noon auctoritee
> Were in this world, is right ynogh for me
> To speke of wo that is in mariage.
>
> III, 1–3

And indeed the Wife of Bath's theme (for it is her cheerful, arrogant voice we hear) is tribulation in marriage – particularly the misery she has caused her five successive husbands. We have here another dramatic expression comparable to the *Pardoner's Prologue*. And as with the Pardoner the term 'confession' may be slightly misleading because at least equally strong an element in the speeches is the much more ancient and human vice of boasting. Yet to represent a vicious person 'confessing' his or her sins in public, or revealing their trickery, as would never be done in real life, is a non-naturalistic but valid device of comic satire; and when the villain is made ridiculously to *boast* of his sins it is even more incongruous, comic and subtle. With the boasting an aggressive element from character, author, and audience, enters into the sympathetic situation, and in the clash humour is born. The person confessing becomes more self-condemned because of his (or her) failure of moral self-awareness. At the same time we respond sympathetically to *anyone* in literature who is vigorous and unrepentant – Falstaff, and Milton's Satan (in the early books of *Paradise Lost*) are only two later and famous examples of such justified sinners and supermen.

Chaucer does not take us quite so far along the road which exalts personal will as the supreme value. Both the Wife of Bath and the Pardoner are ridiculous because they are making a foolish mistake by boasting, which is always amusing in those who normally exploit, to their own advantage, the mistakes, errors and follies of others. The balance in these characters is different, though. The Wife of Bath is predominantly sympathetic because her victims are not only old and rich (which is enough to damn them in the *fabliau* tradition), but also selfish and would be tyrannous. Moreover, the Wife is loving after her lustful, domineering fashion, and we can easily see ourselves in her. The Pardoner by contrast is predominantly satirised.

These 'confessions' create that double image, that intersection of two incongruous planes of reference which is the essence of humour, and which creates that dual response in the reader, by which we recognise comedy, irony, and poetry. 'Confessions' are not straight-forwardly naturalistic, and to seek a straightforwardly consistent 'illusionist' interpretation, especially of those switches of attitude and perspective at the end of *The Pardoner's Tale*, as some critics do, is to be asking questions as mistaken as they would be in a Chaplin classic. Comedy self-evidently has the self-sufficiency which our theories of imitation sometimes fail to credit other writings with.

Self-sufficiency does not mean the absence of realism. Comedy often points very sharply at well-recognised ordinary appearances, again as in a Chaplin film. Intensification and selection of detail constitute both realism and unrealism – another comic duality. The Wife of Bath's secular, boastful 'confession' is in parts marked by such an extremely naturalistic realism of presentation that she is even shown forgetting where she had got to in her ramblings. Yet this is also a taught rhetorical device. The basic structure of what she says is built on the framework, and sometimes the very words, of traditional clerical anti-feminist tracts from St Jerome in the fifth century onwards. Some critics have puzzled themselves as to how she could have known the words of St Jerome and the rest. It has been seriously argued that since she knew no Latin she must have remembered the readings of her fifth husband. The problem and the answers are based on irrelevant novelistic, naturalistic premises, as if she were a real person. As well ask who gave the heroine of an opera singing lessons. The way she speaks is the medium, not the message; the Wife's knowledge of Latin texts is the equivalent of the music in opera; it is the product of the 'composer', not the character. Nevertheless, the Wife's *Prologue* is the *nearest* thing to sustained organic independent-ly dramatic speech in Chaucer. The wife was a favourite with Chaucer's readers years before his death, as well as ever after. In this respect she represents the climax of Chaucer's achievement in that dramatic narrative constituted by the links between the *Tales*, where in general we get nearest to the self-enclosed dramatic structures of later Neoclassical literature, with wonderfully rich realism of ordinary life.

The Wife of Bath's Prologue is in itself a story about her life with her five husbands, how she married them, what a life she led them. This autobiographical thread links many comments on marriage, sex, money, dreams, etc., with realistic touches that evoke the social life of small towns surrounded by fields, the cycle of religious festivities, the easy adult sociability between the sexes in small English medieval towns. There is nothing in the *Prologue* about the Wife's taste for international pilgrimage and her experiences there, nor of her business of cloth-making. Nor is there any mention of family or children. The focus is limited to personal, specifically marital (with a hint of extra-marital) relationships, and in effect to proclaiming a fourteenth-century feminist manifesto. It is not only because of modern feelings for the rights of women that we sympathise with her; it is because of her human enjoyment and gusto, her frank acceptance of life and love and of herself. She accepts the superiority of virginity, but makes a hearty plea for sexual pleasure in marriage. She reflects that sensible middle range of conviction and behaviour represented by the medieval international comic tale, secular, resolutely cheerful, able to give and take hard knocks without resentment. She had tormented her fifth husband, the young clerk Jankin, who had responded by reading anti-feminist stories to her out of his book. She had thrown the book into the fire. He gave her a clout on the ear which left her permanently deaf in that ear. And then they were affectionately reconciled (on consideration that she had the mastery), and loved each other and were true to each other. It is the stuff of the popular comic tale, yet, or therefore, granted some exaggeration, with a delightful sense of life.

Her tale is undoubtedly meant for her and besides being most interesting in itself has a slightly ambivalent ending in relation to her main theme of 'sovereignty in marriage'. It is the nearest Chaucer comes to Arthurian romance and the world of fairyland, though he uses the reference to fairyland to make ironic references to the kind of fairies, in this case friars, found in the world nowadays. The action begins harshly with a knight of Arthur's court who rapes a girl. He is condemned to death for this outrage against women unless he can report to the Queen within a year and a day what women love most. The sense of the Wife dramatically telling the story is strong so far, even as she diverges into Ovid's anti-feminist story of Mida, who could not keep the secret of her husband's two asses' ears. She tells how the knight wanders unsuccessfully and sorrowfully until almost the day of reckoning, when he catches a glimpse of four-and-twenty ladies dancing on a lawn by a forest-side, then meets a poor, filthy and hideous old woman. She will tell him the answer, on condition he will do whatever she asks. The answer is that what women most want is 'sovereignty', domination. The Queen and her court agree that this is right. The old hag asks for her reward, which to the knight's horror is to marry him. He cannot evade it, and in bed she gives him a long lecture on what is true nobility, which does not come from wealth or family, but arises from virtue, witnessed to by noble deeds. Nobility comes from God's grace. Low class, poverty, age and ugliness have nothing to do with the desirability of a wife. Glad poverty is honourable, age deserves reverence, and the ugliness of a wife ensures her faithfulness and humble obedience, for age and dirt are great guardians of chastity. But then the old woman asks, would he prefer to have his wife foul, old, true and humble, or have her young and fair and take the risk? He leaves the decision to her, thus yielding her the sovereignty. She promises to be both fair and good all the time. Cast up the curtain of the bed, she says, and see. They live in joy, and she obeys him in every way that can please him.

The narrative tone, which has become 'general Chaucerian', now reverts to the dramatic *persona* of the Wife of Bath, who concludes with a cheerful parody of the prayer that so often ends English romances, that

> Crist may us sende
> Housbondes meeke, yonge and fressh abedde
> And grace t'overbyde hem that we wedde.   [*outlive*
> And eek I praye Jhesu shorte hir lyves
> That wol nat be governed by hir wyves.

III, 1258–62

This is not quite the moral of her tale, but trenchantly amusing, in Chaucer's vigorous plain style.

The Wife of Bath's Tale is again a version of a widespread traditional tale, and is individually modified. Chaucer's is the only version in which the hero commits rape in the beginning. (The touch of extremism, of forcing things to a limit, as with Griselda and here, is often to be noted in Chaucer.) The answer that the knight eventually finds is the exemplary part of the *Tale*. The answer is well suited to *The Wife of Bath*. It is also a good traditional joke, and from a man's point of view an anti-feminist point. As with the Wife's *Prologue* the answer is poetically paradoxical in that it makes the Wife boast of that very quality, the wish to dominere, for which women have been traditionally condemned; her very defence is her guilt, or her guilt is her defence. The old hag's harangue in bed on the subject of traditional morality is true, but also comic in that situation; and then comes the dilemma between a wife who is old, ugly and true, or the reverse.

Gower also tells the story in *Confessio Amantis* but his version is more decorous. 'Gothic' would seem a mild style if we took Gower as its most characteristic exemplar. He has no nasty rape at the beginning, so he avoids the risk that Chaucer runs of totally losing our sympathy for the knight. At first Gower seems more natural and realistic than Chaucer. If Chaucer's poem were to be regarded as mimetic and naturalistic we might think that a woman of such parts and versatility as the heroine would hardly consider that to have a reformed rapist for a husband would be a satisfactory foundation for a happy marriage based on mutual esteem; even if it was, or especially as it was, some other woman whom he had raped. So Gower did not take that risk. He retains the traditional folktale dilemma between having one's wife beautiful by day alone, or by night alone; so he too is inevitably committed, by this fantasy, to an essentially non-mimetic plot. The situation creates a joke about sexual pride; more generally, a joke, or a series of questions, or propositions, about social reputation and real possession; about the relations between self and society, and social envy; about a particular variation of the broad theme of appearance and reality. Would you prefer to be thought, by your friends, or even more, by your enemies, to be in full possession of something every man desires, although really and secretly you have not got it; or be scorned, or ignored, for not having, what in secret truth you have? How self-sufficient and independent of others' opinions are you? How different is social appearance from personal reality and how much do you value one without the other? Gower's is the traditional folktale dilemma, simpler than Chaucer's, more clear cut. All versions solve it in the same way, by the knight giving the choice to the lady, who having the choice chooses to be beautiful both by day and night. This ending suggests that appearance may be the same as reality if you do not assert yourself too egotistically, and that if you give a woman what she wants, she will give you what you want. It is a good, humane, optimistic, perhaps sentimental, folk solution; non-intellectual, non-clerical, pleasantly feminist. The solution may be a little too easy, partly because the dilemma is too schematic, clear cut, and with little moral implication.

Chaucer sacrifices the clarity of the folktale dilemma presumably because of his strong sense of reality and of the moral dimensions of human relationships. Granted that the story remains fantastic in that the old hag can magically transform herself into a beautiful lady, the dilemma that Chaucer proposes is much more profoundly natural in that it involves no magic alternations by night and day and it is quite possible in ordinary life to choose between marrying an old and therefore constant woman or a young flighty one. More issues, also, are in the balance. Sexual and social pride are involved, as before. But now also personal relationships are more at stake. Physical pleasure is balanced against the love and trust of a stable marriage.

External values represented by youth are set against internal values represented by age. The question of risk arises. Do you want a safe marriage, guaranteed by your wife's age, or will you take the risk of marrying a young woman who may treat you badly, make you a laughing-stock to your enemies and an object of pity to your friends, and who may bear other men's children to inherit your property?

The Knight's readiness to accept his wife's judgement is the ultimate reversal of his brutal assertion of masculine domination by committing a rape. The knight has been educated to move from vile aggression against women to accepting female sovereignty. The significance of the rape is not as an index of character but as part of a pattern of events that show an action and make a proposition. Not its content but its message is significant. The knight is forced, by his situation, to an act of submission to, and faith and trust in a woman, the more striking for his earlier transgression. Though there is no naturalistic characterisation, the nature of actual behaviour is commented upon. The knight now has to treat his wife as a person in her own right, with her own responsibility to decide and act in a moral question of personal relationships; she is not merely a submissive adjunct to himself. He therefore takes a risk, though of a different, less egotistical kind, from the risk he might have taken had he made his wife's choice of what her identity should be for her, instead of properly allowing herself to decide for herself. You need equality (of age, as in other matters, for the knight is young), and you need faith, in order to sustain personal relationships, especially in marriage; if you have equality you cannot have certainty, which is why you need faith. The story says, optimistically, rather like *The Franklin's Tale*, that love that is non-egotistical, that does not seek to dominate, that suffers long, and is kind, must take a risk and trust the beloved, and will be rewarded by a corresponding faith and love. The old wife becomes young and beautiful and promises to be true. Perhaps there is a sense here that the right kind of love *makes* the beloved beautiful and desirable, beauty living in the eye of the beholder. The last word of the story proper is of the lady's obedience, surely very uncharacteristic of the Wife of Bath's sentiments. Then immediately there is a violent switch in perspective, in narrative tone, to the Wife as storyteller – one of the abrupt discontinuities of perspective so characteristic of Chaucer's Gothic art. The Wife gives her own cheerfully coarse interpretation of the story, understandably and comically off-centre, about lusty young men in bed.

The poem has Chaucer's usual range of point of view, subject matter and style. The satirical reference to friars as the only succubi nowadays modulates to the magical glimpse of the four-and-twenty ladies dancing on the grass, associated with the old hag but never explained – an unusual touch of fairy-magic in Chaucer. The comedy of the repulsiveness of the dirty old woman in bed with the shrinking knight is compounded by the noble sentiment and diction of her speech.

THE FRIAR'S PROLOGUE AND TALE

The Friar picks up the Wife's Tale only indirectly, in order to pursue a long-standing quarrel with the Summoner, so he tells a tale about and against a Summoner, which is lightly attached to his character as a Friar, traditionally hostile to Summoners, rather than to his specific personality. The story is a traditional tale with many European versions but Chaucer sets it in a specific social context, in the Friar's 'country', though we do not know where that was, and we may suspect some private joke. A vigorously active archdeacon, who punishes all forms of vice, has a Summoner 'ready to his hand', who is a most efficient and deeply corrupt rascal, using his power to tyrannise over the weak, letting lechers off for bribes in order to line his own pocket. One day, the Summoner, on his way to extort a fine from a poor innocent old woman, falls in with a very smart yeoman in a green cloak, who says he is also, like the Summoner, a sort of bailiff, living 'far in the North'. They immediately become sworn brothers, and confess their malpractices to each other, during which it emerges that the yeoman is really a fiend, whose home is hell. The Summoner is intrigued, not terrified, by such a companion, and asks him various questions about his life, which yield some fascinating information. They agree to work together, each taking whatever he is given. Soon they pass a carter, irritated with his horses, who consigns them to the devil. 'Why don't you take them?' asks the Summoner. The reason is that the carter does not really mean what he says. They go to the poor woman, whom the Summoner threatens with the archdeacon's prison on a trumped-up charge unless she pays him twelve pence. She pathetically pleads her poverty, so the ruthless Summoner says that he will take her new pan. She curses both him and the pan to the devil. The accompanying fiend asks him if he repents, but not he. Since the old woman really means what she says, away he is taken by the devil.

The story is a joke, a satire, an expression of anger against corruption and petty tyrants, a comment on over-confidence, and more fundamentally a story about real intention in speech. When do we really mean what we say? The inner structure of the plot is a popular wild comic fantasy. It embodies an underlying general, human and humorous sense that in the end the biter is bit, wicked men overreach themselves, that corruption corrupts itself; that there is a hope for ordinary inoffensive goodness.

The style is predominantly plain and forceful. A fine example of how effective this style can be, without benefit of elaborate diction, glowing adjectives, or complex syntax, is given by the couplet

> He was, if I shal yeven hym his laude,   [*give him his praise*
> A theef, and eek a somnour, and a baude.
>
> III, 1353–4

To give such praise is ironical; the use of the first person adds feeling and venom; the placing of 'somnour' between 'theef' and 'baude' turns the name itself into an insult, while to have one's function regarded as by definition despicable turns the knife in the wound. This delicately yet deeply cutting invective is powerful poetry.

The couplet is also a brilliant example of metonymy (above p.171). A network of associations, of praise juxtaposed with blame, with theft and sexual corruption, is woven around the summoner and his profession, creating a tapestry of derisive meaning. The regularity of metre, the predominance of monosyllables, with 'somnour' highlighted as the only exception, the concrete yet general nouns, the clinching rhyme, the concision, all reinforce the strength of the couplet. The pleasure of much of Chaucer's poetry throughout his work is to be found in such relatively unobtrusive effects, which generations of colourful Romantic expression of cloudier emotions make it difficult for us consciously to recognise, and may even prevent us sometimes from enjoying.

THE SUMMONER'S PROLOGUE AND TALE

The Summoner on the pilgrimage is angry and insists on speaking against friars, beginning with a coarsely comic popular reference to where friars are kept in hell. This accords with the somewhat scatological nature of his tale, which is also modernistic in its comically arithmetical conclusion (above p. 15).

Although the Summoner, like so many other pilgrims, begins with 'Lordings', and thus demonstrates that his tale was certainly meant for *The Canterbury Tales*, and for its present place and speaker, the poem soon becomes told in the general Chaucerian narrative tone. Although the central incident may suit the Summoner's coarse personality, the varied interest of the subject matter, the subtlety of attitude, in no way correspond to, or express his personality.

A friar, brilliant in preaching and begging, is sarcastically described. He is accompanied by his man who carries a sack for the alms which they collect, and by a companion who writes down the names of those who give, so that they may be prayed for, on an ivory tablet, which is wiped clean as soon as they are out of sight. These companions we hear no more of.

The friar comes to a house where he is always well-received, and where the husband is lying ill in bed in the main living-room. The friar enters, drives away the cat from the most comfortable place by the fire, makes himself at home, and speaks in a most oily, canting way. The wife comes in and is embraced warmly by the friar who

> kiste hire sweet and chirketh as a sparwe   [*chirrups*; *sparrow*
> With his lyppes.

III, 1804–5

She offers a meal which he accepts with amusing hypocrisy:

> Have I nat of a capon but the lyvere   [*chicken*
> And of youre softe breed nat but a shyvere   [*slice*
> And after that a rosted pigges heed –
> But that I nolde no beest for me were deed   [*dead*
> Thanne hadde I with yow hoomly suffisaunce   [*sufficiency*
> I am a man of litel sustenaunce;
> My spirit hath his fostryng in the Bible.

III, 1839–45

The traditional satire on clerical hypocrisy and greediness, common for centuries before and after, is laid on thick. The hypocritical tone of voice is wonderfully hit off. The friar assures the wife that he saw the soul of her child, who she says died two weeks ago, borne up to heaven – the kind of revelation given only to friars, who are superior in this respect even to kings, because they despise worldly pleasure. He goes on in this vein in quite a long speech, expounding a 'glose' on the very words of Jesus which indicates his particular approval of friars (l. 1920), and causes us to remember Chaucer's own contemptuous attitude to 'glosing'. The friar's host Thomas angrily comments on how much he has spent on friars and how little he has got in return. He is answered by an entertaining sermon on not getting angry, full of learned examples, which culminates in an order to Thomas to be confessed. 'No', says Thomas, for he has already been confessed by his local parson (there being always rivalry between the local incumbent, and the wandering friars who were accused of giving easy penances for money). The friar argues about the need for money to build his church, and Thomas is beside himself with anger at the friar's 'false dissimulation'. He promises to give the friar what he has, and the friar is eager. But there is one important condition; that the friar must promise to divide the gift exactly with all the other friars in his convent, convents being usually made up of twelve members. The friar cannot wait, and swears on his faith to divide the gift. He is invited to put his hand down into the bed behind Thomas's back to find the gift, and when Thomas feels him groping around

Amydde his hand he leet the frere a fart   [gave
Ther nys no capul, drawynge in a cart   [horse pulling
That myghte have let a fart of swich a soun.

III, 2149–51

(Some acquaintance with draught horses is necessary to realise the
thunderous effect of the comparison.) The friar starts up like a mad
lion, rushes off to the lord of the manor, and in the most outraged
manner complains to him before all the court of the trick which has
been played on him. The lord's lady would dismiss the grossness as a
churl's deed done by a churl, but the lord is fascinated by the problem
presented – how could a churl have the imagination to set such a
problem? He meditates on questions of reverberation of air in a way
which echoes, if one may put it that way, the Eagle's much longer
disquisition in *The House of Fame*. A squire comes forward with a
ludicrously ingenious solution, about using a cartwheel, which normally has twelve spokes, to the end of each one of which each of the
friars shall lay his nose – the rest may be imagined. The lord, lady and
everybody say that the squire has spoken as well as Euclid or Ptolemy
– and the story comes abruptly to an end.

Although there are literary stories of what we may call the Satirical
Inheritance, and a number of folk-tales about the catching or knot-
ting of broken wind, there are no really close analogues to this tale.
Although it bears all the marks of the international comic popular
tale it is much more original and learned. The portrait of the friar is
broadly satirical, elaborately built up to a masterpiece of hypocrisy,
so that his fall to a crude trick may be the greater. His character as
such is only a broad sketch, but the amount of self-revelatory speech
given to him etches in the few lines very deeply. The long sermon
against anger, besides its intrinsic interest, further emphasises the
self-contradiction when he is so totally unable to control his own. The
wonderfully ingenious comic solution of the cartwheel appears to be
totally original with Chaucer, and a remarkable illustration of what
can only be called his scientific, and specifically his arithmetical
interests. No other poet in English could have invented such a story.

The story in common with most international comic tales both
rejects and asserts. Like *The Friar's Tale* it satirises the abuse of the
powers and values of the official culture by those whose duty it is to
exemplify and maintain them. These tales attack the faulty bearers of
the official culture, rather than official values themselves, by showing
pride going before a fall, the biter bit, the enginer hoist with his own
petard, the satisfyingly comic degradation of those whose moral
quality does not live up to their superior position. The comedy
indulges refreshingly in indecorous invective and fantasy. Such
stories assert the common, common-sense secular values of ordinary
honesty, allowing for a bit of honest deceit of those who deserve to be

deceived. Neither Friar's nor Summoner's story is about sex. Both are placed in the ordinary everyday world of the community.

The style varies from the colloquial realism of the friar's speech and some other plain speaking to the equally effective but surprisingly learned diction attributed to the 'churl' Thomas when he says

> This shaltou swere on thy professioun   [*vows*
> Withouten fraude or cavillacioun.   [*quibbling*
>
> III, 2135–6

This is probably the earliest recorded use of the word *cavillacioun* in English, though it occurs also in *Sir Gawain and the Green Knight* (l. 2275), and must have been 'in the air' at the time. Similarly, the word 'odious' (l. 2190) was just coming into use, and this is one of the very earliest recorded uses. The range of vocabulary extends from traditional earthy Old English words to the most up-to-date new ones.

One of the most interesting uses of words is the friar's mention of 'suffisaunce', already touched on above (p.18). It is one of Chaucer's favourite words, meaning 'satisfaction' or 'sufficiency', first recorded in English in *The Book of the Duchess* (ll. 702 and 1037) and recurring throughout Chaucer's works in *The Parliament* (l. 637), often in the *Consolation*, *Troilus* III, 1909, as already mentioned and elsewhere in *Troilus* and *The Canterbury Tales*. It expresses both a physical and a spiritual comfort and completeness; 'being satisfied'. The phrase in *The Summoner's Tale* 'hoomly' suffisaunce' is itself a paradox which satirises the friar, for 'homely' is a depreciatory word, implying something not very grand. Its juxtaposition with 'suffisaunce' and the phrase's reference to the delicacies which the friar has just so hypocritically ordered make an amusing set of inverted meanings and implicit criticism.

THE CLERK'S PROLOGUE AND TALE

Although there is no explicit connection in the texts, all the manuscripts agree in having *The Clerk's Prologue and Tale* follow *The Summoner's Tale*. There could hardly be a greater contrast (obviously deliberate), yet each is characteristically Chaucerian and it would be hard to say which is the better poem. In the fourteenth and fifteenth centuries the intensity of feeling in the story which the Clerk tells of Patient Griselda was very widely appreciated.

The Host regards the Clerk of Oxford just as many bustling businessmen regard scholars: the Clerk is quiet, so he must be thinking, and in consequence must be miserable.

> For Goddes sake, as beth of bettre cheere!
> It is no tyme for to studien heere.   [*think*
>
> IV, 7–8

He asks for a merry tale, of adventures, without rhetoric. The Clerk 'benignly' answers, and says he has learnt a tale from Petrarch

> whos rethorike sweete
> Enlumyned al Ytaille of poetrie.   [*enlightened*
>
> IV, 32–3

Such was Petrarch's fame in Europe at the end of the fourteenth century. He was the first really widely-known man of letters, whose influence was strong until the seventeenth century. The Clerk represents that side of Chaucer which knows and values rhetorical skill, while the Host represents that other down-to-earth literalistic side of Chaucer which mocks rhetoric. The Clerk refers with admiration which we need not take as ironical to Petrarch's rhetorical introduction to the story, but cuts through this to tell his own version in a beautifully austere style.

The original tale, though Chaucer did not know this, was the last story in the *Decameron*, finished 1353. Boccaccio had fashioned it out of traditional folktale elements. Both Boccaccio and Chaucer, with their rather similar backgrounds of court and city, work readily in the creative tradition of folktale (as Shakespeare, Scott and Dickens could later), while adding more individualistic and learned characteristics. The structure of this story moves away from the everyday domestic world of the popular comic tale into something nearer myth, and for setting it requires a wider range, from peasant's cottage to ducal palace.

The story caught the medieval European literary imagination and there are many versions in several languages for the next few centuries, including stage-plays, one in sixteenth-century England. Its dispersion in the first place was mainly due to Petrarch's late discovery of the tale and his translation of it into Latin prose, 1373–4. This is the version which Chaucer knew and worked from, though he relied heavily on one of the two French translations as well.

So far all versions had been in prose, but Chaucer returns to his favourite rhyme royal, which suits the stateliness and intensity of the story well, without impeding narrative progress. We hear how an unmarried Italian marquis, Walter, of Saluzzo (thirty miles south of Turin) is urged by his subjects to marry in order to secure the succession. They offer to choose him a wife from among the noblest and greatest in the land, but he insists on choosing his own bride. He selects the good and beautiful daughter, Griselda, of the poorest man in the village by his palace. The people are astonished, and no one more so than Griselda and her father. The ladies who must dress her for her wedding hate to handle her old clothes. They have to comb her tangled hair. She becomes a perfect wife, famous near and far for her beauty, goodness and judgement. Soon she bears a daughter.

Now comes a strange desire upon the marquis to test the 'sadness' of his wife. 'Sadness' is not sorrowfulness but stability, firmness, a kind of spiritual solidity, a refusal to complain. It is the key quality which the poem emphasises, and the word 'sad' is a key word, occurring proportionately far more often in this poem than in any other of Chaucer's works. The marquis reminds Griselda of her humble origins, says his nobles resent them, and recalls that she herself when married promised always to assent with patience to whatever he desired. She accepts all this without expressing any grief. The marquis is delighted at her response, but pretends to regard her with disfavour, and commissions a 'serjeant' to take away Griselda's baby. She kisses the child and is heartbroken, but gives her up with Christian resignation, committing her soul to Christ. The marquis ensures that his daughter is well looked after by his sister, Countess of Panico near Bologna, while Griselda in ignorance of this maintains her stoical goodness. Then she bears a son, whom Walter treats in the same way, Griselda also bearing this with 'sadness'. After twelve years more of marriage Walter tests Griselda again by saying that he has now decided to reject her entirely and that she must return to her father's house as humbly as she came. She replies with a noble dignity, far from unfeeling, but without personal resentment, and goes home, clad only in her smock, the people following her weeping. She is faithfully received by her old father, who had always been suspicious of the marriage, and who now covers her with her original old coat.

Then Walter decides to marry again, and tells Griselda to prepare the palace for the new bride, since no one else can manage things as well as she. Griselda prepares for the wedding. The bride and her brother arrive, and all the people now say that Walter is no fool, for the bride is so much younger and more beautiful, and will have finer children. 'O stormy peple, unsad and evere untrewe' (l. 995) comments the poet.

Griselda bears everything, including being asked to praise the new wife's beauty, which she does – 'only' she adds 'do not prick her with tormenting as you have done me. She could not endure adversity as can someone poorly brought up.' Then Walter says 'This is enough'; he embraces and praises Griselda, tells her that the new 'bride' is really her daughter, the brother her son. Griselda only then breaks down into expressive feeling of motherly love, swooning and holding her children so tight that her grip on them can hardly be loosened.

Thus hath this pitous day a blisful ende.

IV, 1121

The story is told, says the poet, still translating closely, not that wives should follow Griselda in humility, for that would be insupportable, but that everyone should be constant in adversity.

That is not quite the end of the affair for Chaucer, but we may pause at this stage to consider this exquisite poem. At the most general level it is a story of suffering redeemed by constancy, like that of Job. God tests Job as Walter tests Griselda. 'Whom God loveth he chastiseth'. These are ancient perceptions, however disagreeable, about both the arbitrariness of suffering and some divine element in its infliction, which causes it to bear fruit if resolutely endured. These always hard sayings are even more so today. This redemptive passive suffering was also seen very much as a feminine virtue (except in the Crucifixion). Gothic 'feminism' is strong in *The Clerk's Tale*. The story is one of the heroism and triumph of Griselda. It is she who overcomes Walter. Nothing, however painful, however irrationally inflicted, can destroy her constant integrity or make her cry out or complain.

It is not too much to recall in connection with this poem the stories of those who have triumphed by endurance in the irrational martyrdoms inflicted in concentration camps in the twentieth century. Suffering and, in a few, the heroic endurance of suffering, are always with us.

The key to the poem is found in the use of the word 'sad'. It is primarily, and paradoxically, an *anti-expressive* word, or rather, perhaps, an expressive word used to signify the absence of the expression of feeling. This is a little unusual in Chaucer, because much of his poetry is concerned with persons, notably Troilus, but also others, who give way to their feelings and express them violently. (Neither *sad*, *sadly* nor *sadness* occur even once in *Troilus and Criseyde*.) The story of Griselda is designed to recommend an heroic Christian stoicism which sacrifices self and personal feeling to steadfast commitment to principle. It is conceived in terms of personal relationships. In order to exalt the nobility of Griselda's commitment to her promise; in order to present a worthy opposite that shall show her virtue to be truly heroic; and in order to show the value of the virtue by its cost in suffering; the story of Griselda sets the virtue of commitment, not against vice, for that is too obvious, in her case too vulgar, but against another virtue, or virtuous feeling, among the best we can know, the love of a mother for her children. This confrontation of two virtues is what makes the exquisite pain of the story. This is why, fantastic as the story is in naturalistic terms, unconcerned with ordinary 'characterisation', it offers a complex model for a genuine life-situation of choice between two goods of different kinds. The story is not, in the end, an account of how an actual husband did, might, should or should not, treat his wife. It is not mimetic. It energises and explores a proposition about life, which is of great importance in the development of religion and civilisation, namely, that 'You should not give way to your feelings'. The story of *Sir Gawain and the Green Knight* makes the same point. That many modern people believe the opposite, or that the story of Griselda is an extreme and one-sided example, of which by his realistic and emotive telling Chaucer increases the tension, need not blind us to its nature or truth. The story is conceived not so much naturalistically as anti-naturalistically. This paradox must surely be what attracted Chaucer to the story. That the subject concerns the *suppression* of natural feelings in the name of a higher obligation makes the story of Griselda, which looks so much like that of Constance, really quite different, for in the story of Constance her natural feelings, especially those of motherhood, are always given free rein. Constance has plenty of sorrow in her life, but to use our present narrow loophole of the word *sad* for surveying this aspect of Chaucer's poetic world, we find that *sad* and *sadness* never occur in Chaucer's *Man of Law's Tale* of Constance, and *sadly* only once, referring to the foolish messenger's heavy drinking (*CT* II, 743). Constance is never *sad*, while Griselda is always so.

The general meaning of the word in *The Clerk's Tale* may be further illustrated by comparing its use in the poem with the sources Chaucer is known to have used. When the fell serjeant comes to take away Griselda's baby daughter, apparently with the intention of murdering the child, the Latin version by Petrarch, the French translation of the Latin, and Chaucer's own version, which relies on both French and Latin, all emphasise that Griselda 'neither weep ne syked' (l. 545). She took and kissed the child, as Petrarch writes, *tranquilla fronte*, which is translated by the French as *de plain front*, and rendered by Chaucer as

> With ful sad face
>
> IV, 552

It is very difficult for a reader of modern English to avoid giving *sad* here the modern sense of 'sorrowful'. But the evidence of the sources, and of the general use of the word *sad* in English in Chaucer's time, all make a clear case for a meaning like 'calm'.

Chaucer's uses of the word *sad* do not depend on any specific word in his source. They are insertions or glosses. Thus when Walter first speaks to Griselda, Chaucer adds the significant biblical allusion to the 'oxes stalle' (l. 291) and the detail that Griselda fell to her knees

> And with sad contenance kneleth stille.
>
> IV.293

Her endurance *so sad stidefast* (l. 564) is part of a generally pathetic addition of Chaucer's own to the scene with the serjeant, and that she continued

> evere in oon ylike sad and kynde   [*uniformly*
>
> IV, 602

is a further gloss on the statement in Latin, French and English, that she never changed. Again, when in all three versions Walter is astonished at Griselda's patience and, but that he knew her love, might have suspected her of hardness of heart or downright cruelty, Chaucer alone adds

> That she hadde suffred this with sad visage.
>
> IV, 693

Each of these last two examples comes at the end of a stanza, where Chaucer is forced as it were to pad out his text so as to give himself room in dealing with the briefer prose of his sources, and takes the opportunity to meet a possible criticism that Griselda may be unfeeling, and to give extra emphasis to the tone and the lesson of stoicism. Here the meaning must be 'calm'. There would be little point in asserting that she endured her afflictions with a face 'sad' in the modern sense. It would sound like a feeble apology, not the bold approving assertion it must be. A failure to realise Chaucer's meaning is the cause of criticism that condemns Griselda or the poem. Chaucer emphasises that she does feel strongly, when Griselda is apparently to be banished in favour of a new wife. She was *tristis* (sorrowful) says Petrarch, and the French says nothing, while Chaucer says *hire herte was ful wo* (l. 753).

But she is unshaken, unchanged, which is further emphasised when Walter sees her *constanciam, la constance et grant pacience*, translated by Chaucer in an unusual image as being

> ay sad and constant as a wal.
>
> IV.1047

She could not be described as always 'sorrowful' as a wall. Chaucer's approval of the quality of being *sad*, his concept of it as stability, constance, calmness, sound judgement, is further emphasised by his independent use of the phrase *sadde folk* (l. 1002), in a passage not based on the sources, to describe those who were not like the *stormy people*, who are, very significantly,

> unsad and evere untrewe.
>
> IV.995

These words occur in an authorial and authoritative interjection which is not to be shrugged off as merely the words of a faceless 'Narrator'. *Sadde* here means 'sound, sensible, stable, unmoved by fickle feeling'.

The word 'sad' is associated for Chaucer with a number of other words, especially 'true' and 'wise', but also 'glad', 'good', 'kind', 'simple', stable' which establish its general aura of wisdom, stability, truth, goodness and even resolute cheerfulness. In Chaucer's work the association with the modern meaning 'sorrowful' is very slight.

Although he translates the story closely, Chaucer thus intensifies in certain respects its spirit. He adds clear religious overtones. He makes additions which cause the story to dig deeper into our feelings by its greater realism and humanity. Griselda is more vividly realised both as a peasant girl looking after sheep and as a sorrowful mother. Walter's relationships with his people are more convincing, the negotiations for his marriage (which was the kind of diplomatic business which Chaucer knew well) are fuller and correspond with actuality. He thus screws the tension up even higher. As poet and Expositor he occasionally gives vent to feeling himself. He says there was little need to test Griselda.

> But as for me, I seye that yvele it sit   [*it ill suits*
> To assaye a wyf, whan that it is no nede   [*test*
> And putten hire in angwyssh and in drede.
>
> IV, 460–3

The comment on the 'stormy people' already mentioned (l. 995) is another example. Fortunately even Chaucer manages to restrain his flippancy in what are for him these rare intrusions.

But it was a strain. Chaucer never withdrew his tender compassion for the sufferings of true and gentle women. But the story imposed a tension on belief, and once finished, it was as if a bent bow was released. The story is immediately followed by an 'envoy' in which Chaucer's natural scepticism, his sense of proportion, his love of anti-feminist satire, all withheld during the tale, are suddenly released, to send a deadly shaft of laughter among the emotions he has raised.

> O noble wyves, ful of heigh prudence,
> Lat noon humylitee *youre* tonge naille,
> Ne lat no clerk have cause or diligence
> To write of *yow* a storie of swich mervaille
> As of Grisildis pacient and kynde,
> Lest Chichevache yow swelwe in hire entraille!   [*swallow*
>
> IV, 1183–8

(Chichevache means 'lean cow', lean because she fed only on patient wives.) In the thirty-six lines of this satirical envoy, which moves as smoothly and easily as any of his poetry, there are only three rhymes. It is an astonishing piece of metrical virtuosity.

The manuscripts all head this piece as 'Lenvoy de Chaucer', and we may assume that Chaucer himself wrote that heading. It begins in his most characteristic 'sententious', in this case aphoristic, vein.

> Grisilde is deed, and eek hire pacience
>
> IV, 1177

and as noted, continues in a typically old-fashioned, popular, teasing, anti-feminist masculine manner, yet not unsympathetically, either. This is not the quiet, thoughtful Clerk speaking, nor a stupid Narrator; it is the poet himself, as the text tells us. Yet the envoy is picked up by the succeeding remarks made by the Merchant and is clearly meant to be part of the tale. In a way it is comparable, even though comic, not serious, in its change of perspective and mood, with the ending of *Troilus*, though more extreme, less grounded in the earlier text. It shows how easily Chaucer could move between the levels of narration. He was not trying to create a consistently naturalistic illusion. He was a brilliantly versatile story-teller ready to exploit any device to stimulate the reader, to change pace, to alter the perspective, amuse, intrigue, delight his audience, and always ready, like all good story-tellers, to leave a core of enigma at the heart of narrative which continues to draw attention.

THE MERCHANT'S PROLOGUE AND TALE

The Envoy jestingly advises wives to make their husbands miserable. The Merchant, quite unexpectedly, takes this up, complaining of the cruelty of his own wife, to whom he has been married only two months. Perhaps this is some contemporary joke about Gilbert Maghfeld (above, p.174), or maybe it is a device to motivate a somewhat anti-feminist tale, though as usual the story cuts both ways.

For some reason this tale, like the Clerk's, is set in Lombardy in Italy (while the Summoner's and perhaps the Friar's are set in the North of England, and the Pardoner's and *Sir Thopas* are set in Flanders.) *The Merchant's Tale* could hardly be more different from *The Clerk's Tale*, and is a deliberate contrast to show an erring wife. The central episode is again one of adult marital domestic comedy with a fantastic core of the kind familiar in the international popular comic tale, enriched by learning of many kinds, and a strongly ironic humour not likely to appeal to the young. The story itself begins and continues without any sense of the Merchant himself telling it.

An old and lecherous knight called January decides at last to marry. The poet with heavy irony puts into January's mouth praise of young wives for old men, and either continues January's speech, or

221

speaks in his own poetic person (and the uncertainty shows how unimportant is the distinction) with general ironic praise for the superiority of marriage over bachelordom;

> For who kan be so buxom as a wyf?   [*obedient*
>
> IV, 1287

A string of not quite relevant examples follows. This is good traditional ironic humour on an ancient theme. January boasts of his youthful feelings – he is only white about the head, and that is but blossom on a green tree. His brother Placebo (Latin for 'I will please'), a flatterer who has been a 'court-man all his life' and who never disagreed with the great lords he has accompanied, confirms all January's opinions. Another brother, Justinus, whose name suggests 'justice', and who is presented as a teller of disagreeable truths, gives the traditional advice to a man who asks if he should marry – 'Don't'. January insists, and only worries that since one is unlikely to be happy both in the present world and the future life, wedded bliss may deprive him of Heaven. Justinus tartly replies that he should not despair; perhaps his wife will be his Purgatory. Remember, says Justinus, the Wife of Bath (who had boasted of being the purgatory of her fourth husband). There is here another amusing confusion of narrative levels, with a character *inside* the story referring to one who is outside that story.

January marries a maiden of tender age and 'small degree', that is, of low rank – not quite a lady. The wedding is splendid, and described with Chaucerian humour and verve, mingling Classical and Biblical allusion,

> And Venus laugheth upon every wight . . .
> And with hire fyrbrond in hire hand aboute
> Daunceth biforn the bride and al the route.   [*crowd*
>
> IV, 1723...8

It is an extraordinary image almost of mythic power. Yet it consorts with sarcastic remarks about tender youth marrying stooping age.

The festivities finish and all rejoice save January's young squire Damyan

> So soore hath Venus hurt hym with hire brond,   [*torch*
> As that she bar it daunsynge in hire hond.
>
> IV,1777–8

The poet, not quite seriously, as Expositor, addresses the perilous fire, the familiar foe, the servant traitor, that January is nourishing, to wit, his squire Damyan in love with his wife.

January and May go to bed. He fondles her and kisses her with his bristly chin. Chaucer creates an extraordinary tactile image of the stiff bristly old face nuzzling the young and tender one. So January labours till day, and then sits upright and sings full loud and clear, all full of fun, a comically disgusting sight.

> The slakke skyn about his nekke shaketh
> Whil that he sang, so chaunteth he and cracketh   [trills
> But God woot what that May thoughte in hir herte,
> When she hym saugh up sittynge in his sherte,
> In his nyght-cappe, and with his nekke lene;
> She preyseth nat his pleyyng worth a bene.   [bean

IV, 1849–54

The apparently impartial plain description of domestic reality, by its selection of detail, combines the visible facts with the responses of January, May, poet and reader and thus forwards the story by implying motive. Although the poet refrains from comment, even claiming ignorance of May's mind, he forms our opinions and expectations. The poet as so often takes up an apparently objective attitude to his story which is actually not neutral.

Meanwhile, Damyan sickens. May in womanly kindness visits his sick-bed with her women (some of the action in this poem being a remote parallel to that in *Troilus and Criseyde*) and he secretly slips her a note, which when she has secretly read she tears up and puts down the privy. These domestic details effectively remove us from the realm of high romance. No such account is given of the disposal of Troilus's letters. Yet we need not think the tale bitter or harsh because of them. It works on the down-to-earth everyday domestic level of the adult comic tale, and though not glamourised shows no deep revulsion.

May is gentle and has pity, like Criseyde and all the best Chaucerian heroines. She writes a nice letter back, tucks it under Damyan's pillow, and secretly squeezes his hand. This is enough to cure his sickness.

January has made a walled garden so private and beautiful that Pluto the king of Fairy Land and his queen Proserpina 'and al hire fayerye' often visit it, and dance about the well-spring in it. Sometimes January makes love to May there.

But, says the poet in a familiar phrase, 'worldly joy cannot last for ever', and accuses Fortune with mock seriousness on January's behalf; for January suddenly becomes blind. He is also jealous. May brings it about that Damyan gets into the garden where alone the jealous January feels sure of May. One day, in June, January lovingly addresses May in words that are a witty parody (by the poet, not by January) of the Song of Songs, and brings May into the garden. She makes a hypocritically tearful declaration of her love for him, and as she does so signals to Damyan to get up a tree, as she had forewarned him in a letter. Meanwhile the Classical god and goddess Pluto and

223

Proserpina enter and wrangle over the nature of women. May implies that she is pregnant and must indulge her fancy for green pears. 'Alas', says January 'that I am blind and cannot help'. May is ready to climb on his back and up the tree where Damyan awaits – and there, says the poet, as he is a rude man, and cannot glose, he must say pretty plainly what happens.

When Pluto sees the wrong which May is doing January he miraculously restores his sight, and when January sees what the poet says may not be courteously expressed (though he does express it a few lines later) he sets up a great roaring. May is not one whit put out. Proserpina has in fact promised Pluto that she shall have an answer. May says she has been instructed that in order to restore January's sight she must struggle with a man in a tree. January has the impression that more than struggling has taken place but is assured that he only thinks so because the recovery of perfect sight cannot be immediate, and so he did not see quite straight. So January finishes up happy. We hear nothing of Damyan, nor how May feels. The focus is on an absurd sequence of improper events, not on characters, and the poet (hardly the Merchant) concludes, with in a sense even greater impropriety

> God blesse us and his mooder Seinte Marie.
>
> IV, 2418

To end such a story so piously seems true Gothic and Chaucerian indecorum, giving a relish of worldly comedy, rather than blasphemy. The nucleus of the story is the traditional proposition spoken by Pandarus: 'Women ben wise in short avysement' (*Troilus* IV, 936). A woman always has an answer.

The central episode called 'the Pear-Tree Episode' is well-known and has many variants. Its origin is probably ultimately in the East, but the twelfth-century learned Latin 'comedy' called *Lydia* gave it impetus in Europe. In some versions God and St Peter discuss the characters' actions. St Peter complains, and God says, in effect, 'You'll see how, if I restore his sight, she'll get out of it'. Chaucer articulates the story much better, connecting the delightfully humanised Pluto and Proserpina much closer to the action, making the whole story a stronger chain of cause and effect. The magical quality of the private garden is also Chaucer's invention, as well as the idea of adding the preliminary discussion of the charms of marriage, even though the material of that is quite traditional. To be sorry either for May at the beginning or January at the end, or Damyan at all, is to sentimentalise a coolly derisive but not embittered story – though the story is reasonably attributed to an embittered pilgrim. In *The General Prologue* we were given licence not to sympathise too greatly with the Merchant. The narrative is spoken by the poet, the general Chaucerian Expositor, and is beautifully adorned with a great variety of interesting description.

THE SQUIRE'S TALE

Some change is needed and with little introductory ado the Squire tells his tale. He is the obvious person to tell a young man's tale of high and sweet romance which will contrast with *The Merchant's Tale*. The metre is the five-stress couplet, and this and the control of the verse, the grasp of courtly situations, and the self-characterisation of the poet all show that it is a work of Chaucer's maturity. His failure to finish also demonstrates that he has grown beyond an interest in youthful love, which is not surprising when we consider the predominance in *The Canterbury Tales* of tales of the adult dilemmas, comedies and tragedies, of married life.

The Squire's Tale is set in the romantic land of Tartary, on the edges of the known world, beyond Prussia. The noble king, Cambyuskan, holds a courtly feast on his birthday in March, and a strange knight comes with a horse of brass, a magic mirror, a gold ring, and a naked sword. All have magic properties and arouse great wonder, though in the end horse and sword are dismissed by the poet somewhat peremptorily.

The story turns to the king's daughter Canacee, to whom has been given mirror and ring. She is up early, on a beautiful morning, and the ring allows her to understand what the birds are saying. She hears the piteous story of a female falcon, betrayed in love. It has been a theme dear to Chaucer as we have seen, and it is told with some vigour. After the complaint the poet promises to continue the tale to tell how the falcon won her love back, and how he will recount adventures and battles – very untypical Chaucerian subjects – but the story immediately fades out unfinished. Chaucer's mature imagination does not sustain it. The account of the falcon's lost love is pale and thin after the superb introductory descriptions of how the wonderful horse of brass came to the court, of the behaviour of the people, and of the court festivities. Perhaps the nearest we shall ever get to a full description of a great fourteenth-century festival at court is the description here of people high and low buzzing around the new wonders, the music, the orderly bustle of the feast, the wine, the form of dances, the secret interchange of looks, even to the hangover on the following morning. The description of Canacee is both realistic and charming. She has not revelled the night away.

225

> She was ful mesurable, as wommen be,
>
> V, 362

and she rises fresh at dawn

> As rody and bright as dooth the yonge sonne.   [*red-cheeked*
>
> V, 385

When she sees the misery of the falcon (with whom she can converse because of the virtue of the magic ring) she asks her:

> Is this for sorwe of deeth or los of love?
> For, as I trowe, thise been causes two
> That causen moost a gentil herte wo;
> Of oother harm it nedeth nat to speke.
>
> V, 450–3

Such a comment harks back to the dilemmas presented by Machaut.

The poem shows Chaucer's mature awareness of and interest in the conduct of the story, and possibly an anxiety that this one is not quite coming off. He comments on how important it is to get to the 'knot' of a story, by which he probably means what we should call the 'point', and urges himself to get on with it (ll. 401–8). He also uses the favourite rhetorical device of describing by refusing to describe and says of the courtly celebration

> Heere is the revel and the jolitee
> That is nat able a dul man to devyse.   [*describe*
> He moste han knowen love and his servyse
> And been a feestlych man as fressh as May,   [*festive*
> That sholde yow devysyen swich array.
>
> V, 278–82

But the Squire is *just* such a man, so described, even with the reference to May, in *The General Prologue*, who the poet says he would have to be to recount revel and jollity. The story-telling attitude here clearly dramatises the teller as the dull man ignorant of love, the *persona* that Chaucer himself as poet loves to assume, and whom the Squire is not. The passage is an example of Chaucer's usual 'ignorance formula', nothing to do with the Squire as a character but part of the poet's normal battery of narrative devices as Expositor.

A most interesting possibility is that an astronomical structure underlies this curious poem. There is no doubt that such a structure underlies *The Complaint of Mars*, as we have seen, for it is made obvious. Dr J.D. North has argued that such astronomical allegories underlie several other poems. He bases the argument on a number of mysteriously precise astronomical references that occur in many poems – for example, in *The Merchant's Tale* and in *The Franklin's Tale*. That these must have had significance for Chaucer, is hardly to be disputed. They relate to Chaucer's general scientific interests. In general they are likely to be additional enrichments rather than structural determinants – even if we could understand what structures they might represent. The problem is highly technical, but it does seem as if Chaucer in *The Squire's Tale* took the name of Cambyuskan's queen, Elpheta, from the name of a star, and that Cambyuskan has some relation to Mars. Chaucer may have ingeniously dabbled in some of these correspondences, rather in the spirit of composing a crossword puzzle, and then found it got too complicated, or at any rate had carried it as far as he cared to. How many people would have appreciated his ingenuity?

THE FRANKLIN'S PROLOGUE AND TALE

It may be that Chaucer, not wishing to finish *The Squire's Tale* began to think he would have another character cut it short, as the Knight had *The Monk's Tale* and the Host *Sir Thopas*. At any rate, the manuscripts follow the unfinished *Squire's Tale* immediately with effusive praise from the Franklin 'considering thy youth', which perhaps is meant to stifle any continuation. The Franklin wishes his own son were a man of such judgement as the Squire, and there seems no irony here.

>   Fy on possessioun
> But if a man be vertuous withal.

V, 686–7

He wishes his son could learn 'gentillesse'. Perhaps the Franklin is presented as a bit of an old buffer. At any rate the Host rudely replies 'Straw for youre gentillesse', and abruptly calls for a tale. The Franklin responds peaceably, first disclaiming in a rather rhetorical manner any knowledge of rhetoric. He says he will tell a 'Breton lay', though it is little like the handful of earlier Middle English poems that may be claimed to be such. The action is however set in Brittany. The story is about *trouthe* and *gentillesse* and presumably the Franklin's earlier remarks about *gentillesse* and his son were given to account for the fact that it is he to whom the tale is attributed, and to link it with *The Squire's Tale*. Chaucer places the tale here for further variety. It is about love, as *The Squire's Tale* was meant to be, but about love, and the problems of love, in marriage, which at this stage of his life Chaucer found much more interesting than the sorrowful moo-ings of calf-love. He had already told several of the normal popular tales about love in marriage, which are all comic, and which culminate in *The Merchant's Tale*. After this it is time for sweetness and light,

227

without evading the threats to happiness that life, and particularly love, offer. Hence *The Franklin's Tale*, one of Chaucer's most original poems, not comedy, not exactly romance, certainly not satire, nor irony, yet with elements of all these, and unashamedly a celebration of *trouthe* and *gentillesse*.

In Armorica, now called Brittany, we are told, a knight called Arveragus fell in love with a lady, Dorigen, and served and suffered long. At last she, for his worthiness, and especially for his meek obedience, took pity on him and agreed to take him for her husband and her lord (of such lordship as men have over their wives). Apart from the touch of mature flippancy in the last remark this is the normal Chaucerian ideal of love leading to marriage, briefly dealt with in some dozen lines. In order to achieve full happiness Arveragus agrees that even as husband he will obey Dorigen except that in public, for honour's sake, he takes the 'name' of sovereignty. This is the first premise of the tale. The second premise is Dorigen's corresponding promise always to be humble and true to him. We begin where *The Wife of Bath's Tale* ends. The third, immediately arising out of the proposition of mutuality just expressed,

> That freendes everych oother moot obeye   [*must*
>
> V, 762

is that

> Love wol nat been constreyned by maistrye.   [*constrained by force*
>
> V, 764

So much for mastery, even sovereignty. The free spirit of love, which desires liberty, not to be a thrall, demands also patience, a high virtue, which conquers where rigour fails (as Griselda may be thought to illustrate). 'Lerneth to suffre' (l. 777), that is, to be patient – for like it or not, everybody in this world misbehaves at some time, for some reason, and every wrong that is received cannot be avenged. This sensible, sententious passage is the foundation stone of the story, and can only be taken as said by the poet. It is indeed part of the foundations of the whole of Chaucer's thought. Other characters and stories illustrate it. Not only Griselda overcomes by patient endurance: so does Palamon. Even Criseyde expresses this traditional pacifist wisdom: 'Men seyn, "the suffrant overcomith", parde' (*Troilus* IV, 1584).

Arveragus and Dorigen are happy, but the pursuit of honour requires Arveragus to go and dwell in England a year or two. He writes regularly to Dorigen, but she is sad and in particular worries about the threat of the rocks on the coast to the safety of the ship in which Arveragus will eventually return. In a long speech she questions the wisdom of God in creating something so evidently evil and irrational.

> Eterne God, that thurgh thy purveiaunce   [*providence*
> Ledest the world by certein governaunce,
> In ydel, as men seyn, ye no thyng make.   [*in vain*
> But, Lord, thise grisly feendly rokkes blake   [*fiendish*
> That semen rather a foul confusion
> Of werk than any fair creacion
> Of swich a parfit wys God and a stable,
> Why han ye wroght this werk unresonable?

V, 865–72

Her friends try to cheer her up, and on 6 May bring her into a beautiful garden, where all sing and dance save the melancholy Dorigen, and here when she is on her own a young squire, Aurelius, who has long loved her, expresses his feelings and asks for her mercy, or he will die. Dorigen is not in the least tempted to be untrue; nor is she shocked, and in order to make her refusal less harsh, though not less absolute, says 'in play' that she will be his love if he removes the rocks which she feels endanger her husband's life. 'It is impossible', he says, and he must die. He goes home distraught and since these are pre-Christian times prays to the gods, then falls sick. Arveragus returns safely and he and Dorigen resume their happy life. Meanwhile Aurelius's brother remembers his studies at the university of Orleans, and they both go there where they meet as by magic a clerk who can perform magic deeds, and who will remove the rocks on the coast for a thousand pounds. All this is done, with much scientific comment from the poet about tides and astronomy, with the result that the magician produces, not the fact, but the illusion, to all people, for a week or two, that the rocks have disappeared.

Aurelius, with fearful heart and humble expression then courteously recalls to Dorigen how she plighted her 'trouthe' in the garden, and announces that he has fulfilled the condition. Dorigen is horrified. She goes home in fear and sorrow, and weeps and wails a day or two. She then expresses her sorrows in a long 'complaint' against Fortune, formally introduced. She gives a long list of ladies who have committed suicide rather than lose their virtue.

> Why sholde I thanne to dye been in drede?

V, 1386

And thus she laments, always intending to die rather than give herself to Aurelius. But she cannot bring herself to it. Arveragus, who has briefly been away, returns and asks the cause of her sorrow, which she immediately confesses. This husband, with cheerful face, says the poet,

> Answerde and seyde as I shal yow devyse.   [*tell*
>
> V, 1468

She must keep her promise, for

> 'Trouthe is the hyeste thyng that man may kepe'
> – But with that word he brast anon to wepe.   [*he immediately burst
>   out crying*
>
> V, 1479–80

After this agony Dorigen obeys, 'as if she were half mad' with sorrow, so that Aurelius has so much compassion on them both that he cannot bring himself to commit

> so heigh a cherlyssh wrecchednesse
> Agayns franchise and alle gentilesse.   [*generosity*; *nobility*
>
> V, 1523–4

She thanks him on her bare knees. Aurelius curses the day he was born, hard put to it to pay his debt for which he has had no gratification. But he too vows to keep his 'trouthe', and asks the clerk of Orleans time to pay off his debt in full. The philosopher himself will not be outdone in *gentillesse* by knight and squire, and releases him from his debt. The tale ends with the question, who was the most generous?

It is as usual a traditional tale with many folk-tale elements, adorned with considerable though not burdensome scientific knowledge about tides, and deepened by philosophical questioning. The central narrative episode is a version of what folklorists call the Rash Promise – examples are stories such as that of Jephtha (*Judges* XI), or, with a happy ending that of Rumpelstiltskin. Chaucer probably carved the essential elements of this story out of a much longer one in Italian prose, by Boccaccio, in his series on 'questions of love' called *Il Filocolo*, though there is another version of the same story in the *Decameron*. But Chaucer made considerable changes.

Stories of this kind do not rely on plausible motivation or consistent illusion, as we have seen already. The characters are clear-cut types with recognisable human feelings, but the power of the story lies in its inner structure, based on, but not 'imitating', real-life situations, and usually concerned with personal relationships and the values which govern behaviour. The obvious examples are fairytales and Biblical parables, which often contain implausible elements, combined with surface realism, in order to make important points.

What is the point of *The Franklin's Tale*? Obviously, at the level of conscious values, to teach the importance of love, freedom, patience, generosity, *trouthe*. But it would not do this if the inner structure were not powerful. It is built on paradoxes, composed of opposite but complementary compulsions which both support and oppose each other, and in so doing create interest and illustrate the nature of life. Honour, *trouthe*, love, safety are part of each other, yet are also in conflict.

The structure of *The Franklin's Tale* rests on Dorigen's love for her husband, her consequent fears for his safety from the rocks in the sea, and her paradoxical and good-natured jest to Aurelius that if he can remove the threat to her husband she will give herself to Aurelius. The proposition is self-contradictory, and the impossibility of removing the rocks guarantees the impossibility of her loving Aurelius. That is why Dorigen allows herself to make the joke, to soften her refusal. (Unlike Criseyde she *can* say no, but sentimental-ises it a little.) She knows the true hardness of the rocks and of the world. When Aurelius produces an *illusion* that the rocks have disappeared he reveals an unsuspected relationship between the rocks, and love, and faith. The structure of events shows that the physical materiality of the world, as represented by the rocks, may be harsh, but if you deny it you lose the spiritual values of love and faith. You cannot have advantages without disadvantages, or without risk. The rocks do not *symbolise* honour; that is either too materialistic a view or not materialistic enough. They represent *rocks* – harsh physical materiality. They also represent the price you have to pay for honour: physical danger for the husband, physical chastity for the wife.

The story goes further, when, none of them knowing that the rocks are covered only by magical illusion, Dorigen's husband Arveragus says she ought to keep her word and give herself to the squire Aurelius. Arveragus sacrifices his own feeling of his own honour, as reputation, to its deeper aspect as *trouthe*, which is loyalty, keeping one's promises, integrity, an inner value. There is no extravagance of sacrifice. Arveragus would not have Dorigen's unfaithfulness known, but the nature of unfaithfulness is the opposite of solitary. Dorigen's *trouthe* to her husband conflicts with her *trouthe* to her own plighted word. The survival of society depends on individuals keeping their promises, but which of two conflicting promises should be kept? Chaucer reveals the ambivalence of deep values, or that values good in themselves may be incompatible with each other – a good Gothic point illustrated again in *The Clerk's Tale* and in *Troilus*. *The Franklin's Tale* also includes propositions about appearance and reality. When the sea apparently covers the rocks, appearance takes over from reality. Physical reality is harsh and dangerous, but it is better not to conceal it from oneself, or worse, spiritual, dangers ensue; and then moral integrity, represented by Dorigen's faithful-ness as a wife, may be shipwrecked. Reality is better than illusion, even when painful.

The happy ending reflects the 'moral optimism' of Chaucer, of

Gothic feeling, of the Romance *genre*, and of Christianity; of the faith (in the Boethian language of *Truth, Balade de Bon Conseyle*), that 'trouthe thee shal delivere'. The adherence of Arveragus and Dorigen to *trouthe* calls forth in the others the *gentillesse* which we are told in *The Wife of Bath's Tale* derives from Christ, the type of self-sacrificing love.

Another major point in the story is the *connectedness* of all experience, whereby Chaucer reveals his traditional, archaic feeling for the unity of experience, as against the fragmentation of experience which is characteristically modern. In *The Franklin's Tale* we see that the moral laws governing behaviour have some connection with the physical laws governing matter. Disturb one and you disturb the other. Dorigen attempts to change the environment irresponsibly. She does it in jest, so the outcome is only a fantasy, and is redeemed. The modern world does indeed change the environment on a scale quite as large as Dorigen envisages, and ecologists now begin to warn us of the consequential but unforeseen and dangerous effects. Magic is the technology of folktale. Chaucer puts into Dorigen's mouth a very modernistic accusation of God for allowing all the suffering, danger and evil in the world. In modern thought the recognition of evil often leads to the denial of the existence of God, the denial therefore of value and purpose in the universe independent of mankind's preferences. Of course, if objective value is denied, evil also cannot exist – it is just another irrational purposeless accident for which nothing and nobody can be blamed. Good and evil are themselves inextricably linked. One cannot exist without the other. The story structure of *The Franklin's Tale*, like that of *The Clerk's Tale*, illustrates this traditional notion. It is notable that the danger from the rocks, and Dorigen's questioning, are entirely original with Chaucer. He articulates modern feelings and insights. The answer to all this questioning is the assertion, and exercise, of the archaic complex of moral qualities evoked at the beginning of the tale. In these matters Chaucer carries further, and deepens, the concepts of honour already examined in connection with Criseyde (above, p. 133). *Trouthe* meaning faithfulness, integrity, promise-keeping, is the part of honour which takes its origin from inner integrity, not outward social reference. The balance between the inward and the outward pulls of honour makes it a potentially ambivalent quality, with an element of inherent self-contradiction. When the self-contradiction becomes too strong, for Chaucer the inner pull, personal integrity, *trouthe*, should prevail.

One of the strangest things of many strange things in modern Chaucer criticism is that this penetrating and generous-spirited tale has been read as totally ironical, a cynical send-up of a silly old Franklin who is obsessed by social climbing. Such a reading is produced by applying novelistic assumptions to traditional literature, and by adopting anachronistic attitudes that disregard or are ignorant of the historical nature and value attributed to chastity, honour, bravery, etc. The cynical reading also bases itself on Dorigen's long formal complaint, which is regarded as so long, and in the end so irrelevant to her situation, as to be self-evidently silly and therefore a mockery of Dorigen. This judgement itself assumes that Chaucer never nods. It is indeed the case that Dorigen's complaint to some extent gets out of Chaucer's control. It is on a subject he was always inclined to dwell on. A list is always attractive to him. But there is no signal whatever that Chaucer *intends* Dorigen to be made to look ridiculous: at worst there is a minor artistic failure.

The general interest of this extraordinary and original, yet traditional tale is so great that there is no space here to comment on its wealth of knowledge and the felicity of diction.

The Franklin's Tale concludes a long and fascinatingly varied but connected series that can reasonably be held to begin with *The Wife of Bath's Prologue*, and which, though it also contains *The Friar's Tale*, *The Summoner's Tale* and *The Squire's Tale* is sometimes called The Marriage Group, and is believed to conduct a kind of debate about marriage. It might as well be called the '*Trouthe* and *Gentillesse*' group. Certain themes do recur, and three out of the seven tales do indeed deal with married people, with *The Wife of Bath's Tale* in addition commenting on sovereignty in marriage. There is good evidence that Chaucer in his maturity is interested in marriage as little 'high' literature has been till the twentieth century, though the international medieval comic tale deals often with the subject and reflects Chaucer's own interest. But to refer to a 'Marriage Group' or 'Marriage Debate' is to impose a desire for systematic thought and exposition on Chaucer which the whole of *The Canterbury Tales*, from *The General Prologue* onwards, shows him avoiding. Chaucer, more influenced by systematic scientific thinking than any other major English poet, seems specifically to reject systematisation of human relationships and moral concepts. His modernity is profound and exceptional, but partial.

THE SECOND NUN'S PROLOGUE AND TALE

The Second Nun's Prologue begins the Fragment numbered eight, and is not connected in the text with any preceding tale. It has already been briefly discussed (above, p.78). *The Prologue* refers to the writer as 'unworthy son of Eve' (1. 62) and it and *The Second Nun's Tale* are written in rhyme royal.

The Life of Saint Cecile is referred to in the *Prologue* to *The*

Legend of Good Women and must therefore have been composed before *The Canterbury Tales* period proper, and inserted without revision. The tale is a devout saint's life, which betrays no sign of impatience in the composition, but little liveliness either. It was probably translated from a single Latin text, and Chaucer asks the reader to

> Foryeve me that I do no diligence
> This ilke storie subtilly to endite.
>
> VIII, 79–80

It is indeed not subtly composed, whether for reasons of piety (but then, why apologise?) or as some kind of penance, since in the preceding stanza Chaucer refers, in what are admittedly traditional phrases, to his own sinfulness. The reference in the *Retractation* at the end of *The Canterbury Tales* to his writing of the lives of saints as being to his credit makes one suspect that he wrote this poem for the good of his soul. So we must forgive the lack of artistry and pass on.

THE CANON'S YEOMAN'S PROLOGUE AND TALE

The Canon's Yeoman's Prologue is certainly late, mature work, and as certainly linked to *The Second Nun's Tale*. It was composed so late that though there can be no doubt of its authenticity on grounds of sheer style, manner and greatness, it did not even get into all the manuscripts. The Canon and his Yeoman are described as coming up on horses sweaty with the haste they have made to join the pilgrims. They are clearly a happy afterthought of Chaucer's. The *Prologue and Tale* seem to be motivated partly by his interest in alchemy, partly by his strong suspicion that it was bogus, partly by the fascination of tricky or downright dishonest practices and persons. That led to thinking about those who had been deceived, and fed his lately discovered vein of self-revelatory speeches or soliloquies. Hence the Canon's Yeoman's long and passionate outburst. The whole fitted into his mature interest in the world and people around him, and in the scientific and philosophical problems which lie beneath the surface.

The Canon's Yeoman's Prologue makes a fascinating little drama on its own. First we see the sweaty horses, and the curious canon who had ridden so fast, apparently for no more than the pleasure of the pilgrims' company.

He hadde ay priked lik as he were wood   [*spurred*; *mad*
A clote-leef he hadde under his hood   [*burdock-leaf*
For swoot, and for to keep his head from heete.   [*sweat*
But it was joye for to seen hym swete!

VIII, 576–9

That last line is pure Chaucer, pure pleasure in essential animated life of whatever kind, such as leads him elsewhere to write of a 'manly man', 'a wommanliche wyf', a 'horsly hors'; and to praise the pilgrim Yeoman for dressing his tackle 'yeomanly'. The Canon's Yeoman, in answer to the Host's questioning at first praises the Canon's 'heigh discrecioun', his judgement, and says the Canon if he wished could turn the very ground to silver or gold. He is, in other words, an alchemist. Why then, asks the Host, is he so shabby and dirty, 'so sluttish'? At this the Canon's Yeoman breaks into quite another vein. Of the Canon he says he is too clever by half; they live in squalor, and his own face is strangely discoloured because of his work at the alchemical furnace, where the Canon's experiments are false and always fail. The Canon comes up on this conversation and tells his Yeoman to be silent, but the latter now has the bit between his teeth. The Canon flees away for sorrow and shame, while the Canon's Yeoman begins his tale by disburdening his heart of all the lost labour and deceit of 'that slidyng science', of which Chaucer shows considerable knowledge, satirically deployed. Chaucer must have studied it, though there is no reason to suppose that he had himself ever been seduced by it. The Canon's Yeoman is in somewhat different case. He is bitterly disillusioned about alchemy.

Whoso that listeth outen his folie,   [*wishes to show*
Lat hym come forth and lerne multiplie.   [*practise alchemy*

VIII, 834–5

He describes the infatuation of men so desirous of the fabled riches to be won by alchemy that they reduce themselves to poverty and ill-health in their mad pursuit. He drives the lesson home by a wonderful *chiaroscuro* sketch of the experimental shop of his master the Canon – the materials, the explosions, the disappointments, disagreements and arguments of the experimenters. Chaucer takes a great delight in the list of strange and resounding names of chemicals and processes. The Canon's Yeoman after showing the ill-success of his own Canon then proceeds to tell of the downright trickery of another alchemical Canon, describing a confidence trick which Chaucer may have learnt from life, though a few comparable anecdotes have been noted. It is too complicated a plot for an orally based folktale, but it is very much of the same nature as the medieval international comic tale. The dupe is laughed at, and though the trickster, the 'cursed Canon', is condemned, there is no serious satirical and didactic purpose. The narrative of the complicated conjuring trick is a masterpiece of clarity and ingenuity. The interest and aesthetic satisfaction normally founded on a shapely and complex plot are here based on the convolutions of the confidence trick itself, which is of course related to the characters of the subtle alchemist and his stupid victim. We smile at the ingenuity of the trick, and the disappointment of the dupe, who is an idle and selfish priest on whom we need waste no sympathy.

The tale is rounded off with a hundred lines of consideration of the *pros* and *cons* of alchemy, where it is Chaucer rather than the Yeoman who is speaking. There is a characteristic avoidance of an extreme position either for or against. Alchemy, though never intellectually so respectable as astrology, was nevertheless a well-established and accepted science. Chaucer's objections to it are not scientific; he is prepared to believe that the experts are right. In so far as he objects, he objects on practical and religious grounds. First, it is no good for the non-scientist to practise alchemy, because he is too ignorant:

> Lat no man bisye hym this art for to seche,
> But if that he th'entencioun and speche
> Of philosophres understonde kan. [*scientists*

VIII,1442–4

And secondly, since, according to Plato, scientists are sworn not to disclose or write the central secret of their art, because it is so dear to Christ, that He does not wish it to be generally known,

> I rede, as for the beste, lete it goon. [*advise*
> For whoso maketh God his adversarie,
> As for to werken any thyng in contrarie
> Of his wil, certes, never shal he thryve,
> Thogh that he multiplie terme of his lyve. [*practise alchemy all his life*
> And there a poynt, for ended is my tale.
> God sende every trewe man boote of his bale. [*remedy for his evil*

VIII,1475–81

As with *The Pardoner's Tale* the actual narrative is a jewel within a rich setting of comment and example, as well as of realistic description, dialogue and character. There are occasional touches which suggest a special audience, and since we know from Chaucer's poem to Bukton that at least *The Wife of Bath's Prologue* circulated, perhaps separately, in Chaucer's lifetime, it is quite possible that he used various Canterbury poems to suit special occasions, even if he designed them originally for inclusion in the Canterbury series. He may have been called on for special recitals and have produced individual parts of *The Canterbury Tales* on such occasions.

In this last of the comic tales we see, appropriately enough, in the subject of alchemy, the height of Chaucer's interest in what may be called the 'materiality' of matter. Many popular comic tales are based on the intransigence of matter to emotional or spiritual pretentions – the equivalent of a dignified man slipping on a banana skin, or having a custard pie thrown in his face. *The Miller's Tale* and *Summoner's Tale* are particularly good examples of human dignity comically reduced by brute materialism. The human condition itself, seen as a spirit stuffed into a bag of skin and bones and dung is in this respect a comic anomaly, or from a different point of view, a tragic one. Alchemy, however, was built on the premise that matter somehow could be made to obey laws similar to those of the spirit. It was fundamentally unlike modern science because its intellectual system was really an analogy of psychological and emotional structures, which is why the modern psychoanalyst Jung found it so interesting to study. (That alchemy led to modern chemistry is pure accident, and alchemy may have in reality held the development of real chemistry back, for chemistry developed much later than physics.) Alchemy is based on the notion, ultimately, that matter behaves as if it were like mind and feeling. It is archaic, and scientifically confused. It is also morally confused. Its practitioners were either almost literally half-baked idealists, like the Canon's Yeoman, or swindlers, like the canon in his story, or simply stupid, greedy men, like the priest in the story. It might be said that *The Canon's Yeoman's Prologue* and his long after-speech set out to reveal the confusion of mind and matter involved in alchemy, and to show that it must be ridiculous. In so doing, matter and mind are distinguished. The confusion is a perversion of the connectedness that *The Franklin's Tale* shows validly exists between matter and mind, because alchemy is followed in a spirit of selfish acquisition, not of *trouthe*. *The Canon's Yeoman's Tale* itself, the comic anecdote, is a story of a trick whose comedy lies in the revelation of trickery, the disappointment of greed, and the implicit reassertion of clear social, intellectual and moral rules which have been foolishly muddled and infringed by those who have thus been appropriately punished. The confidence trick is itself a clarifying comment on the nature of alchemy. The comic contradiction which is both presented and sorted out is summed up in the pregnant line

> Bitwixe men and gold ther is debaat.

VIII, 1389

The style at first also plays the game of spiritualising matter by using alchemical terms so freely, but the story of trickery is very lucidly explained. The comic story and the discussion of alchemy each come to the same conclusion: have nothing to do with alchemy. The style in every sense makes this plain: avoid 'multiplying'.

This cautious attitude may be seen to develop further in the following tale by the Manciple, though it is on a very different subject. Caution is carried still further again in *The Parson's Tale*. Chaucer is moving towards his end.

THE MANCIPLE'S PROLOGUE AND TALE

The next section, numbered nine, stands on its own, not yet connected with other tales, but beginning with a reference to 'Bob-up-and-down' which may be a facetious reference either to Harble-down, or to 'Up-and-Doun Field' near Boughton, in either case no more than a mile from Canterbury, and an unrealistic place to start even a short story. There is some entertaining comedy between the Manciple and the drunken Cook but *The Manciple's Tale* to which it leads is less genial and more pointed.

The story exists in a number of versions but Chaucer takes it from Ovid where it is told of Phebus (who became god of the sun), when he dwelt on this earth as the flower of young knights. Phebus has a beloved wife, who in his absence betrays him with a much less worthy man. A white crow, kept in a cage, and capable of speech, tells Phebus what has happened and in a passion Phebus kills his wife with an arrow. Then he deeply regrets his impatient anger, and condemns the crow evermore to be black and to have a discordant cry.

The poem is remarkable even for Chaucer for its sententious commentary, some lines of which are sharp, original, radically critical, and with important implications for Chaucer's notion of the relation of word to meaning. The words are put very clearly into the Manciple's mouth, but his speech expresses that love of literalism which accompanies Chaucer's almost equally strong taste for rhetorical elaboration and exaggeration. It is worth noting, however, that Chaucer's view here is that the word should 'agree with the deed', which is very different from the view, current from the seventeenth century onwards, that 'the word should represent the thing'. Chaucer is not advocating a *literalistic* theory which sees words as merely 'labels' of 'things'.

The Manciple says,

> If men shal telle proprely a thyng
> The word moot cosyn be to the werkyng.
> I am a boystous man, right thus seye I, [*plain*
> Ther nys no difference, trewely,
> Bitwixe a wyf that is of heigh degree [*high rank*
> If of hir body dishonest she bee [*unchaste*

> And a povre wenche, oother than this –   [*poor*
> If it so be they werke bothe amys –
> But that the gentile, in estaat above,   [*noble*
> She shal be cleped his lady, as in love;   [*called*
> And for that oother is a povre womman,
> She shal be cleped his wenche or his lemman.   [*sweetheart*
>
> IX, 209–20

The poem concludes with fifty lines, also clearly spoken by the Manciple, beginning 'Lordynges' (l. 309), which most sententiously repeat his mother's advice, with the frequent address 'My sone', not to speak too much.

It is a curious speech. Although it is not stirring poetry, and is unquestionably presented through the Manciple, it is so emphatic that it deserves attention. It may well be very late work. It is as if Chaucer is indirectly already telling himself to 'shut up'.

> My sone, be war, and be noon auctour newe   [*new teller*
> Of tidynges, wheither they been false or trewe.
>
> IX, 359–60

Never to repeat a story is a strange message from the author of *The House of Fame*, so eager for tidings, let alone the author of *The Canterbury Tales*. The Manciple twice says 'I am noght textueel' (ll. 235, 316), that is, well-read (though quoting Plato, which need not bother us). The only other time this word is used in Chaucer is in the immediately following *Parson's Prologue*. If any one was 'textueel' it was Chaucer himself, but in his divided consciousness, where old is set against new, unified against specialised, contemplative against analytic, it begins to look as if the old, the 'archaic' contemplative element, dependent on few texts, is beginning to get the upper hand of the discursive, widely-ranging modern. *The Manciple's Tale* perhaps unconsciously reflects Chaucer's deepening distrust, as he gets older, of undue verbalisation, of irresponsible story-telling. *The Parson's Tale* shows that distrust becoming decisive.

THE PARSON'S PROLOGUE AND TALE

The reference to the Manciple in the first line of *The Parson's Prologue*, which begins the final Fragment, numbered ten, is not absolutely certain, since the best manuscript, Hengwrt, has it written above an erasure, and a few other manuscripts use different names. My guess is that the process of revision was still going on as Chaucer was drawing his material together in his now contracted scheme. He wanted *The Manciple's Tale* where it now fits, for the reasons I have suggested, but came late to that placing. There were other adjustments still to be made. The astronomical timing described in *The Parson's Prologue* shows that it was about four o'clock in the afternoon, on 20 April, whereas the Manciple's tale, begun only a mile from Canterbury, was started explicitly in the morning. There is also an oversight in the astrology, though Chaucer might not have worried about that.

The Parson's Prologue is as full of interest as all the others though of a different kind. The Parson expresses a rigidly hostile attitude to 'fables', but says he will tell of 'morality and virtuous matter' in order to give lawful pleasure. But he is a Southern man

I kan nat geeste 'rum, ram, ruf' by lettre,	[*tell tales*
Ne God woot, rym holde I but litel bettre:	[*rhyme*
And therfore, if yow list – I wol nat glose –	[*if it pleases you*; *deceive*
I wol yow telle a myrie tale in prose.	[*pleasant*

X, 43–6

The Parson's condemnation of alliterative verse which usually tended towards solemn edification, *and* of rhyme, in which many pious works are written, is surprisingly severe. It can only be explained by assuming that in Chaucer's mind prose was coming to be thought of as the only vehicle for serious, non-fictional writing, and that verse was becoming associated only with fiction, and usually secular fiction. This actual situation was not fully realised in English till late in the sixteenth century, but Chaucer is here as usual in advance of his age. At the end of the Parson's 'tale', which is a religious meditation, the distrust of fiction becomes complete. On the other hand, the Parson must still at this stage, before his tale, be allowed some dramatic freedom and autonomy. Chaucer need not have agreed wholeheartedly with the words he puts in the Parson's mouth, though it would not seem that he is mocking the Parson.

The Parson likens their journey to the perfect glorious pilgrimage which is called the heavenly Jerusalem – another late thought of Chaucer's, and a further turning away from the secular realism of daily life. All the pilgrims, including the Host, are glad to hear him, though the Host asks, very sensibly, that he should speak 'in little space'. Many of the themes touched on in the *Tales* are summed up in this long tract. The Parson reminds his hearers of the Day of Judgment, and the torments of Hell. God orders and controls all things, and a man's first duty is self-mastery. Honours, wealth, delights, even love of family, though good in themselves can seduce him from his eternal destiny. There is a long passage about the Seven Deadly Sins, where many things are held up to condemnation, as 'superfluitee of clothing and horrible disordinat scantness'; great households (such as John of Gaunt's, though Chaucer does not say so); 'bakemeats and dishmeats, burning with wildfire and painted, and castled with paper' (as they were in court festivities), and so forth. The commonplace that Christ is the only source of 'gentilesse' is reiterated. One of many shrewd remarks is that inordinate desire for knowledge or glory may be regarded as a form of avarice. Extortion and oppression are roundly condemned, and while 'degree' is upheld, it is a lord's duty to give his dependants cause to love him. Throughout there is a continual insistence on 'reason'. The sermon is a forthright call to repentance; it pulls no punches, leaves few aspects of ordinary living untouched.

The immediate source of this powerful diatribe against the joys of life is unknown and there seems no reason why we should not attribute to Chaucer himself sufficient originality and conviction to have composed it, as he composed so much else, from traditional elements themselves well known, mainly deriving ultimately from thirteenth-century Italian originals written in Latin by laymen. Chaucer may well also have worked from French texts of the same tradition. He produced at any rate a work of polished artistic prose, not cramped or made awkward by close translation. Chaucer's acquaintance with sermon literature has been amply demonstrated by Professor Wenzel. His position in this religious stream of oral and written tradition is comparable with his position in the stream of traditional comic tales. He accepts the tradition, but is innovative, especially in his use of the English vernacular.

The date is remarkably early in England for a layman to compose a religious treatise, especially in prose. If *The Parson's Tale* is not the very first instance, then probably the prose treatise *The Two Ways*, by Chaucer's friend and poetic disciple Sir John Clanvowe, is actually the first, but composed under Chaucer's influence at a very similar date around 1390. Clanvowe's treatise has some touch of Lollardry; not so Chaucer's, but each is essentially a devout layman's serious attempt to come to terms with the self-discipline, the social codes, the asceticism and other-worldliness of monk-dominated medieval Christian spirituality. Much of it seems more sour and more absolute than is necessary for laymen or than would have been endorsed by the great medieval theologian St Thomas Aquinas, who seems to have made more allowance for natural affections. For us this does not much matter for two reasons. One is that the whole mixed 'Gothic' nature of *The Canterbury Tales* implicitly juxtaposes *The Parson's Tale* with other tales which though they may, as Chaucer later expresses it, 'sownen into synne', qualify and modify *The Parson's Tale* by implicitly or explicitly expressing a quite reasonable different view of a decent life and social norms. Even the international popular comic tales imply, by the laughter caused by their infringement, the sensible rules of quite a good society. One kind of writing is comic and fantastic, the other serious and devout, but neither sermon nor comic tale can be a *total* statement of a world-view, even if *The Parson's Tale* claims to be.

The other reason why a claim by *The Parson's Tale* to absolute assent need not worry us is that no one need now take literally the devotional injunctions of six hundred years ago, when social and intellectual conditions were so different. For *us* the tale must be a kind of fiction, because the passage of time turns all documentation, even lists of stores, into fictions. On the other hand, it would be grossly anachronistic to believe that this strenuously devout work was in any way consciously fictional, or ironical, or not serious, to Chaucer. We must not confuse our fictions with his, or allow modern abstruse speculation about the nature of reality to confuse a perfectly clear literary-historical situation. The works of Chaucer, so multiple in point of view, conducted on so many fictional levels, are powerfully attractive to speculations about the nature of fictions, of the relation between word and deed, of teller to tale, and so on. Such speculations should not wantonly obscure the broad historical truths about which there cannot be reasonable doubt. One of these truths is that such a devotional work as *The Parson's Tale* was serious and literal in intention. There is no question of a Narrator, stupid, ironical, anti-Christian, or even Christian. Nor is the *persona* of the writer important here. He is virtually invisible – simply the accepted producer of the text on which we focus all our attention without regard for the speaker. There is equally no sensible doubt that the *Retractation*, in which Chaucer 'revokes' all his secular works, is serious, literally meant, by Chaucer the man. We shall return later to it.

First, we may here, almost at their end, cast an eye back over *The Canterbury Tales* as a whole. Their protean variety defies summary: they have to be seen as a Gothic miscellany. The dominant impression is of liveliness. The fundamental image of pilgrimage is one of movement, opening horizons, changing forms. The portraits of *The General Prologue*, both traditional yet broken into new possibilities, reflecting both ideal and real people, are characteristic of the whole. And the place the poet gives himself in *The General Prologue* is equally representative. He is perfectly at home even in that place of transience, an inn. He is familiar with all classes, friendly to all, in no sense a rebel or an Outsider. Yet a part also of him is withdrawn, as an observer outside the group, a little aside. He is not Knight, Clerk, Parson nor Ploughman. He alone of all the pilgrims is of undescribed status and has no function, no work, attributed to him. Yet he is there, partly inside; not only as an invisible omniscient author but part of his own subject matter. He occupies socially and artistically a perfectly secure but marginal, exploratory, even transitional position. Transition is often that brief period when experience is most intense, when we are momentarily conscious of two states of being, related yet different, between which we move, conscious of both states, appreciative of both, as we cannot be when we are firmly ensconsed in the one or the other. This transitional quality may well be as much inherent in everyone's experience as is that other different experience of the archaic timeless moment, of intense peacefulness and rest, which we often imagine in the past or in the future, and so rarely, if ever, experience in the present. Chaucer anxiously sought such archaic stability of felicity in Boethius. He did not find it at the end of his early poems, and only doubtfully at the end of *Troilus*. He may have found it at the end of *The Canterbury Tales* and of his life, but if so it was only by rejecting that peculiarly transitional, ambivalent willingness to be in two worlds at once, to accept both of two apparently incompatible points of view, which is the source of so much of his liveliness and his humour.

It remains to survey briefly his later years, and a few of the shorter poems, some of which express that more settled view of life, which Boethius and much Christian teaching strove for.

Chapter 14

THE LAST YEARS

The outlines of Chaucer's career after 1386 can be clearly traced. Much the same pattern of courtiership and public service as before is repeated.

Having lived in Kent since 1385 and been free from office since 1386, he presumably devoted himself to his writing and to his duties as Justice of the Peace. Doubtless the exercise of such duties further enriched his knowledge of men. He did not enjoy or endure a stationary tranquillity for long, for in July 1387 he was granted protection for a year to go to Calais in the retinue of Sir William Beauchamp, although as his name does not appear on the list of Sir William's Controller it is not certain that Chaucer went, or if he went, how long he stayed. Also in 1387 the payments to his wife ceased, and it is probable that she died in that year. Perhaps the loss of her annuity caused Chaucer to live beyond his income, for he began to be sued for debt in April 1388, and sold his crown pension for a lump sum about the same time. Other matters made the first half of 1388 unpleasant. The 'Merciless Parliament', controlled by the barons hostile to the court and Lancastrian factions, sat from 3 February to 4 June 1388, and pursued the leaders of the court party with relentless hostility. Sir Nicholas Brembre, formerly Lord Mayor and one of Chaucer's colleagues as a Collector of Customs, who was leader of the Victualling guilds and the most important leader of the court party in the City, was tried, found guilty and executed in February in a barefaced travesty of justice not to be condoned by his own violent and unscrupulous character. Thomas Usk, Chaucer's admirer and also a member of the court party, was executed early in March. After a long and bitter struggle Sir Simon Burley, the principal leader of the court party and one of Richard's tutors, was condemned and executed on 5 May. Richard risked his very throne in his opposition to Burley's fate; his queen is said to have gone on her knees to Richard's uncle, the surly and quarrelsome Duke of Gloucester, to save him; but to no avail. With him perished three other knights of his party. Truly, 'the wrastling for this world axeth a fal'.

Burley's death seems to have slaked the Merciless Parliament's desire for blood, and the tension of hostility relaxed. Richard had no choice but to lie low and make friends. A year later, in May 1389, Richard made a dramatic gesture of self-assertion, and after ridding himself of some of his main enemies began to appoint some of his own nominees. Chaucer was small fry, but it may be that he owed his next official post to Richard's new ascendancy. On 12 July 1389 he was appointed to the responsible position of Clerk of the King's Works. Since Gaunt was not in the country until October of this year, it cannot be to his influence that Chaucer owed the appointment. As with his position at the Customs, the clerkship was not a sinecure, a reward for mere courtiership. He had general responsibility for repairing and maintaining the Tower, Westminster Palace and other royal buildings, and was granted wide powers to obtain materials, control expenditure, and in some cases to impress workmen. In 1390 he was given a special assignment to erect scaffolding for the jousts at Smithfield, and another for repairs to Saint George's Chapel, Windsor. In the same year he served on a commission led by Sir Richard Sturry (another of the court party and one of those friends who favoured Lollardry). The commission's task was to survey the walls, ditches, bridges and sewers along the Thames between Greenwich and Woolwich. In September 1390 Chaucer was robbed no less than three times in four days. On one of these occasions he was assaulted and beaten, and seems to have lost twenty pounds of the king's money, with some of his own.

This is evidence that he had real work to do, being in charge of the king's money, the loss of which he was excused. He gave up the Clerkship eight months later, on 17 June 1391, probably because of his appointment, made before 22 June 1391, as subforester of the king's park in North Petherton, Somersetshire. He was apparently appointed by Sir Peter Courtenay, who was Constable of Windsor Castle while Chaucer was in charge of the repairs to Saint George's Chapel. (Sir Peter Courtenay seems also to have been a knight agreeable to the king.) So far as is known Chaucer retained this office to the end of his life, and it was obviously less arduous than the Clerkship of Works. Its value is unknown.

Whatever travelling was required by the subforestership, Chaucer retained his dwelling at Greenwich, which may be the 'solytarie wildernesse' of which he complains in the *Envoy to Scogan*. His favour remained strong at court and he received in January 1393 a gift of ten pounds for good service; in February 1394 an annuity of twenty pounds; and in December 1397 the grant of a butt of wine yearly. During these years he often borrowed small sums of money in advance from the Exchequer, and in 1398 was sued for debt, though this was an action probably arising out of transactions during his clerkship, since he was sued by the widow of one of his former subordinates. His favour at court again stood him in good stead, and he was able to obtain letters of protection against this suit for two years. We do not know the outcome of the affair. The chances are that he was not poor, though he may have lacked ready money at times. The dilatory methods of the Exchequer (often badly in arrears with payments) and the general shortage of currency in the four-teenth century could easily account for small borrowings.

During these later years Chaucer seems also to have established firmer relationships with John of Gaunt's son Henry, Earl of Derby and afterwards Henry IV. At Christmas 1395 and in February 1396 Chaucer delivered ten pounds to Henry, and received a valuable scarlet robe, trimmed with fur, as a gift. No one at this time thought of Henry as future king. Chaucer had always been associated with the Lancastrian faction, especially through his wife, although his main associates and interests seem to have lain with the court party. Moreover, Gaunt had been much out of the country in the past few years. Now Gaunt had returned, and although Henry had been associated (in the absence of his father) with the baronial party in the year of the Merciless Parliament, he seems, by virtue of his Lancas-trian affiliation, to have become by 1396 a member of the new court party in which his father was active. To be loyal to Henry was not yet to be disloyal to Richard. Chaucer's friends Scogan and Bukton (if the latter was Sir Peter Bukton from the Holderness mentioned in *The Summoner's Tale*) were also close adherents of Henry of Derby. Two other friends of Chaucer similarly had a footing in both court and Lancastrian factions: Sir Lewis Clifford, who brought Des-champs' poem in praise of Chaucer from France; and Sir John Clan-vowe, the probable author of the Chaucerian poem *Cuckoo and Nightingale* and the prose tract, *The Two Ways*. Both these were distinguished men and favoured the Lollards.

Apart from such of the *Canterbury Tales* as were written in this last decade of the century and of Chaucer's life, there are some minor poems which may belong here. They make a mixed bag. *Trouthe, Gentilesse, The Former Age, Lak of Stedfastnesse, Fortune*, all express in varying degrees a keen sense of 'This wrecched worldes transmutacioun', with its corollary that

> No man is wrecched, but himself it wene,
> And he that hath himself hath suffisaunce.

Fortune, 25–6

The power of mind, the need for self-sufficiency, for internalised values, are again emphasised. *The Former Age* praises the archaic past, expressing a longing for peace and calm, finishing

Allas, allas! now may men wepe and crye!
For in oure dayes nis but covetyse,
Doublenesse, and tresoun, and envye,
Poyson, manslauhtre, and mordre in sondry wyse.

60–3

The strain of contemplating the actual world is always severe, but these poems emphasise evil rather than joy. They have none of the readiness of earlier works to see the good, and to hold good and evil together.

There are also two humorous poems to younger friends, Scogan and Bukton. To Bukton, perhaps on the occasion of his marriage, Chaucer writes mockingly of marriage, bidding him 'read the Wife of Bath'. In the *Envoy to Scogan* he asks in pretended dismay:

Hastow not seyd, in blaspheme of the goddes,
Thurgh pride, or thrugh thy grete rekelnesse,   [*rashness*
Swich thing as in the lawe of love forbode is,
That, for thy lady sawgh nat thy distresse,   [*because*
Therfore thow yave hir up at Michelmesse?

15–19

He gravely reproaches him, for the god of love may extend his displeasure with Scogan to include those who are 'hoary-headed and round of shape'; once more the image of the portly Chaucer arises before us, now grey-headed. He makes an interesting reference to his poetry

That rusteth in my shethe stille in pees.
While I was yong, I put hir forth in prees;   [*thrust her eagerly forward*
But al shal passe that men prose or ryme.

39–41

There is a note of melancholy here, but it is followed by a reference to his distance from the head of the stream of grace and honour and worthiness, by which he presumably means the king's court. He says he lives in 'solitary wilderness', 'as dull as death', and desires Scogan to keep him remembered 'where it may fructify' – perhaps in the mind of the king, or of Gaunt, or of Gaunt's son.

The handful of short poems of this period includes also the delightfully witty *Merciles Beaute*, in which Chaucer commits with exquisite skill the very 'crime' of which he had accused Scogan. After praising the beauty of his lady, and complaining in the usual terms that her lack of pity will be his death, he concludes:

Love hath my name ystrike out of his sclat   [*slate*
And he is strike out of my bokes clene
For evermo; ther is non other mene.   [*way*

> Sin I fro Love escaped am so fat,   [*since*
> I never thenk to ben his prison lene;   [*prisoner*
> Sin I am free, I counte him not a bene.   [*not worth a bean*
>
> 34–9

This shows an agreeably carefree spirit in age. The requests in *Scogan* and *Fortune* may suggest that by this time Chaucer's active life as a 'working courtier', so to speak, was over. No such poetical requests for favour have survived from his earlier, more active years. It may be that the favours he undoubtedly received are to be associated with these poems.

Towards the end of the decade King Richard became more and more unpopular, while divisions increased within the court party. The most famous of these quarrels was that between Gaunt's son Henry and the Duke of Norfolk, which in 1398 culminated in the abortive trial by combat at Coventry and the exile of both. John of Gaunt died in February 1399, and Richard, who was badly in need of money, confiscated the whole of the huge Lancastrian inheritance. This confiscation, combined with many other acts of extortion and despotism, thoroughly alarmed everybody. When Richard set sail for Ireland in May 1399, complete with minstrels and crown jewels, to crush the Irish revolt, he left behind him his own country ripe for rebellion. When the new Duke of Lancaster arrived in England to claim his rights such numbers of Richard's discontented subjects hastened to join Henry that many had to be sent home again for lack of food. Even Henry's eventual seizure of the Crown did not destroy his popularity.

In the last five years Richard had completely alienated the affections of his subjects from the great lords to the London rabble, and many of his most loyal and efficient officers stayed on to serve his successor equally loyally and efficiently. It must have been a relief to serve a king more capable and less capricious than Richard, while Henry's claim to be the true successor of Henry III together with the façade of legalism of Richard's deposition were a sufficient sop to the conscience of most. There can be little doubt, too, that Henry's might helped to confirm whatever seemed shaky in his right. Richard's cause attracted few martyrs, and the Revolution was achieved with remarkably little fuss and bloodshed. Henry IV was received as king by Parliament on 30 September 1399, being in the official terms which Chaucer repeats,

> conquerour of Brutes Albyon,
> Which that by lyne and free eleccion
> Been verray kyng.

Chaucer, an old man as the times went, and with a lifelong association with the House of Lancaster, acquiesced in the change, and addressed the lines just quoted to the new king in a poem entitled *The Complaint of Chaucer to his Purse*, a graceful punning request for reward as witty as anything he ever wrote. There was nothing servile or unusual in such a poem by a court poet, and doubtless other courtiers, less talented, were accustomed to make similar requests in plain prose. Such demands were part of the system by which a great man or a king obtained and paid for the services of the retinue which was as necessary to him as he was to his dependants. Henry IV was careful to obtain support wherever he could, and was as inclined to foster the arts as Richard had been. It is pleasant to record that he speedily granted Chaucer an annuity of forty marks on 19 October and a few days later confirmed Chaucer's former grants from Richard. The ostensible reason for this confirmation was that the earlier letters patent from Richard had accidentally been lost, but maybe as a practised courtier Chaucer felt that it would be no bad thing, while Henry was in a giving mood, to have new letters under the new seal.

In December 1399 Chaucer took a lease of a house in the garden of Westminster Abbey. His last recorded payment from the Exchequer was on 5 June 1400, and on 25 October 1400, according to the inscription formerly on his tomb, he died. He was buried in the Abbey, and this may have indicated that he was held in special honour by the king, for the Abbey was primarily a burial place of royalty. (The first commoner to be buried in the Abbey was John Waltham, Richard's Treasurer and Bishop of Salisbury, who had died as recently as 1395. This signal honour was paid to him as a mark of Richard's special regard, and many people had objected.) Unfortunately the chronicler Walsingham, who tells us about Waltham, does not notice Chaucer's death, so we do not know what people thought. But it is certain that for some years Chaucer had been recognised in both the English and French courts as the great poet of England.

The final honour (if such it be) of his burial gives a greater, indeed an ironic interest, to the last chapter of all his writing, the *Retractation*. This short passage of prose comes at the end of the *Tales*, but refers to the whole of his life's work, and in it he asks mercy and forgiveness of Christ for just those 'translations and indictings of worldly vanities' which had earned him fame. He revokes them in some detail – *Troilus and Criseyde, The House of Fame, The Legend of Good Women, The Book of the Duchess, The Parliament, The Book of the Lion* (now lost), those *Canterbury Tales* which tend towards sin, 'and many a song and many a leccherous lay'. He gives thanks for his translation of the *Consolation*, saints' legends, homilies, and other books of morality and devotion.

There seemed something morbid to the earlier critics about this wholesale and as we feel unnecessary denunciation of the secular works, and some critics thought it spurious. Later critical opinion accepts it as genuine, though it is not in all the manuscripts. Works such as *Troilus* are not condemned for anything immoral in them; Chaucer's followers united to praise his morality, and the reader may judge of it for himself. The works' fault lies in their 'this-worldliness'. As death approached, Chaucer's mind reverted to the narrowest and strictest definitions of the good life. The attempt of his mature years to have the best of both worlds, Heaven and Earth, is not unreasonably abandoned, since he must now inevitably lose this present world. That *contemptus mundi* found in *Somnium Scipionis*, the *Consolation*, and *The Parson's Tale*, with its longing for stability and joy is no longer contradicted by the experience of glad youth, or the excitement of intellectual adventure into new worlds of thought. That contempt of the world produced by a vivid sense of the bliss and eternity of heaven had always been an important element in Chaucer's thought, and the evidence of some of his later short poems may suggest a hardening in his attitude to the world. Now, with both experience and authority, Chaucer's twin masters, advocating the way of rejection, that way was necessarily chosen.

Sir Launcelot, who was the noblest knight of all the world, and with one exception the most virtuous, ended his days in religious retreat and repentance. There is even a suggestion in Dante's *Convivio* that this was the natural development of a man's life; and in fourteenth-century England an old age of retirement in the shade of a monastery was by no means an uncommon end to life. We must remember, too, the commonplaces of Christian thought accepted by Chaucer; that however good a man's actions, if they are not performed for the sake of God, they shall avail him nothing. If one remembers also the uncomfortable duality of the conception of the world's goodness and badness forced so sharply upon medieval thinking, it may well be thought that to spend one's active days in the world and one's retirement in pious repentance and preparation for death is a very human and by no means foolish way of resolving the duality inherent in both 'experience' and 'authority'. It was worth while to remember the next life; the conception of Heaven was glorious, and there were terrible accounts of the torments of the damned. For Chaucer, divided between two worlds, the concept of Purgatory seems never to have meant much, except as material for a joke.

There is therefore nothing that need surprise us about the *Retractation* and no reason to reject it. The fifteenth-century tradition of Chaucer's deathbed repentance, recorded by Dr Thomas Gascoigne, Chancellor of Oxford University 1434–44 might easily have been suggested by this very *Retractation*.

Chaucer's family prospered in the fifteenth century. His son Thomas who had received favours from Richard continued to receive them from Henry throughout a distinguished career. He married about 1394–5 and his daughter eventually became Countess of Suffolk.

Chaucer's poetic reputation also flourished. In the middle of the sixteenth century it was even fashionable for courtiers to 'talk Chaucer'. Only about the eighteenth century did he become thought of as predominantly a comic, even a ribald poet. Throughout the nineteenth century his works continued to attract the attention of men and women of general education and interests. His variety reflected much of the variety of that century.

There is no hope of summing up in a few words, after so long a book, the greatness and diversity of Chaucer's works, and their inexhaustible interest, set as they are within the rich culture of an extraordinarily interesting as well as troubled period. The peculiar mixture of old and new, of participation with detachment, of protean sympathy with irony, of multiple points of view, all of which give variety, yet for which he seems able to preserve a basis of certainty, is surely Chaucer's outstanding artistic characteristic.

The great risk for Chaucer's kind of writing, as of Gothic art in general, is fragmentation, or a serial dissipation of effect, or a schizophrenic duality, presenting unresolved dichotomies and self-contradictory, self-destructive inconsistencies. The attempt at variety, the implication of several possible points of view, may shatter unity; yet most of us rarely feel that Chaucer is disintegrated, even when our rational processes reproach him for his inconsistencies. It is not with Chaucer's world, as it seems with ours, that 'the centre cannot hold'. In the form of the poems the poet's speaking voice, for all the different levels of meaning which may be implied, holds together the poem and his audience in a complex pattern of relationships. The poem is a script for the poet – more, a script for *Chaucer*. This is their uniqueness, more profound that their 'ordinary' uniqueness of genius. Milton's or Wordsworth's poems have both the ordinary uniqueness of genius and a highly personalised style, but as products of print culture they emanated originally from an essentially unknown author; the printed book is designed to be bought by strangers, and no amount of biographical knowledge can change their nature. On the other hand, the poem of a truly oral culture has an equally impersonal quality of quite different origin and nature. It is in a real sense, because traditional, a creation and possession of many people.

In the manuscript culture of the Gothic period the poets fumbled towards a situation different again, although partly traditional, in which Chaucer almost fully achieved the art of writing poems in which he not only created the story, the style, the audience, but also himself. In a sense, in fiction he 'imitated', with varying realism, but more 'organically' than he imitated anything else, his own real self.

When we 'read Chaucer', that expression takes on more meaning than the normally convenient brief designation of a particular body of writing. We ourselves have to act out in our imaginations his own script. It is we, as readers, who hold, or do not hold, together the disparate points of view we allow ourselves to entertain. It is we who imitate the reading poet-in-his-audience, who project our ironies, to take responsibility for all the various things that may be said, or hinted, or even thought. In a curious way this highly dramatic and least egotistical or assertive of writers sucks us up more completely into his own world than any such varied monsters of egotism as Donne or Milton or Wordsworth. And yet we are still the audience, too. Thus we are made to embody multiple points of view, bound together in unity of story, story-teller, audience. As he says when all is ready for Criseyde to come to Pandarus's house:

> *Us* lakketh nought but that we witen wolde   [*We lack nothing*; *know*
> A certeyn houre, in which *she* comen sholde.

III, 531–2

We are all joined together in the reading, under the eager guidance of Chaucer the Expositor, who shares, yet manipulates our feelings. How far is this Master of Ceremonies himself and actor? The degree of acting varies during the course of his works, and sometimes he speaks more in his own voice, and with one voice, than at others. Finally, at the end of the performance, he abandons his roles altogether and comes forward as a simple earnest human being, as anxious as the rest of us. In some ways the 'real' man must be smaller than the variety of rôles and the many scenes he has presented to us. That is natural, for he has been deploying for our pleasure the riches of ancient and complex cultures, the products of many human minds.

Here we may find a further, final clue to that sense of unity which we experience in Chaucer's script for himself which embodies so much variety. Although it is his own script, his own verbal realisation, the material which he uses, even when he transmutes it, is traditional narrative, traditional motifs, traditional attitudes. Although he manipulates it with unique artistic genius, the material is the product of long, general human experience. Chaucer's authorial modesty towards the given story and other matter, as towards the audience or reader, reflects a genuine humility which allows him to accept, and thus in some way to hold together, with either amusement or pain, joy or sorrow, the bewildering variety of the world. By his general acceptance of tradition, even though he changes and occasionally subverts it, he retains and expresses a unifying sense of common humanity.

SELECT BIBLIOGRAPHY

Place of publication London or New York except where otherwise
indicated.

A. BIBLIOGRAPHIES AND DICTIONARIES

Baugh, A.S. (1968), *Chaucer*, Appleton-Century.
Benson, Larry D. (1974) A Reader's Guide to the Writings of
Chaucer, in Brewer, Derek (ed.), *Geoffrey Chaucer*: (Writers and
their Backgrounds), Bell.
Crawford, W.R. (1967) *Bibliography of Chaucer 1954–63*, University
of Washington Press.
Griffith, D.D. (1955) *Bibliography of Chaucer 1908–1953*, University of
Washington Press.
Hammond, Eleanor P. (1908) *Chaucer: a bibliographical manual*, re-
printed Peter Smith, Gloucester, Mass., 1933.
Magoun, F.P. Jr. (1961) *A Chaucer Gazetteer*, University of Chicago
Press, Chicago.
Tatlock, J.S.P. and Kennedy, A.G. (1927) *Concordance to the Com-
plete Works of Chaucer*, reprinted Peter Smith, Gloucester, Mass.,
1963.
Watson, G. (1974) *New Cambridge Bibliography of English Litera-
ture*, vol. I, 600–1600, Cambridge University Press.
See also the edition of J.H. Fisher, Section C.

B. LIFE AND TIMES AND GENERAL BACKGROUND

Brewer, Derek (1978), *Chaucer and his World*, Eyre Methuen Ltd.
Crow, M.M. and Olson, C.C. (1966) *Chaucer Life-Records*, Oxford Univer-
sity Press.
McFarlane, K.B. (1972) *Lancastrian Kings and Lollard Knights*, Clarendon
Press, Oxford.
McKisack, M. (1959) *The Fourteenth Century*, Clarendon Press, Oxford.

Manly, J.M. (1926) *Some New Light on Chaucer*, reprinted Peter Smith, Gloucester, Mass., 1959.

Rickert, E. (1948) *Chaucer's World*, ed. Olson, C.C. and Crow, M.M., Columbia University Press.

Thrupp, S. (1948) *The Merchant Class in Medieval London*, University of Michigan Press, Ann Arbor and Toronto.

C. EDITIONS

Brewer, Derek (1960) *The Parlement of Foulys*; reprinted Manchester University Press, 1976.

Donaldson, E.T. (1958) *Chaucer's Poetry: an anthology for the modern reader*, Ronald

Fisher, John H. (1977) *The Complete Poetry and Prose of Geoffrey Chaucer*, Holt, Rinehart and Winston. (With very full recent bibliography.)

Price, D.J. (1955) *The Equatorie of the Planetis: with a linguistic analysis by R.M. Wilson*, Cambridge University Press.

Robinson, F.N. (1933) *The Works of Geoffrey Chaucer*, Cambridge, Mass.; 2nd ed., Oxford University Press, 1957, (The standard text.)

D. RECEPTION

Brewer, Derek (ed.) (1978) *Chaucer: The Critical Heritage*, 2 vols, Routledge and Kegan Paul.

Spurgeon, C.F.E. (ed.) (1914–24) *Five Hundred Years of Chaucer Criticism and Allusion 1357–1900*, 3 vols.; reprinted Peter Russell, 1961.

E. LANGUAGE AND METRE

Baugh, A.C. (1959) *A History of the English Language (revised edn)*, Routledge and Kegan Paul.

Baum, P.F. (1961) *Chaucer's Verse*, Duke University Press.

Burnley, J.D. (1980) *Chaucer's Language and the Philosopher's Tradition*, D.S. Brewer, Cambridge.

Davis, Norman (1974) Chaucer and Fourteenth-Century English, in *Geoffrey Chaucer* (Writers and their Backgrounds, ed. Derek Brewer), Bell.

Davis, N., Gray, D., Ingham, P. and Wallace-Hadrill, A. (1979) *A Chaucer Glossary*, Clarendon Press, Oxford.

Elliott, R.W.V. (1974) *Chaucer's English*, Deutsch.

Jones, Charles (1972) *An Introduction to Middle English*, Holt, Rinehart and Winston.

Kökeritz, H. (1962) *A Guide to Chaucer's Pronunciation*, Stockholm and New Haven, Conn.; paperback, Holt, Rinehart and Winston.

Roskow, Gregory (1981) *Syntax and Style in Chaucer's Poetry*, D.S. Brewer, Cambridge.

Strang, B.M.H. (1970) *A History of English*, Edward Arnold.

Ten Brink, B. (1901) *The Language and Metre of Chaucer*, 2nd ed., rev. Kluge, F., transl. Bentinck Smith, M.

F. GENERAL LITERARY BACKGROUND

Brewer, Derek (1983) *English Gothic Literature*, Macmillan.

Boitani, P. (1982) *English Medieval Narrative in the 13th and 14th Centuries*, Cambridge University Press.

Burrow, J.A. (1982) *Medieval Writers and their Work*, Oxford University Press.

Ford, Boris (ed.) (1983) *The Pelican Guide to Medieval English Literature*, Harmondsworth.

Pearsall, Derek (1977) *Old English and Middle English Poetry*, Routledge and Kegan Paul.

G. SOURCES AND LITERARY TRADITIONS

Benson, Larry D. and Andersson, T.M. (eds. and trs.) (1971) *The Literary Context of Chaucer's Fabliaux*, Bobbs-Merrill Company Inc., Indianapolis.

Bryan, W.F. and Dempster, G. (eds.) (1941) *Sources and Analogues of Chaucer's Canterbury Tales*, Routledge and Kegan Paul, 1958.

Havely, N.R. (1981) *Chaucer's Boccaccio*, D.S. Brewer, Cambridge.

Lewis, C.S. (1964) *The Discarded Image*, Cambridge University Press.

Minnis, Alastair (1982) *Chaucer and Pagan Antiquity*, D.S. Brewer, Cambridge.

Rickard, P., Brewer, Derek and others (1973) *Medieval Comic Tales*, D.S. Brewer, Cambridge.

Spearing, A.C. (1976) *Medieval Dream Poetry*, Cambridge University Press.

Wimsatt, J.I. (1982) *Chaucer and the Poems of 'Ch'*, D.S. Brewer, Cambridge.

Windeatt, B.A. (1982) *Chaucer's Dream Poetry: Sources and Analogues*, D.S. Brewer, Cambridge.

H. SOME GENERAL AND CRITICAL STUDIES

(a) Collections of Essays

Brewer, Derek (ed.) (1974) *Geoffrey Chaucer* (Writers and their Background), Bell.

Brewer, Derek (1982) *Tradition and Innovation in Chaucer*, Macmillan.

Brewer, Derek (1984) *The Poet as Storyteller*, Macmillan.

Brewer, Derek (1985) *Chaucer's Mentality*, D.S. Brewer, Cambridge.

Donaldson, E.T. (1970) *Speaking of Chaucer*, Athlone Press.

Rowland, Beryl (ed.) (1979) *Companion to Chaucer Studies*, revised edn., Oxford University Press.

Salu, Mary (1980) *Essays on Troilus and Criseyde*, D.S. Brewer, Cambridge.

Schoek, R.J. and Taylor, J. (eds.) (1960) *Chaucer Criticism*, 2 vols., University of Notre Dame Press, Indiana.

Spearing, A.C. (1972) *Criticism and Medieval Poetry*, revised edn, Edward Arnold.

(b) Other Works

Burrow, J.A. (1971) *Ricardian Poetry*, Routledge and Kegan Paul.

David, A. (1976) *The Strumpet Muse*, California University Press, Berkeley and Los Angeles.

Howard, D.R. (1976) *The Idea of the Canterbury Tales*, California University Press, Berkeley and Los Angeles.

Hussey, S.S. (1983) *Chaucer: An Introduction*, revised edn., Methuen.

Kean, P.M. (1972) *Chaucer and the Making of English Poetry*, 2 vols., Routledge and Kegan Paul.

Mann, J. (1973) *Chaucer and Medieval Estates Satire*, Cambridge University Press.

Muscatine, C. (1957) *Chaucer and the French Tradition*, University of California Press, Berkeley and Los Angeles.

Muscatine, C. (1972) *Poetry and Crisis in the Age of Chaucer*, University of Notre Dame, Indiana.

Robertson, D.W. Jr. (1962) *A Preface to Chaucer: Studies in Medieval Perspectives*, Princeton University Press, Princeton.

I. RECORDINGS

Readings in the original pronunciation
Troilus and Criseyde (abridged), Argo ZPL 1003–4.
The General Prologue, Argo PLP 1001.
The Knight's Tale, Argo ZPL 1208–10.
The Miller's Prologue and Tale, CUP Cassette 211859.
The Wife of Bath, CUP Cassette 212197.

The Merchant's Prologue and Tale, CUP Cassette 211875.
The Pardoner's Tale, Argo ZPL 1211.
The Nun's Priest's Tale, Argo PLP 1002.
The Wife of Bath's Prologue and Tale, Argo ZPL 1212/13.

INDEX